GW00683551

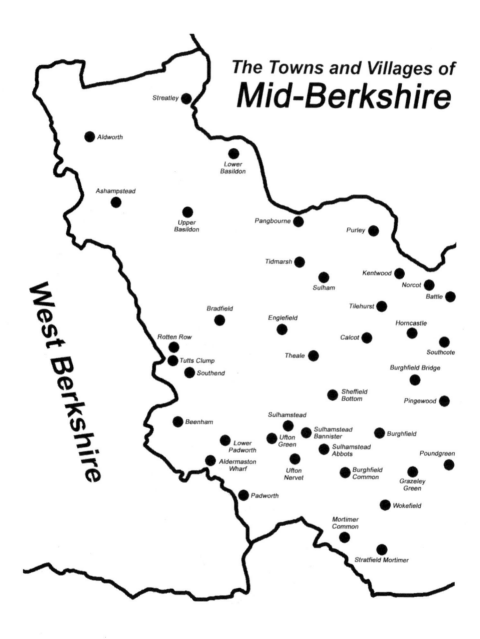

The Towns and Villages of
Mid-Berkshire

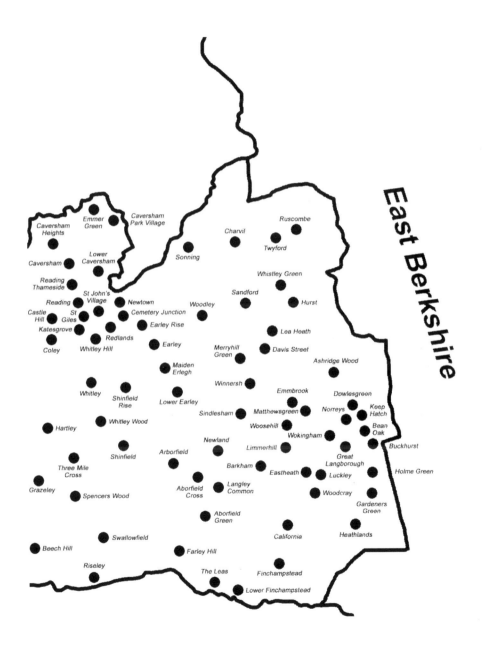

MID-BERKSHIRE TOWN and VILLAGE HISTORIES

including Reading, Caversham, Woodley and Wokingham

Berkshire Town and Village Histories
Volume 2

David Nash Ford

Nash Ford Publishing
Wokingham, Berkshire

All illustrations and photographs are from the Nash Ford Picture Library unless stated otherwise.

Some of these village histories were first published in an earlier form on David Nash Ford's Royal County of Berkshire History Website at www.berkshirehistory.com between 1996 and 2017.

ISBN 978-1-905191-02-4

Front cover: Pangbourne, Bradfield and Sonning
Back cover: Town and Village History Coverage

Nash Ford Publishing
Wokingham, Berkshire
www.nashfordpublishing.co.uk
www.berkshirehistory.com

For my Mum, a Tilehurst girl

Other Volumes in this series:

Volume 1: East Berkshire Town and Village Histories
Volume 3: West Berkshire Town and Village Histories

Contents

List of Illustrations

All photographs, maps and illustrations are taken or drawn by David Nash Ford or are antique prints from the Nash Ford Picture Library except: Figure 42: Chalk Caverns beneath Emmer Green which is the copyright of @forgottenheritage and Figure 140: The Museum of Berkshire Aviation which is the copyright of my friend, Tony Wright. Many thanks to both of them for allowing me to use their images.

Introduction

At the heart of Mid-Berkshire lies Reading, the largest town in the United Kingdom. In previous centuries, Wokingham was a rival market centre, but by the industrial Age, Reading was out in front. Since the early Anglo-Saxon period when the ancient woodland in this area was cut down, however, the surrounding countryside has been part of the county's agricultural breadbasket, with Windsor Forest to the east and the higher grazing land of the Berkshire Downs to the west.

The Anglo-Saxons have left their mark on the area through the names of their early tribal chieftains, Redda, Sunna and Wocca, represented in the place-names of Reading, Sonning and Wokingham. The remains of banks and ditches surrounding Roman Silchester show how their arrival was not welcomed by the local people. However, the chieftains easily made their way into the area down the River Thames. Later, the Vikings were to choose Reading as their base from which to conquer the South of England and they engaged in nationally important armed clashes in the region.

In addition to the Rivers Thames and Kennet, there were soon roads leading west out of London, which for their day were considered major, if badly maintained. It is not surprising therefore to find that the region saw the march past of many armies heading out from the capital. After the Battle of Hastings in 1066, when William the Conqueror's soldiers failed to cross London Bridge in order to take London, they marched west through Mid-Berkshire in search of a Thames crossing controlled by a potential ally. Troops constantly passed through the local area during the Civil War of the 17th century, as Reading lay halfway between the parliamentary headquarters in London and the royalist one in Oxford. The town itself was besieged for some time.

Figure 1: An Old Cottage such as Mary Russell Mitford would have known.

As well as its strategic importance, Reading held other attractions in centuries past. The great abbey with its hand of St James was a huge draw for medieval pilgrims both rich and poor. It seems always to have incorporated royal accommodation, enabling our medieval monarchs to satisfy their spiritual needs only a brief ride by horse or boat from their residence at Windsor Castle. Reading would sometimes be filled to overflowing with the royal entourage and those attached to associated lords. The increase in customers would benefit tradesmen not only in Reading but in all the surrounding villages. The kings even installed royal stud farms at local manors.

The 'turnpiking' of major roads in the area during the 18th century resulted in better quality road surfaces, at the price of a toll. The travel and hospitality industry thrived, with regular coaches travelling out of Reading and Wokingham. The A4 or Bath Road became a key thoroughfare, with places like Twyford experiencing rapid growth.

Local towns in the area became satellites for polite society outside London, where artistic and literary pursuits blossomed. Mid-Berkshire is especially known for the works of the early 19th century author, Mary Russell Mitford, who wrote charming short essays on village life, based on her experiences at Three Mile Cross. Her descriptions conjure up images of a different age, still visible in the villages of today, despite changes in the pace of life:

"The prettiest cottage on our village green ... stands in a corner of the common, where the hedge-rows go curving off into a sort of bay round a clear bright pond, the earliest haunt of the swallow. A deep, woody, green lane, such as Hobbima or Ruydsdael might have painted, a lane that hints of nightingales, forms one boundary of the garden, and a sloping meadow the other: whilst the cottage itself, a low thatched irregular building, backed by a blooming orchard, and covered with honeysuckle and jessamine, looks like the chosen abode of snugness and comfort. And so it is."

From the early 18th century, the building of the Kennet and Avon Canal and later the Railway made Mid-Berkshire and the surrounding countryside a great place to establish industry. The towns had always been centres for the wool trade. Breweries now became particularly popular because of the large amounts of water available from the rivers. H & G Simonds of Reading became one of the largest and best-known in the World. Brickworks were also a staple of the area, the most prominent being S & E Collier of Tilehurst.

Despite the dissolution of the County Council, the Boroughs of Reading and of Wokingham and parts of the District of West Berkshire still form the central portion of the county, which as a whole is represented by the Lord Lieutenant and High Sheriff. Prior to 1844, Mid-Berkshire was much more fragmented. In Norman times, the Earl of Salisbury owned extensive lands in Berkshire and administered them from his central estate at Amesbury in Wiltshire. As a result, in older records, specific areas of the parishes of Wokingham, Hurst (including Twyford), Swallowfield and Shinfield were considered to be in Wiltshire rather than Berkshire. These areas were not even attached to one another and did not cover the whole of each parish. The exact boundaries seem to have changed over time, adding still further to the confusion.

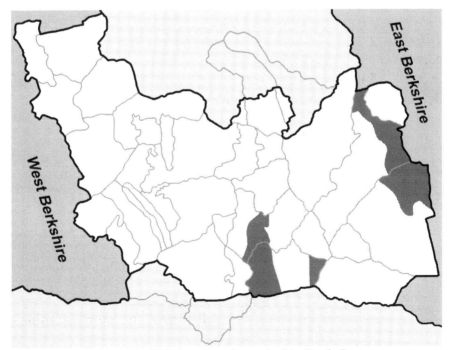

Figure 2: Wiltshire Lands marked in Dark Grey

Aldermaston Wharf

The village of Aldermaston Wharf straddles the border between the parishes of Aldermaston, Beenham and Padworth. Lying mostly in Padworth, this busy wharf adjoining Aldermaston Lock, was largely used by the timber trade. The Lock was built during the cutting of the first section of the Kennet and Avon Canal between 1718 and 1723 by John Hore of Newbury. It was enlarged in the mid-18th century with the addition of the attractive scalloped brick walls. Today there is a café and canal visitors' centre on site.

Figure 3: The Swing Bridge at Aldermaston Wharf

The canal obtained a transportation rival in 1847 when the Berks and Hants Railway (part of the Great Western Railway) came to Aldermaston Wharf. The station has always been simply called Aldermaston Station, although it is some way to the north of Aldermaston. The Victorian buildings there were mistakenly demolished in the 1970s due to a mix-up with Alderminster in Warwickshire.

The lock was once known as Brewhouse Lock, as the Aldermaston Brewery stood alongside in the Swan Drive/Kingfisher Close area. The Brewery was founded in 1770 and was run by the Stephens family, who also owned the Mill Lane Brewery and the Stephens, Harris and Stephens' Bank in Reading. The Stephens family pulled out of brewing in the 1830s to concentrate on their more lucrative banking efforts and the Aldermaston Brewery was sold to the Strange family in 1833. The business eventually became named WJ Strange and Sons and operated for nearly a century. After the outbreak of the Second Boer War, the volunteer Imperial Yeomanry was formed to support of the British Army in South Africa. In January 1900, their Berkshire contingent visited Aldermaston Wharf on their ride from Reading to Newbury before deployment. The troopers were entertained with ale, cigars and cigarettes by John Strange at the brewery, who received an address in his honour and great cheers of thanks. After the brewery's eventual demise in 1952, the site became a factory for Sterling Cables but, after 1990, was redeveloped for housing.

The Strange family used to live at Bridge House on the other side of Mill Lane (now part of Alder Bridge School). Both this house and the malthouse next door survive, overlooking the canal. The latter is attached to Malthouse Cottage which, in the 1920s, became the home of Richard Aldington, the First World War poet and friend of TS Eliot and DH Lawrence.

Aldworth

A popular story says that, in ancient times, Aldworth was the home of giants. They used to fight with one another and threw around many of the larger rocks to be found in the Thames Valley and on the Berkshire Downs. However, they were not thought to have dug ditches and the extensive Bronze Age Grim's Ditch, which crosses the Downs and ends in Aldworth and Streatley, is instead named after the chief of the Anglo-Saxon gods, Woden, whose nickname was Grim. It was probably some sort of boundary ditch and bank. Aldworth was first settled by pagan Anglo-Saxons in the Dark Ages and the name means Old Farm. In AD 871, King Alfred's great victory over the Vikings of Reading at the Battle of Ashdown is identified, by some, as having taken place on the prehistoric Ridgeway below Dean's (or Dane's) Bottom and Lowbury Hill, in the north of the parish.

Figure 4: The Four Points Inn at Aldworth

At the time of the Domesday Survey (1086), Aldworth was owned by Theodoric the Goldsmith. A German, he became famous in the reign of Edward the Confessor as the finest gold and silver worker in London, if not the country. His main country residence was at Kennington in Surrey. Later, William the Conqueror was so keen to retain his services, that he gave him several estates, including five in Berkshire where there was good woodland for smelting the metal. Aldworth manor covered two 'hides' (perhaps 250 acres – although it had previously been five hides) and was worked by five plough-teams (each with four oxen). The village included ten serfs and villeins (tenant farmers), as well as four bordars (cottage dwellers) and their families. There was woodland enough for ten pigs to feed there and the whole was valued at £5.

Figure 5: Sir Nicholas de la Beche and other Aldworth Giants

Aldworth is a small and rather charming village with its late Victorian well-house over the (now sealed) 370ft deep well at the centre. Adjoining this is the busy Bell Inn, apparently named from a badge of the De Ferrers family who were lords of the manor in the 14th and 15th centuries. The present pub is contemporary with them and of cruck construction. The original structure was built to serve travellers on the Ridgeway and was popular with sheep drovers attending the famous East Ilsley Sheep Fair. However, today the parking around it can be quite cramped. The beautiful rose-covered thatch of the Four Points Inn, just south of the village is much easier to access.

The main manor house of Aldworth stood next to the church but tended to be owned by absentee landlords like the De Ferrers. Village life was therefore dominated by the lords of the lesser manor centred on La Beche Castle. This small fortified manor house stood on the site of De la Beche Farm and was first crenellated in 1338. It took its name from the De la Beche family who lived there when not exerting their influence at the Royal Court. They were said to be descended from the ancient giants, for several of them towered above their medieval contemporaries. Sir Philip De la Beche fell from grace for supporting the Earl of Lancaster in his rebellion against King Edward II. His son, Edmund, later rescued other adherents locked up in Wallingford Castle, despite being a man of the cloth. His brother, Sir Nicholas, was close to King Edward III and was tutor to the Black Prince and his siblings. Perhaps some of the royal children even visited Aldworth. Nicholas, however, mostly served as a soldier in campaigns during the Hundred Years' War in France and Brittany. The family are all buried in the parish church. Their memorials, known as the 'Aldworth Giants', constitute the largest collection of medieval effigial monuments to one family in an English parish church. The Earl of Leicester is said to have ridden down from Cornbury Park (Oxfordshire) to show them to Queen Elizabeth I. Nine effigies survive, three of which are nicknamed John Long, John Strong and John Neverafraid. There is said to have been a tenth, called John Everafraid, under the, now blocked, arch on the outside wall to the right of the porch. He is said to have sold his soul to the Devil in return for earthly riches. His soul would be taken wherever he was buried inside or outside the church. So, John conspired to cheat the Devil by being buried under the church wall, below the arch. The De la Beche estates eventually passed to the Langfords who moved their chief seat to Bradfield Place. La Beche Castle was left to decay and, by the time of the Civil War, was in ruins. Only traces of the old moat survive today.

A few years before the Civil War, in July 1607, the eccentric inventor, William Bush, passed through Aldworth on his way from Lambourn to Streatley. He was travelling across the Berkshire Downs in a wheeled ship as part of his attempt to travel by air, land and water in the same vessel. The air part had already been completed from the tower of Lambourn Church. Aldworth was part of the land section and he later planned to sail on the Thames. It must have been an extraordinary sight. Other visitors to and residents of Aldworth have included several members of literary society: the novelist, Richard Graves, was vicar in the 18th century; the poet, Laurence Binyon from Westridge Green, and the in-laws of Alfred, Lord Tennyson are both buried in the churchyard. Tennyson's official title was Baron Tennyson of Aldworth. Nearby stands the once famous 1,000-year-old Aldworth Yew, under which priests preached before the church was built. It still clings to life despite being much reduced in size by a huge storm in 1976.

Arborfield

Excavations on the site of the old Whitehall Brick and Tile Works – in what is now the Tyler Drive area of Arborfield Green – have revealed that this area was the site of a small Iron Age farmstead and metalworking community. Low-grade locally-dug bog iron ore was being smelted with charcoal in domed furnaces to produce blooms of the metal. These could eventually be processed into the tools and weapons from which the period takes its name. Occupation continued into Roman times when the industrious locals also turned to pottery production.

However, Arborfield is essentially an Anglo-Saxon village, the name being originally Edburgefeld meaning Edburga's Field. Edburga was quite a widespread Anglo-Saxon lady's name. The best known of such individuals locally were St Edburga of Winchester and St Edburga of Bicester. The 'field' was one of several areas of open land lying in a band across Mid-Berkshire and marking the western boundary of Windsor Forest. It was originally part of the huge parish of Sonning and as such was owned by the Bishop of Salisbury. The old mill pool supplied him with eels for his dining table. Sadly, the picturesque castellated mill is long gone. It stood on the Loddon, next to Hall Farm and the old manor house and church, both of which have also been demolished, though a small ruin of the church survives.

Figure 6: William Standen and his home, Arborfield Hall

The first building on this site was a small 13th century wooden chapel-of-ease to the mother-church at Sonning. The replacement stone building, erected about 1300, is at the core of what stands today. In the mid-19th century, its roof timbers were judged unsafe and a new church was built nearer the village in 1863. For many years, the north aisle remained roofed to house the church's many monuments. Chief of these is the fine renaissance effigial tomb chest to William Standen (died 1637), his wife and his wife's grand-nephew, the young son of the regicide, Nicholas Love. Thankfully this was moved to the new church in 1939 before too much damage was incurred.

William Standen was almost certainly the builder of the old manor house known as Arborfield Hall, described by Mary Russell Mitford (of Three Mile Cross) in the 1820s as the "Old House of Aberleigh" in her classic work, 'Our Village'. A once fine Jacobean mansion with Dutch-gabled wings, it was by then in a dilapidated state, open to the elements on one side. It is said to have had an entrance hall big enough to drive a carriage through. The last of the Standen line, Edward – the man who fell for Molly (or Sally) Mogg, the barmaid of literary fame from the Rose in Wokingham – died without children in 1730.

George Dawson eventually took on the hall but having estates in both Berkshire and Yorkshire was swamped with debts. Though he loved Arborfield, in a rash moment in the 1820s, he declared "Pull it down" and his steward eagerly obliged. Dawson's son built a replacement many-gabled Neo-Tudor building and lived in a cottage (now Arborfield Grange) on the estate while the work was in progress. However, it was still unfinished when he sold it to Sir John Conroy, the Controller of the Household of HRH the Duchess of Kent and her daughter, Princess Victoria. When Victoria came to the Throne in 1837, Conroy, whom she despised, was banished to Arborfield. The house was finally demolished, in 1956, after being wrecked by both British and American forces during the Second World War.

All these buildings stood at or near the Church Lane/Greensward Lane junction on the Reading Road. This is officially the village of Arborfield: although the more substantial settlement is Arborfield Cross, slightly to the east. The Cross itself, with the village war memorial, has been a roundabout since 2004. The village pond once stood before White's Farm in the angle between the Reading Road and Sindlesham Road. It is said that the ghost of a local 18th century witch used to emerge from the pond to terrorise the village until bound under a large slab at its bottom by seven priests.

Figure 7: The old Swan Inn at Arborfield before closure

Across the road stands one of three well-known and historic pubs in the parish. The Bull Inn – once a stop-over for Queen Victoria – is named after the Bullock family who were lords of the manor for several centuries before the Standens. In the early 16th century, Thomas Bullock was Gentleman Usher Extraordinary to

King Henry VIII. The old Swan, further into the village, is now sadly closed despite having been the more picturesque, especially when lit up at Christmas. It was built in 1661 and is supposed to have played host to King George III, presumably whilst on a hunting expedition. The old Bramshill Hunt, on the edge of the former garrison, was the traditional meeting place of this hunting party from nearby Eversley in Hampshire.

Arborfield Garrison started life as a remount depot for horses in 1904 and operated throughout the First World War, and afterwards, until 1937. It later became an Army Technical School and the headquarters and training centre for the Royal Electrical and Mechanical Engineers (REME). During the Second World War, part of the Royal Artillery was based there just prior to D-Day and it was subsequently used for the assembly of allied troops bound for Europe. The Garrison closed in 2015 and is now a housing development called Arborfield Green, despite most of the site being in Barkham parish.

Ashampstead

There is some evidence of Neolithic, Mesolithic and Bronze Age occupation in Ashampstead, including a Grim's Ditch in Bowyer's Copse. The naming of this feature dates from the Anglo-Saxon period as it was the nickname of their chief god, Woden. It was late in this period that a proper settlement began to develop in the parish. This is when the manors of Ashampstead in the west and Hartridge in the east seem to have been established. It is thought likely that William the Conqueror's army marched this way en route for Wallingford, where they were to cross the Thames before seizing London. The army would have needed feeding and seem to have devastated the local farmland so that its value was considerably reduced by the time of the Domesday Survey in 1086.

Figure 8: The old post office at Ashampstead

Hartridge manor is certainly found in the Domesday Book and Ashampstead may possibly be the otherwise unidentified manor of Ashdon also found there. All these names are Anglo-Saxon. Ashdon means Ash Tree covered Hill, being replaced by Ashampstead, meaning Ash Tree covered Homestead, as the settlement grew. Hartridge means Stag Ridge and, interestingly, Ashampstead and Burnt Hill Commons, in the south of the parish, were converted into a deer park in the early 13th century. They had earlier been dedicated to woodland used for pasture, with a late 12th century pottery kiln supporting a thriving pottery industry. The bank and ditch for the park pale has been identified and there was also a pond, as well as two lodges for the parker. This may have been the park attached to Bradfield manor established by Roger de Somery in 1240. It seems to have gone out of use in the mid-16th century when it was turned to common grazing land with gates at each entry point. Any stray animals were rounded up and taken to the pound on Pike's Hill.

Ashampstead was the original home of the well-known Tilehurst and Reading family of Zinzan. Alessandro Zinzano is believed to have been a master horseman who came over to the court of King Henry VIII from Italian governed Albania in the 1540s. His sons and grandsons often competed in the jousts and other royal entertainments. Alessandro may have attached himself to the retinue of Sir John Norreys from nearby Yattendon Castle, whose illegitimate daughter he later married. It was Sir John who gave them their Ashampstead estate, although its exact location is not clear.

The parish commons were slowly enclosed from about 1680. When use of the commonland declined in the late 19th century, local landowners tried to turn it into more attractive parkland with exotic trees like Wellingtonias and Monkey Puzzles. The villagers resisted but they were ultimately unsuccessful as the parker kept a special pocket down his trouser leg from which to surreptitiously plant a sapling unnoticed. Many of his trees can still be seen today. During the Second World War, the commons were used as concealed convoy camps with semi-permanent buildings for the army heading to the south coast for D-Day. In 1971, what remained of the commons was handed over to the Yattendon Estate. Locals may still collect firewood and leaf-mould but no longer have grazing rights.

The church at Ashampstead was built in the late 12th century on the site of an ancient yew tree whose stump can still be seen in the church wall. It was a chapel-of-ease to Basildon and did not become formally detached with its own parish until 1847. A hundred years after it was built, the interior walls were covered in beautiful wall paintings possibly by Benedictine monks from Reading Abbey. These colourful pictures were used by the priest to help instruct the congregation in many different Bible stories, including the Annunciation, the Visitation, the Nativity and the appearance of Gabriel to the Shepherds. Over the chancel arch is depicted Christ and the Apostles, along with souls being dragged down to Hell on one side and admitted to Heaven on the other. After the Reformation, the Puritans of Edward VI's reign did not approve of this iconography and had them all plastered over. However, they were rediscovered by the Reverend Vyvyan Moyle when some of this plaster fell off during a storm in 1886. Moyle was an interesting character who was vicar between serving time for two convictions for fraud. He used his discovery to promote the church and then steal donations meant for the upkeep of its fabric.

Figure 9: The Medieval Wall Paintings in Ashampstead Church

Next door, the 13th century cruck-framed St Clement's Cottage, hidden behind a 17th century façade, was reputedly built as a 'hospitium' (or hostel) for medieval travellers heading from

Reading to Oxford. It retains 16th century chevron wall paintings inside and a 300ft deep well outside. The old Fleece and Feathers pub (aka the New Inn, but now a private house) in Bottom Road was another stopping point in the village, this time for drovers bringing sheep to market in Reading. Anti-mechanisation 'Swing' rioters also drank there when marching from Yattendon to Basildon in November 1830, pressing local labourers to join them and smashing farm machines as they went. They were eventually stopped by troopers from Reading and scattered when eleven of the party were arrested.

The local witches of Ashampstead are also said to have travelled to Basildon, for meetings with their sister coven there. At a certain get-together, an argument broke out between the two groups. They came to blows and the Ashampstead ladies were chased home amongst a barrage of spells. Immediately they crossed the parish boundary, however, their powers grew stronger. Their leading warlock thrust his staff into the ground and stopped the pursuers in their tracks. The staff grew into a great elm tree which stood (until blown down) at Witch Elm Bottom, the junction of Long Lane and Bottom Road.

Ashridge Wood

Ashridge Wood, on the Forest Road, is the nearest to a village that developed in Ashridge manor. It became the northern part of Wokingham Without parish in 1894 and has since been transferred to Hurst. In the late 13th century, the Earl of Lincoln wanted to cut down the trees and turn the land over to agriculture, but an inquest decided that this was the King's hunting route between the parks of the Bishops of Winchester (at Billingbear) and Salisbury (at Bearwood) and so needed to be kept as woodland. In 1299, the Carmelite Friars from London were allowed to take a number of oaks from Ashridge Wood, presumably for building work at their priory; and, the following century, it was turned into a proper deer park.

The old Forest Road was made into a turnpike toll road in 1770 through subscriptions from the local gentry whose land it passed through. Their names are recorded (though now unreadable) on a large contemporary oval monument near the present termination of the road created by the building of the M4. This used to stand at the Binfield end, in the grounds of Marchfield House, and heading the list of contributors was the Countess of Leicester who lived there. She was the sister of Countess Gower from Bill Hill.

Figure 10: The Warren House Inn at Ashridge Wood

The building now called Ashridge Manor (formerly Ashridgewood House) was rented by Sir Arthur Sullivan, of the Gilbert and Sullivan operatic writing partnership, in the Summer of 1899. Whilst there, he completed his last comic opera, The Rose of Persia, written with Basil Hood. During the First World War, it was the home of Frederick de Vere Allfrey, who had grown up at Stanbury Park in Spencers Wood. His only son and heir, Frederick de Vere Bruce Allfrey, was killed in Europe's last lance-on-lance battle in 1914. He went to the aid of a friend who had been unseated in the charge but was shot dead whilst trying to remove a broken lance from his comrade's leg.

At the eastern end of Forest Road, the Warren Inn has a core dating back to the 1680s when it was a farm called the Warren House. The site probably started out as the home of the warrener who looked after the rabbits for the medieval manor of Ashridge. The house appears to have become a pub in the 1770s and, during the Regency period, it was well-known for the May Day Revels held there, including sack races, cudgel fights and shooting at cheese-rounds.

At the western end of the road stands Bill Hill, a fine blue and red brick house built for Lord Blundell in 1723 to replace an old hunting lodge. A decade later, it was sold to Lady Harold who subsequently married Earl Gower. Although the Countess survived into her 80s, she ultimately met a terrible death from burns when her clothes accidentally caught fire. Her son, Rear-Admiral Leveson-Gower, then had to take his elder half-brother, from the Earl's first marriage, to court in order to prove that Lady Gower had owned Bill Hill in her own right and it therefore belonged to him. In the 1790s, the house was rented out to the young Marquess of Blandford (later 5th Duke of Marlborough). He was a party animal, spendthrift and collector who started a fine assemblage of unusual and exotic plants at Bill Hill before moving on to Whiteknights in Earley. His eldest son, the future 6th Duke, was born at Bill Hill in 1793.

Barkham and Langley Common

Barkham is an Anglo-Saxon word meaning Birch Tree Home. It is recorded in a charter of AD 952 as having been given by King

Edred to his thane, Aelfwine, who passed it on to Abingdon Abbey. In the 1240s, the manor was owned by a family who took their name from the place. They probably built the moat at Church Cottages to surround their manor house next to the church. However, in 1248, John de Barkham conspired with a certain John de Bendinges of Winchfield (Hampshire) to have a band of robbers attack two Brabant merchants in Alton Woods (also in Hampshire). They relieved them of 200 marks (£133-3s-4d). The two Johns were arrested soon afterwards and tried in Reading. John de Barkham managed to escape to Scotland, but he was still outlawed and Barkham manor was confiscated by the King. The manor's income helped to pay for the rebuilding of Windsor Castle.

Figure 11: The Bull at Barkham named after the Bullock Family

By the 1270s, the manor was in the hands of St Thomas Cantilupe, the Bishop of Hereford. He was Chancellor of England and may have dropped in at Barkham on his journeys to see the King in London. His main home in the area, however, was in Earley and he soon sold Barkham to his valet, William Neville (of a different family from the Nevilles of Bisham and Billingbear). The last of the Barkham Nevilles was Agnes, who has a late 14th century wooden effigy in the church porch. She had either a saintly or witch-like reputation in the village, depending on who you spoke to. Having married Gilbert Bullock, Agnes brought the manor to this important Arborfield family, uniting the two manors for several centuries. It was during their ownership, in the 1350s, that Barkham appears to have become some sort of depot for the transportation of timber from Windsor Forest to Westminster Abbey, where it was used in the rebuilding of the choir roof. The Bullocks built themselves a late 15th century hall house, called Barkham Court, which remains at the core of Church Cottages. It may have been used as an overflow home for their large family based at Arborfield. The family name is also reflected in the name of the Bull pub.

Figure 12: Agnes Neville at Barkham Church

The Bullocks were not the only prominent family in the medieval parish. The Kingsmills were a well-known local family who, after the Dissolution of the Monasteries, lived at Sydmonton Court in North Hampshire. However, their original home was Langley Pond Farm – sometimes erroneously called Langley Manor – at Langley Common. Barkham is also often quoted as being the home of the ancestors of President George Washington's mother, Mary Ball. There was certainly a well-to-do family of Ball living in Barkham from at least the late 15th century until well into the mid-17th century. The most famous member was William Ball, a well-known roundhead lawyer who wrote a number of political pamphlets. He was a relative of the Standens of Arborfield Hall. However, he was not the man who left for Virginia in 1650 and eventually became great grandfather of the famous Mary Ball. The Barkham man died in Holborn in 1647 with a family of at least seven. The eldest, William, eventually returned to Berkshire and settled in Bracknell.

There was at least a chapel in Barkham from the 1220s, although a formal parish church may not have been built until the 1310s. By 1689, however, repairs were required for "the wind and weather did beat in through" the roof and the bell-ringers were often "forced to let go the ropes and run out from under the ... steeple for fear of its falling". The old church was totally rebuilt in 1860-1 by John Berry Clacy, the man who laid out the Forbury Gardens in Reading. He was from an old Barkham family and chose to retain the elegant Louis XVI-style font in which his ancestors had been baptised for many years. The loss of the medieval building was much bemoaned by Peter Hempson Ditchfield, the historian, archaeologist and prolific writer, who was Rector of Barkham some 25 years later. However, Clacy's church is a beautiful example of early medieval rustic Gothic revival architecture.

Ditchfield is buried in the churchyard, near the southern nave wall, not far from his predecessor, David Davies. Davies had been a well-known social reformer and slavery abolitionist in Regency times. A great advocate for a minimum wage, he had witnessed the mistreatment of slaves at close hand when working in Barbados before arriving in Barkham to administer to the local population, 80% of whom were barely surviving on poor relief. The beautiful and famous churchyard cedar tree, under which Ditchfield and Davies were interred, had been planted by Davies' friend, the lady of the manor, Mrs Leveson-Gower, in 1788. Unfortunately, it succumbed to honey fungus disease in 1996.

Historically, the village of Barkham was the ribbon development along Barkham Street from Barkham Square and the church up to the Bull Inn, Spark's Farm and Barkham Manor. Modern Barkham, around the post office, developed from a small hamlet on Coppid Hill called Dowle's Barn in Wokingham parish. The name survives in Dole's Farm House and Doles Lane on whose corner it sits (and also at Dowles Green in Keep Hatch). The settlement started out around the roundabout at the bottom of Bearwood Road and developed northwards from the 1920s.

Battle

Battle is the Oxford Road area of Reading, adjoining the town centre mostly west of the railway (where Reading West Station opened in 1906). It is best known through the names of Battle School, Battle Library and previously the Battle Hospital. This was a manor created just after the Norman Conquest from the lands of the old Anglo-Saxon nunnery based at what became St

Mary's Church. The last abbess held it before 1066, although it is likely that she was an abbess in name only as the nunnery had been destroyed by the Vikings forty years earlier. William the Conqueror gave this western side of Reading to his new foundation of Battle Abbey which had been built on the site of the Battle of Hastings in East Sussex between 1070 and 1094 – hence the name. The Abbot's estate was centred on a monastic grange at Battle Farm, on the site of Barnwood Close. In later years, part of the old Portman Brook there was used as an ornamental canal and a lake created. The tree-lined drive joined it to the Oxford Road approximately at the Beresford Road junction, with an entrance lodge on the western side.

Figure 13: The First World War Hospital at Battle

Long after the Dissolution of the Monasteries, Queen Elizabeth I granted the lease of the Reading Battle estates to her Treasurer of the Royal Household, Sir Francis Knollys (the 'Great Knollys'). She also let him live at Abbey House, her palace in the ruins of Reading Abbey, although he did own Caversham Park and Greys

Court (in Rotherfield Greys) as well. Battle became the main land-holding of his sixth son, also Sir Francis, who spent his youth as a privateer (or pirate) alongside Sir Francis Drake but later became "the ancientest Parliament man in England," having been MP for Oxford, Berkshire and Reading almost continuously for over 75 years. The family later bought the estates but, after they had to give up Abbey House, they moved to Lower Winchendon (Buckinghamshire), Thame (Oxfordshire) and then to Fern Hill Park in Winkfield. When they died out in 1775, there was a nationwide search for an heir. After many claimants came forward, the Battle lands were eventually allocated to an extremely distant cousin who then changed his name from Weldale to Knollys. The names were later used for streets built on the eastern part of the estate.

The old hospital, built just west of the old farm in 1866-67, began life as the Reading Union Workhouse, where the destitute were given board and lodging in return for work. It consisted of receiving blocks, an infirmary and a fever block. Later additions included vagrant accommodation built in 1892. During the First World War, it was requisitioned as a War Hospital and became Battle Hospital in 1929. It closed in 2005 and the buildings were replaced by a large supermarket and the Battle Place housing estate, accessed via the attractive old entrance lodges.

This area was once a leafy fashionable region of Regency Reading lined with several villas belonging to the local gentry. Opposite the workhouse was the estate of Elm Lodge, a large country house built in 1834 for George Higgs, the former Reading Mayor and owner of the Katesgrove Tannery. He was the nephew of the founders of the Simonds' Bank in Reading. The house still survives today as offices called Marsh Lodge in

Wilton Road. From 1902, it was the St Andrew's Home for Waifs and Strays, accommodating 40 boys and, from 1948, girls as well. It closed in 1975. The old Reading Football Ground was built in the surrounding park in 1896 – hence its name, 'Elm Park'. The club moved to the Madejski Stadium in 1998. Just east of the railway bridge was another villa, Oxford Lodge, which also survives, though much altered and hidden behind a motorcycle shop. From Gower Street, immediately opposite, you can still see the top of the gabled wings above and behind the shop.

Figure 14: St Andrew's Home for Waifs and Strays in Wilton Road

One of the earliest of these small estates belonged to the Zinzan family who are remembered through the naming of Zinzan Street. Originally well-known as exceptional sporting horsemen, from Italian-ruled Albania, they regularly performed at the Royal Court. Later, they settled down at Calcot Park. However, when this was sold in 1686, they purchased a small estate off the Oxford Road. The mansion stood between Zinzan Street and Waylen Street, about a third of the way along. The last of the family line was a well-known Reading doctor who inherited

Beenham House with his first wife. His second wife lived off the Oxford Road until 1811 and Zinzan Street was built over her land in 1852.

Figure 15: Butler and Sons of Chatham Street

In 1896, Kensington Road, on the edge of Elm Park, was the home of the notorious child-murderer, Amelia 'Annie' Dyer. She had apparently moved to Lower Caversham and then Reading to escape an abusive husband and began to make her living by taking in illegitimate children, whom their mothers wished to hide from a judgemental society. Not long afterwards, the body of a baby girl was found floating in the Thames. Bizarrely, she was wrapped in brown paper marked with Dyer's address in Lower Caversham. However, because Dyer had moved, it took some time to track her down. In the meantime, two more little bodies appeared in the river. She was eventually arrested, tried and hanged at Newgate for the murder of seven children. There were probably at least four others, perhaps many more.

Fifty years earlier, in the early 1840s, more crime had been suspected in the area when the 'Father of Photography', William Fox-Talbot, set up the first mass production photographic laboratory in Russell Terrace. A plaque on his house records this. He was producing the first book of photos, but the locals thought his assistants were forgers. More extensive industries still remembered in the area range from alcohol to pump production. The Butler (previously the Baker's Arms) in Chatham Street survives today as an attractive old public house despite the surrounding terrace houses that it once served having completely disappeared. It started life as a simple 'beer-shop' in 1830 when Charles Butler and Sons started business there. Until 1976 the pub and adjoining off-licence were popular for their 'Reading Abbey' brand of wines and spirits, all bottled on the premises; but especially fondly remembered is their Reading Abbey Mountain Wine.

Before 1986, the Reading Retail Park, in the angle between the Oxford Road and Norcot Road, was the Nine Elms Iron Works (named from an earlier location in London), home of the Pulsometer Engineering Co from 1901 and called Sigmund Pulsometer Pumps (SPP) after 1961. As the name suggests, they were particularly well-known for their pistonless pumps and were, at one time, one of the largest pump manufacturers in Europe. Next door, on the site of Branagh Court, was the Berkshire Printworks, owned by the Brooke family of Brooke Bond Tea, which moved there from King's Road in 1932. The Brooke Bond packaging, including their famous tea cards, was printed there for many years. Sadly, the printworks closed in 2002.

The Brock Barracks, which are just over the old Tilehurst border, were built in the late 1870s in the 'Fortress Gothic Revival' style as the headquarters of the Royal Berkshire Regiment. They were named after Major-General Sir Isaac Brock KB who defended Canada against the Americans during the Napoleonic Wars. Its cenotaph was made by Sir Edwin Lutyens (whose grandparents lived at Southcote House). It is an exact replica (reduced in size) of his famous cenotaph that stands at the heart of Whitehall. Since the regiment's successor ceased its connection with the barracks in 1982, it is now used as a territorial army base.

Bean Oak

Bean Oak is one of the most easterly suburbs of Wokingham, named after the old farm whose fields the estate was built upon. The farmhouse, dating from the late 18th century, stands opposite the northern end of Plough Lane. It was also an area of brickmaking. Thomas May of Bean Oak Farm was making bricks as early as the 1860s and the Victoria Brick and Tile Co was operating behind the old Plough Inn on the east side of Plough Lane during the First World War.

The first hamlet to develop in the area was Froghall Green, on the London Road, named after a large country house known as Frog Hall. This, in turn, was named from the amphibians in this boggy region of the town. The house was converted into a pub in the 1760s and its remains are believed to be incorporated into the present Three Frogs. No doubt, this is why the pub is so named, despite bizarre tales concerning three Napoleonic prisoners of war or a Belgian landlord serving up frogs' legs to his customers. The present house (now flats) called Frog Hall is a Queen Anne building just to the south. Its original name is unclear but, after 1815, it certainly became known as Waterloo Lodge. In the 1840s, it was bought by John Walter II of Bearwood, proprietor of the Times Newspaper. His son, John Walter III, lived there with his family. A later owner, Vaughan Stokes, is erroneously said to have drowned himself in the large fishpond there. Another local pub, the old Plough at Bean Oak, now a fish restaurant, was built in 1924 on the other side of Plough Lane from its predecessor. For sixty years through the late 19th century it had been run by the Rance family who gave their name to Rances' Lane.

Figure 16: The Three Frogs at Frog Green

In November 1864, Mrs Ann Rance, landlady of the old Plough, was one of the many witnesses called to the Court of Common Pleas in London to help resolve the case of a huge "Clerical Scandal at Bracknell" which had been centred around Pocket (or Pocock) Copse on Bean Oak Farm. The Perpetual Curate (or Vicar) of Bracknell, the married Reverend Herbert Taylor Howes, had had his services boycotted and was made the target of 'rough music' from his parishioners (the banging of pots and pans to show disapproval of adulterers or wife-beaters). He brought a case of slander against Leonard Barber, the farmer at Bean Oak, who he believed had spread rumours about the nature of Howes' relationship with Miss Mary Beechey, the daughter of a Wokingham schoolmaster. Howes was 34 and the lady was 30. Barber had discovered the couple trespassing on his land, apparently lying partially undressed together, embracing and kissing (if not more), but Howes claimed they were doing no such thing. He had bumped into Miss Beechey on his way into Wokingham but decided to leave his horse at the old Plough and, instead, escort her to Bracknell via a shortcut to Binfield across the fields north-west of the London Road. The two promptly got lost and Miss Beechey took off her coat to sit down while Reverend Howes surveyed the surrounding landscape. It was at this point that Farmer Barber had arrived and evicted them from his land. Several witnesses appeared to confirm that they had often seen the couple surreptitiously disappearing into the local woods together. However, the jury were unable to come to a verdict. The case was dismissed and Barber was forced to pay all legal costs, amounting to £250 (about £15,000 today). It seems the local people disliked the curate so much that they collected enough money from the local gentry, including the Marquess of Downshire, to pay off most, if not all, of the debt. Howes was moved on to St Alban's Church in Holborn.

Beech Hill

It is not known whether there were any Romans resident in Beech Hill, but they would certainly have passed through, along the Camlet Way between St Albans and Silchester. It joined the Devil's Highway at Fair Cross on the southern border of the parish. Perhaps travellers would have stopped at the 'Trunk Well', immediately north-west of the present village, to refresh themselves. This may have been named by the Anglo-Saxons as the Vigorous Spring, although, if the first element is the Celtic for 'face', it might suggest it was decorated with the sculpture of an ancient god. Trunkwell House stands near the site today. In Tudor times, the manor house was the home of a branch of the widespread Noyes family from around Andover (Hampshire) who later lived at Southcote Lodge. When the diarist John Evelyn's friend, Henri le Coq, lived at Trunkwell, he found the place so delightful that he often referred to it as 'Tranquille'. He was a French Huguenot refugee whose father had fought with William III's Dutchmen against James II's Irish troops at the Battle of Broad Street (in Reading). When he was naturalized in 1698, he took the name St Leger instead, as this was his family estate near Poitiers. The present building at Trunkwell was built as the Trunkwell Farm House in 1878 and renamed when the adjoining manor house was demolished in 1898.

Figure 17: Margery de la Beche kidnapped from Beaumys Castle

Beech Hill appears to be a Norman name given to the place by the De la Beche family from Aldworth, although the village sign incorrectly displays the arms of De la Beche of Wokingham, a different family. The residents of La Beche Castle in Aldworth had a secondary home at Beaumys Castle on the edge of Beech Hill. All that remains of it today is a dry and overgrown moat next to the A33 just over the border in Swallowfield parish. It was once fed by the River Loddon. The original 13th century house there was owned by Geoffrey Le Despenser from Martley in Worcestershire. The moat was dug for his nephew, Hugh Le Despenser, the favourite of King Edward II. When disgraced by Queen Isabella in 1322, Hugh fled the court and her lover, Roger Mortimer, raided many Despenser lands including Beaumys.

Figure 18: Beech Hill House, home of Henry Lannoy Hunter

Finally, in 1335, the castle came into the hands of the De La Beche family. Sir Nicholas, sometimes erroneously considered to have been Lord De la Beche, was made Constable of the Tower of London and Seneschal (or Governor) of Gascony. He oversaw the education of Edward III's son, the Black Prince, but died childless in 1345. His widow, Margery, remarried twice in short succession and her husbands are believed to have died of the Black Death. It was while staying at Beaumys with Prince Lionel and several other royal children that this widowed lady was abducted by her childhood sweetheart, Sir John Dalton. He broke in with sixty-four Berkshire and Lincolnshire squires and made off with Margery to Scotland. It is suggested they were actually lovers and had arranged the abduction together for the sake of appearances.

Adjoining this stronghold, on the Beech Hill side of the border, lived a hermit to whom the lords of Beaumys were probably patrons. In 1170, the old hermitage was given to Vallemont Abbey in Normandy and they established a small priory there. It only ever housed a couple of monks however and seems to have been a simple medieval hall-house with a chapel dedicated to St Leonard. It passed into secular hands in 1399 because of the problems inherent with non-native monasteries. A 1648 house stands on the site, with a contemporary dovecote and granary. It was built by a branch of the Harrison family from Finchampstead and is still known as The Priory. The monastic foundation was always known as Stratfield Saye Priory, a reminder that, until 1866, Beech Hill was the Berkshire part of Stratfield Saye, a parish which, like Stratfield Mortimer, crossed the county boundary. The parish church at Beech Hill was not built until the following year, 1867. Beech Hill House is the other major country house in the parish. It was built in around 1720 for Henry Lannoy Hunter, a Levant Company merchant trading in the Holy Land and the Ottoman Empire. His family lived there for many generations until 1950, but it is now divided into flats.

Beenham

The Anglo-Saxon name for the village means Bean-Growing Home, one of a number of crop-based place-names in the district of West Berkshire. It is sometimes mistakenly given the suffix of

Valence through confusion with Benham Park near Newbury. The main manor seems to have been based at Beenham Grange (aka Beenham Farm, aka Manor Farm) in the south of the parish. It was owned by Reading Abbey from the time of its foundation. The Abbot rented it out to tenant farmers, perhaps to the De Beenhams in the 13th century, certainly later to the Carters who remained there after the Dissolution of the Monasteries and through to the 1730s. Thomas Carter was Sheriff of Berkshire in 1535 and his probable son, William Carter (died 1586), once had an elegant memorial brass in the church.

A second manor based around Beenham House may have first emerged in the 1340s. The old timber gabled house preceding the present one was built by Henry Perkins in the 1590s. He was from the well-known recusant Catholic family of Ufton Court and a nephew of the notorious Lady Marvyn. Stories of a tunnel between Beenham House and Ufton Court were probably based on an escape route out of the extensive cellars through which persecuted Catholic priests could quickly leave unnoticed if the authorities arrived unexpectedly. By the 1650s, however, the Beenham branch of the Perkins family had converted to Anglicanism. In 1703, they sold the house to Sir Charles Hopson, Sir Christopher Wren's master joiner who was responsible for much of the woodwork at St Paul's Cathedral. The present house was built by his granddaughter and her husband, Reverend Doctor Bostock, the Vicar of Windsor (and descendant of an old Abingdon family), in the 1740s and expanded by their son in 1794. It is actually a red-brick house, but has been painted white, leading to the mistaken belief that it was built as a twin to Sulhamstead House, across the valley.

During the Civil War, when the King's army were returning from the Battle of Lostwithiel in October 1644, the parliamentary army marched out from Basingstoke and Reading to meet them at the Second Battle of Newbury. Two days before the battle, Major-General Waller's troops arrived in Beenham and camped on the heath west of the village. Strong local tradition has it that the soldiers kept their horses in Fodderhouse Copse and one of them murdered the barmaid at the Black Horse pub (now 2 Forge Cottages near the Six Bells). The locals later strung him up but the girl's ghost still haunts the area. The army's commander, the Earl of Essex, whose men were encamped at Bradfield Southend, was not well and had to retire to Reading. However, he may have discussed battle strategy at Beenham before he withdrew, including the bold march north around Donnington to outflank the Royalists. They ultimately defeated the King but gained little advantage from the battle.

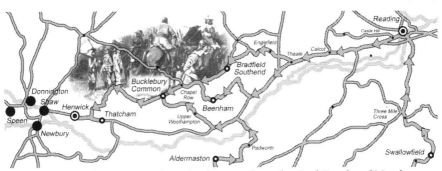

Figure 19: Parliamentary Army's Approach to the 2nd Battle of Newbury

Around the same time, a group of nine parliamentary soldiers, separated from their regiment, half-starved and desperate, attacked Hall Place Farm (aka Hildersley's Farm aka Parker's Farm) in the south of the parish. They broke down the door and terrorised Mrs Richard Hildersley (or Ilsley) and her family who lived there. She managed to send word to her husband, who was presumably out in the fields or in the village. He quickly returned with his neighbours and they chased the soldiers away. This was a younger branch of the prominent Catholic Hildersley family of East Ilsley and the farm (now a private house) retains 16th century elements from their time. In the 18th century, the Iremonger family from Bucklebury moved to the old farm. They are commemorated on some of the most intricately carved and informative of Berkshire's gravestones which stand near the porch in Beenham churchyard. One of them shows Old Father Time and another a trumpeting angel. Their name is also reflected in the incorrectly spelt Ironmongers Copse, just over the border in Bucklebury parish.

Figure 20: Elaborately Carved Gravestones to the Iremonger Family

Beenham Church retains only small details of its 13th century original, for it has been rather prone to fires. It was first burnt down in 1794. After the flames had abated, the villagers collected enough bell metal to considerably reduce the bill for casting six new bells. The Six Bells pub in the village commemorates the event. Luckily, the church's brick tower survived the second disaster in 1859. In the 1730s, the vicar was Thomas Stackhouse, a prominent theologian who wrote 'The History of the Bible from the Beginning of the World until the Coming of Christianity'.

A hundred years later, in 1830, there were ugly scenes at Beenham when 2000 Berkshire machine rioters from Thatcham marched through the village. They gathered new recruits and attacked both Sticks Farm and the Grange, destroying the threshing machines there. After a fight at Brimpton, the following day one of the Beenham men was sent to prison and the other two transported to Australia, despite the vicar pleading for clemency.

Bradfield

The little known holy well of St Andrew behind Bradfield Church was probably first named after Anu, the Celtic goddess of the Countryside. A Roman pottery kiln has been excavated just north of the village at Barn Elms Farm. It was used to make large grey storage jars. However, it was not until the late 7th century that the Broad Field began to develop as a proper settlement. At that time, a thane called Edfrith built a minster on the site of Bradfield Church. A minster was filled with priests who went out preaching in the surrounding countryside, but it probably later became a monastery and the home to a more isolated community of monks. Their early history is thought to have been preserved in documents later attributed to Abingdon Abbey. An old story tells how the last of the Bradfield monks sallied forth to oppose William the Conqueror's army after the Battle of Hastings. This adds weight to the theory that, in order to cross the Thames at Wallingford, his soldiers took the route from Southwark through Bradfield to avoid the narrow Thameside paths. Having failed in its defence against the invader, the monastery was dissolved and the wounded had to retire to Abingdon.

In the mid-14th century, Bradfield was owned by the De La Beche family from La Beche Castle in Aldworth. When the Langford family inherited their estates in 1364, they made Bradfield their principal seat and built a house there called Bradfield Place. A description of the site when granted as a dower house to Joan Langford in 1390 shows that, as well as a large hall house, there was an extensive complex of barns, stables, dovecotes, wells, kitchens and servants' quarters. Small portions still survive at Bradfield College: the ruined 'Tom o'Bedlam's Hole' was part of a small bastion on the boundary wall, walls of the 'great grange' tithe barn are incorporated into the buildings at the corner of Ashampstead Road and Rectory Lane and the so-called 'monastery wall' was part of the old manor house itself.

In Tudor times the manor passed to Thomas Stafford, a cousin of William Stafford who married Queen Anne Boleyn's sister, Mary. During the time of Thomas' grandson, Sir Edward, as the local lord, his maternal uncle, Sir Henry Docwra (later Baron Docwra of Culmore) also lived at Bradfield Place. He had retired from a military career in Ireland where he had made efforts to develop Derry and is sometimes described as its founder. Mary, the wife of Sir Edward Stafford, became sole lady of the manor upon her husband's death in 1623. She subsequently married her fourth husband, Elias Ashmole, Windsor Herald from the College of Arms. He was an antiquarian, best known for leaving his collection of curiosities to Oxford University, which then became the core of the Ashmolean Museum. Ashmole was a favourite at the court of King Charles II but was, nevertheless, hated by Mary's brother, Sir Humphrey Forster of Aldermaston House, and her second son, Humphrey Stafford. Stafford even tried to murder the poor man. Forster was caught up in a prolonged lawsuit with Ashmole which he eventually lost. He later tried to disrupt one of Elias' manorial courts held at Bradfield but was promptly arrested. Mary and Elias Ashmole were eventually hounded out of the village and forced to move to London, at which point their relationship broke down.

Figure 21: Bradfield College including remains of the old tithe barn

During the Commonwealth, the rector was one John Pordage, an astrologer and mystic, who claimed to have experienced the most extraordinary visions of both angels and demons. He supposedly fought a dragon in his driveway for several hours. The authorities eventually removed him from office after a prolonged trial in Speenhamland and Reading. In 1679, the manor was purchased by Sir William Thompson, a rich London merchant who wanted a country estate. Bradfield Place was divided up and partly rented out as a farm, while Thompson built himself a new house (that no longer stands) in the area of Greathouse Wood, alongside the motorway.

In 1740, the right to appoint the Rector of Bradfield was held by Francis Blandy, the Henley solicitor who was infamously murdered by his daughter, Mary. He appointed his brother-in-law, John Stevens, to the post and John's brother, Henry Stevens, purchased the manor in 1755. The Stevens family came from Culham Court in Remenham and retained both manor and church positions together at Bradfield for the next three generations. In 1837, they built a new manor house back on the present college site and, thirteen years later, Reverend Thomas Stevens gave this to his new foundation, St Andrew's College, now Bradfield College. The college has some interesting features, including a chapel with 17th century panelling from the old manor house; a dining hall with stained-glass windows by pre-Raphaelite artist Sir Edward Burne-Jones; and a 1,600-seater Greek theatre based on that at Epidauros and built in a disused chalk pit by the first headmaster in 1890.

Thomas Stevens was also responsible for the rebuilding of the parish church and for the building of the Bradfield Workhouse in Union Road. Perhaps not surprisingly, he finally went bankrupt in 1881. Stephen Wilson of Bradfield Hall at Rotten Row had built the Bradfield Poor House (now the almshouses in Marriners Lane) in 1810. Stevens' workhouse that superseded this in 1835 was a large complex, built in a Y-shape, spreading back from an entrance block at its base. 250 inmates, from across some 29 local parishes, could be housed in separated male and female accommodation. If the poor could not support themselves, they were now obliged to move to the workhouse and, if able bodied, work for their keep. Bradfield also had a 'school of industry' where 111 children were engaged in needlework and straw plaiting. It later became the Wayland Hospital but, in 1996 all but the entrance block (which was converted to apartments) was demolished and redeveloped as Wayland Close.

Buckhurst and Great Langborough

Figure 22: Buckhurst Lodge now St Anne's Manor, Heelas Family Home

Just south of the Coppid Beech roundabout on the A329(M) at Wokingham stands St Anne's Manor. Originally called Buckhurst House or Lodge, this is the manor house of Buckhurst, a name still prominent today at Buckhurst Meadows and Buckhurst Grove. In Tudor times, it was owned by the Wokingham branch of the widespread Barker family whose memorial brasses may be seen in Sonning Church. It was officially a detached part of Wiltshire until local government reforms in 1844. John Heelas built the present house in the late 19th century, after he moved to what was a mere farmhouse in the early 1840s. Fifty years earlier, his father, William, had set himself up as a linen draper in the town. William Heelas Way is his memorial. John's sons later opened similar premises in Reading that became the Heelas Department Store (now John Lewis). The name Buckhurst changed to St Anne's when the house became a nursing and convalescent home run by the Sisters of Bon Secours in 1939. It was converted into an hotel in the 1970s. The Montague Park housing estate was built over the land of Buckhurst Farm in the mid-2010s.

From the late 19th century, the area slightly further west became a popular site for the building of country villas for the Wokingham gentry, notably Starmead and Mertonford along the Easthampstead Road. Starmead has gone, although the name is reflected in Starmead Drive where it once stood. Mertonford is now flats. It was built for Henry Bilson Blandy in 1896. He was one of the directors of Blandy and Hawkins' Castle Brewery in Reading. Later, in 1920, the house was purchased by Eric Simonds, director of the rival H & G Simonds' Seven Bridges Brewery.

St Crispin's School was built on farmland immediately to the west of the Buckhurst estate between 1951 and 1953. It is a pioneering piece of architecture. As the post-war baby boom began to put pressure on the government to build more schools while reducing costs, prefabricated modular buildings were seen as the way ahead. St Crispin's has a steel frame infilled with concrete panels and a flat roof, the first of many similar designs erected all over the country. As such, it is a Grade II listed building. The dominant four-storey central tower is locally understood to have been built in such a way that it could be easily converted to a hospital in times of national emergency, but evidence of this is sadly lacking. Inside, the structure was decorated with a number of delightful murals depicting the four seasons by Fred Millett. Happily, they were restored in 2011 after having been covered over in the 1970s.

To the south-west of St Crispin's is Great Langborough. This area originally covered some of the common fields of Wokingham, shared by the people since the Norman Conquest by dividing them into strips, each farmed by an individual. They were enclosed and allocated to local landowners in 1817. The name presumably refers to the Long Borough stretching along Peach and Denmark Streets just to the north.

Burghfield

The name Burghfield is Anglo-Saxon for Hill Field. The village is built on the lower slopes of Burghfield Hill, but the name could also refer to a prominent Bronze Age burial barrow rather than a hill, like the one discovered on Burghfield Golf Course.

Figure 23: The Six Bells & Fowler's Grocery Store

From pre-Conquest times, the parish was divided into three manors: Burghfield Regis, Burghfield Abbas and Sheffield. Burghfield Abbas was owned by Reading Abbey. The manor house was at Burghfield Place, which had a medieval moated site north of the present house which was only put up around 1905. The Tudor manor house, however, may have been at Culverlands near Burghfield Common. Burghfield Regis was the main manor. Its manor house, known as Nether Court, stood on the site now occupied by the Old Rectory. In the time of King Edward the Confessor, it was owned by his mother, Queen Emma. It was one of the nine manors which she eventually gave to Winchester Old Minster (or Cathedral), supposedly in thanks for successfully passing through an ordeal by fire. This had proved her innocence when accused of having a torrid affair with the bishop. It was confiscated from the diocese after the Norman Conquest and came into the hands of the Mortimer family. Their eventual heir, King Edward IV, gave the manor its royal title of Regis.

These owners were absentee landlords however and the effective lords of the manors were their under-tenants. These were the family of Thomas de Burghfield who proudly took his name from the village sometime before 1175. Sir Roger de Burghfield of Burghfield Regis was the most prominent member of the family. A Knight of the Shire (Member of Parliament) for Berkshire in 1301, he was long remembered as a patron of Burghfield Bridge. However, he is best known locally for his superb wooden effigy displayed in the parish church. This was, unfortunately, stolen in 1978, but was later recognised in a Belgian antiques' market and repurchased for £10,000 raised by public subscription.

Burghfield Parish Church was entirely rebuilt by local architect, John Berry Clacy, in 1843 in the most extraordinary Romanesque style, although it appears to have something of the Italian Renaissance about it too. The old building was rather attractive, with a stepped wooden tower. It is featured in one of the present building's stained-glass windows.

Figure 24: Wars of the Roses Hero, the Earl of Salisbury, at Burghfield

There are two further important effigial monuments inside. In the porch are the stone figures of Richard Neville, 5th Earl of Salisbury, and an earlier Montacute Countess of Salisbury (it is difficult to tell which, as several died around the same time). They are somewhat past their best but you can easily imagine their original magnificence, for the painted colours of the Earl's emblazoned tabard can still be clearly seen if you get down on the floor and look underneath. He was the father of the great 'Warwick the Kingmaker' and played his own vital role in the Wars of the Roses before being executed after the Battle of Wakefield in 1460. It is not known why the two effigies are preserved at Burghfield, for these two characters were buried at Bisham Abbey, at the eastern end of the county, and it was there that their monuments must originally have stood. Tradition has it that the effigies were dragged "from Newbury" behind a galloping horse and that the lady turned over en route. Hence her extremely worn state.

Another survival from the old church is the memorial brass to Nicholas Williams (died 1568) and his two wives (though the figure of one has been lost). Sir John Williams, a direct descendant of Iestyn ap Gwrgant the last Prince of Morgannwg (Glamorgan), had married Elizabeth Moore, a considerable Burghfield heiress, around 1495. She was presumably a descendant of Gilbert de la More who had granted some land in Burghfield to Reading Abbey in 1261. Their second son, also John, had risen to be Keeper of the King's Jewels and he purchased Burghfield Abbas after the Dissolution of the Monasteries. He was later made Lord Williams of Thame in Oxfordshire where he was eventually buried. His main residence was nearby Rycote Palace. He may, however, have often stayed at Burghfield because it was closer to London. Williams' sons all predeceased him and his estates were inherited by his eldest daughter, Margery, and her husband, Henry, Lord Norreys of Rycote. It was Henry who granted Burghfield to his wife's cousin, Nicholas, who appears on the brass. The Norreys family and their heirs, the Earls of Abingdon, later rented the manor out to tenants until they sold up around 1803.

For AWE Burghfield see Grazeley; *For Burghfield Bridge see* Pingewood, Burghfield Bridge and Sheffield Bottom

Burghfield Common

Burghfield Common or Heath was the shared grazing ground for the people of Burghfield parish. It sat on the higher ground of Clay Hill, Man Hill and Burghfield Hill, where the Clayhill Brook, the Teg and the Burghfield Brook rise. Burghfield Hill is sometimes known as Hermit's Hill. Records of this name only date back to the 1840s but it could indicate that, in earlier times, a medieval hermit had a small cell in the area and was sustained by the locals.

In the early years of the Civil War, the Common must have seen considerable troop movements, as soldiers headed to and from Burghfield Bridge. By 1644, the bridge had been destroyed but Colonel Gage's 700-strong royalist army still crossed the Common on their return to Oxford in the October after relieving the Siege of Basing House in Hampshire. They had a hundred prisoners with them and probably found the Common a convenient stopping point. In 1872, the Common was certainly the headquarters camp site for the Third Division of the British Army, consisting of several thousand men. Military manoeuvres were taking place across the south of England and people travelled from miles around to view such an exciting spectacle.

Figure 25: Culverlands at Burghfield Common

It was while crossing Burghfield Common on foot, in 1785, that a Farmer Smith from nearby Silchester in Hampshire was held up by a highwayman. The farmer had spent a busy day at Reading Market buying and selling to earn his living. Unwilling to give his goods up to some lazy ruffian, the canny Silchester man attacked the unsuspecting thief and pulled him off his horse. Grabbing the bridle, he at once mounted the beast and rode off, making his trip to market even more profitable than he had hoped.

Burghfield Common was enclosed in 1853 and the common land allotted to various landowners. It consisted of "dark fir forests interspersed with heathery and furze-grown scraps of clearing. At rare intervals there occur[red] a solitary cottage". There were, however, two pubs, the Three Fir Trees and the Rising Sun, with farms around the edge and the Burghfield Brick and Tile Kiln run by Michael Thorn at Benham's Farm. Further dwellings began to be built not long after enclosure, initially at the Reading Road/Mans Hill junction and around the arc of School Lane and Bunce's Lane. One of the more recent expansions, at Great Auclum Place, at the end of the 20th century, covered the site of a large country house of that name. It had been built in the 1930s for Neil Gardiner, a grandson of Alfred Palmer of Huntley and Palmer's Biscuits. Between 1947 and 1973 (and briefly in 1939), this estate was the venue of the Great Auclum National Speed Hill Climb, an important hilly speed trial on the motor sport calendar.

Another fine country house called Culverlands (also once known as Burghfield Hill House) stands on Mans Hill, just to the east of Burghfield Common. The name is an old field name, probably meaning Dove Lands. In the Regency period, it was the English country estate of Sir Gilbert Blane, the Scottish physician who instituted health reforms in the Royal Navy, particularly the introduction of lemon juice to prevent scurvy. His son rented the house to the local curate, Reverend Charles Smith Bird. He was a theological and entomological writer who kept what was then considered "one of the finest cabinets of specimens" of butterflies and moths at Culverlands. The house was remodelled in a stuccoed Italianate style for the Thursby family in 1879. The monkey-puzzle trees on the estate were the first in England to be raised from seed. In the Victorian era, the foundations of an older brick house in an adjoining orchard were thought to have been those of the 'Abbot's House' where the Abbots of Reading Abbey stayed. This was presumably an early manor house for Burghfield Abbas, before it was moved to Burghfield Place near the present day Atomic Weapons Establishment.

Figure 26: HMS Dauntless at Burghfield Common

Hillfields on a northern spur of Burghfield Hill is a large polychromatic villa built in 1862 for Horatio Bland. He was something of an antiquarian collector and, after his death in 1876, his collection was given to the town of Reading and formed the impetus for the establishment of Reading Museum. It afterwards became the home of the Willink family, well known today for the local school and leisure centre named after them. Hillfields is currently the headquarters of the Guide Dogs for the Blind Association.

During the Second World War, a Royal Ordnance explosives filling factory was built on the Grazeley Green-Burghfield border where AWE Burghfield now stands. Huts to accommodate the workers were erected in what is now the Chestnut Drive/Rowan Way/Elm Drive area. After the War, these were converted into an entry training establishment for the Women's Royal Naval Service called HMS Dauntless. It remained in service until 1981, by which time 30,000 women had received basic training there towards becoming a Wren.

Calcot and Horncastle

Calcot is the lower part of old Tilehurst parish, lying down by the Holy Brook and the River Kennet, along the Bath Road to the west of Reading. The original village of Calcot Green was some way south of the road, around Calcot Mill. The area became part of the ecclesiastical parish of Theale in 1832 and the civil parish of Theale in 1894 but now stands within the new parish of Holybrook. It is divided into a number of residential areas: Calcot, Beansheaf Farm, Calcot Row, Calcot Place, Horncastle and Ford's Farm. The name Calcot means Cold Cottage – possibly a stopping point where Anglo-Saxons could keep out of the cold on the road out of Reading. There are also signs of an even older Roman village at Pincent's Manor.

The main Pincent's Manor site dates back to the early 14th century when Edmund Pincent acquired it by swapping land in Sulhamstead with the Abbot of Reading. It later passed to the Sambournes, then the Lords Windsor and the Blagraves, but was always more of a farm than a manor house and none of them ever lived there. The present farmhouse is of 17th century date. The other manor in Calcot was Beansheaf manor, based at the farm of that name that stood in the Blackwater Rise area. It was named after the Beansheaf family who appear as jurors in Reading as early as 1241.

Figure 27: The Berkshire Lady met her future husband in Calcot Woods

Most of the history of Calcot is associated with Calcot Park, the manor house of Tilehurst. In the medieval period, the manor near the church had been a monastic grange, providing agricultural produce to Reading Abbey who also owned Calcot Mill. After the Dissolution of the Monasteries, it was eventually sold to Sir Peter Vanlore, a Dutch banker working in London, who leant a vast fortune to King James I. He probably built the first Tudor mansion at Calcot where he raised a large family. The house later passed to the Zinzans, a family of master-horsemen, who may have altered or rebuilt the house at the end of the 17th century. There is an interesting old story about this mansion which, by the 1690s, had come into the hands of Sir William Kendrick after he sold Whitley Park in order to move further out of town. His eldest daughter and chief heiress was the celebrated 'Berkshire Lady'.

The real name of the gentlewoman who was given this outstanding nickname was Frances Kendrick. She was an extraordinary woman who could ride, hunt, shoot and fence as well as any man. She was also extremely beautiful and her suitors were many. However, she had her sights set on a poor barrister named Benjamin Child. Frances had met him at a party in Reading, but he had taken little notice of her, so she sent him an anonymous letter challenging him to a duel. The confused lawyer arrived at the rendezvous expecting to find some hot-headed dandy. Instead he was faced by a masked lady with a rapier pointing his way. Then came the icing on the cake, for she posed him a question: "Fight or marry me?" After some deliberation, Benjamin decided discretion was the better part of valour and accepted her proposal. He was whisked off to Wargrave, where the two were quickly wed. It wasn't until afterwards, on arrival at Calcot, that Benjamin discovered the identity of his new bride.

Figure 28: The Mary Lyne Almshouses at Horncastle

The two later fell deeply in love and, when Frances died, her husband could not bear to stay at Calcot Park alone. He sold the house to Sir John Blagrave but subsequently found that he could not bear to leave either. Having purchased the house, the Blagraves had to strip the lead from the roof to literally flush him out. However, the weather did so much damage that they were forced to totally rebuild the mansion (1755) as we see it today. The Blagraves lived there until 1929 when the estate was converted into a golf course with the house providing a magnificent club house. It has since been converted to private residential flats, but is still surrounded by the golf course.

Where the name Horncastle came from is something of a mystery. It may have been named after the pub of this name (now a pet supplies shop) which is supposed to have received this nickname as the home of a local family called Horn. Horn's Copse in the area is recorded as early as 1583. The most attractive building in the locality is the mock-Tudor Mary Lyne Almshouses, with lozenge patterned brickwork (now individual homes). They were built in 1851-2 for "six widows without encumbrances or unmarried of 60 years or upwards belonging to the Church of England and of respectable character" from Tilehurst and/or Burghfield. Mary Lyne was an 86-year-old spinster whose leather-dealing father had moved to Reading from Malmesbury in Wiltshire. She was living at Moatlands Farm in Burghfield through the generosity of the widow of her sister's nephew, Reverend William May-Ellis. She obviously wished to make sure that other less fortunate women could find a comfortable place to live.

California

California is the northern part of Finchampstead parish, bordering on Wokingham. Despite what is marked on many modern maps, it is not called Wick Hill. It was originally the very western portion of Windsor Forest called Finchampstead

Bailiwick and consisted mostly of woodland and the heathland of the Long Moor where the monarch hunted red deer. This area is well known for its 'rides' rather than roads. The oldest ones were created by Queen Anne when she became too large to hunt on horseback and needed to ride in her carriage instead. King George III later added more including the famous Nine Mile Ride which starts at the site of the royal buckhounds' kennels at Swinley Lodge, near Forest Park, and terminates at the Park Lane junction by the Robinson Crusoe Park in California.

The name California comes from a brickworks and saw mill established on the Luckley Estate along the Nine Mile Ride in the early 19th century. The name seems to date from after the estate was broken up in 1849, although why 'California' was chosen for this industrial site is unclear. It stood at the junction with Kiln Ride, which was named in its memory, and once had its own railway to take the bricks onto the main line. There seems to have been a small hamlet there in the mid-18th century when the junction just to the north was known as Three Oaks, presumably from a trio of prominent trees.

The largest Bronze Age burial mound in the county is a bell barrow, 100ft in diameter, hidden in the woods down Warren Lane; while Kingsmere, off the Nine Mile Ride, is sometimes said to be a Roman lake. However, both this and Queensmere (previously Silverstock Pond), off the Sandhurst Road, were created in the 1880s as boating lakes for John Walter III of Bearwood House. The beautiful timber-framed house called Queensmere was built overlooking the latter lake in 1926 by George Harry Gascoigne, an important engineer and innovator in the production of reinforced concrete. The framework and brick infill came from a huge old 16th century tithe barn at Billingbear Park in Waltham St Lawrence.

California is best known for its country park. Longmoor Lake in California Country Park used to be a small pond, but it was expanded in the early 1870s when John Walter III had clay dug from it to make 4½ million bricks to build Bearwood House and the associated estate houses in Sindlesham, as well as his Times Newspaper Building in Printing House Square, London. Housing first began to appear in the area when much of the Bearwood Estate was sold off to pay for death duties after the First World War. The cheap land attracted ex-servicemen who set up a number of smallholdings, but rising prices forced many to sell up after only a few years.

Figure 29: California Snake Train and Ballroom

Longmoor Lake was purchased by Alfred Cartlidge who organised mystery coach trips there for Londoners. In 1931, he created the 'California in England' Day Park there which became highly popular with holidaymakers. The large art-deco ballroom, that stood behind the surviving gazebo in the car park, is fondly remembered for its tea room and glass floor (recycled from the Crystal Palace) that lit up in different colours. This was partly used as an aircraft engineering factory during the Second World War, whilst also holding entertainments for local servicemen. Chalets were later built and the place became a full holiday camp in the 1950s. Attractions included an amusement park, circus, zoo, swimming pool, boating lake and miniature railway. Its speedway motorcycle track held national championships and drew large crowds. The park even had its own team called the California Poppies. The old ballroom eventually became a night club but, unfortunately, burnt down in 1976 and the holiday camp closed. Cartlidge's daughter later established Drayton Manor Theme Park in Staffordshire.

Castle Hill

The Castle Hill area of Reading adjoins Coley on its northern edge. The name may suggest it was the location of the elusive Reading Castle, although the only reliable reference to this suggests it was a short-lived wooden motte and bailey construction, built during the 'Anarchy' civil war of King Stephen's reign, somewhere near Reading Abbey. The so-called 'castle' on Castle Hill may have been an old Roman villa or some other nondescript ruin mistakenly thought to be a castle.

Castle Street and Hill were part of the old medieval main road from London to Bristol. By the 1650s, stage coaches started running through the town and the Reading Turnpike Trust was established in 1714 to keep Castle Street, Castle Hill and what now became the Bath Road in good order, initially as far as Sulhamstead and later beyond. The toll gate was set up at the Tilehurst Road/Coley Avenue junction and the elegant King's

Arms (formerly the New Inn) was built immediately to the east around the same time. It quickly became one of the town's major coaching stops. In 1797, the place was, however, briefly commandeered as accommodation for over 200 refugee Roman Catholic priests, escaping the aftermath of the French Revolution. Today it is divided into several homes. In the 18th century, houses on the north side of Castle Hill did not reach past the King's Arms and, on the south, not past Coley Place.

Figure 30: Castle Hill showing the old King's Arms Inn

However, in the Victorian era, the upper reaches of Castle Street and Castle Hill itself became lined with beautiful villas for the town's rich businessmen: Bath Place, Downs House, Ripon Lodge, Freemantle Lodge, Falconer Lodge and many others. The best known is perhaps Yeomanry House (formerly Castle Hill House) which until 2017 was the town's registry office. Few others survive. On the opposite side of Castle Hill, Downshire Square was developed in the 1860s, including the Church of All Saints, for the local community.

Caversham and Caversham Heights

Extensive and deep underground chalk mine caverns in the Emmer Green area of the parish indicate that Caversham's name may be fairly self-explanatory: Caves' Home. They were probably worked from the 17th century and perhaps much earlier.

A very early lord of the manor was Walter Giffard, the Earl of Buckingham. He was an important official at the royal court and may have found Caversham a convenient boat ride away from the royal palace at Old Windsor. It was probably Buckingham who established an important statue-based shrine to 'Our Lady of Caversham' in a chapel dedicated to St Mary, probably near the church at Caversham. It is first recorded when in 1106 his widow, Countess Agnes, presented it with the "principal relic of the realm": the spear that pierced Christ's side on the Cross. Her lover, Prince Robert Curthose, Duke of Normandy, had acquired this whilst on crusade in the Holy Land, though it was later said to have been brought to Caversham by an angel with one wing (probably a statuette which held the relic). Sixty years later, her son gave both the chapel and Caversham Church to the Austin Canons of Notley Abbey at Long Crendon in Buckinghamshire, near Thame. They established a small cell around the chapel which, though it had no official rank, was often known as Caversham Priory.

During the Middle Ages, Our Lady of Caversham's Shrine was one of the great pilgrimage centres of England. In the worship of the Virgin Mary, it was second only to the great shrine at Walsingham in Norfolk. It was centred around a wonderful jewel-encrusted and crowned statue of the Virgin but, as well as the spear, it acquired a whole collection of other important holy relics, including a piece of the rope with which Judas hanged himself, and the knives that killed both the holy King Henry VI and St Edward the Martyr. The latter may have been brought from Reading's Anglo-Saxon nunnery. Pilgrims visiting the shrine from the south would first stop half-way across Caversham Bridge at the apsidal Chapel of St Anne, jutting out onto Piper's Island. It is long gone, but similar bridge chapels are still to be seen at Bradford-on-Avon (Wiltshire), St Ives (Huntingdonshire), Wakefield and Rotherham (both Yorkshire).

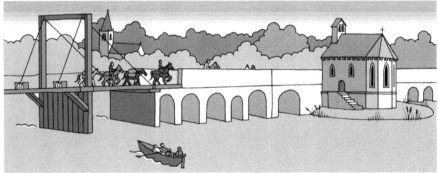

Figure 31: Medieval Caversham Bridge with Chapel and Drawbridge

Caversham Bridge was probably first built in the 1220s. It was a wooden structure, later replaced by one of stone, at least on the Caversham side of the river, until the whole thing was rebuilt in iron in 1869. At this time, the ferryman's house, which had replaced the old chapel, was successfully moved 'en masse' eight feet eastwards, reputedly with Mr Piper the ferryman and his family still inside. Not even a window was broken. The present bridge was built in 1923-6. There was always a medieval ferry for poorer people who could not afford the bridge tolls, as well as for pilgrims, crossing between the footpath to the Thames behind the Rivermead Centre and the Warren by St Peter's Church. This was retained well into the 20th century, particularly for cattle going to market.

Figure 32: Old Caversham Court remodelled by Pugin

Upon landing, the pilgrims would head up to the top of Priest Hill, where they could visit St Anne's Holy Well which was said to cure many afflictions. This may be a very ancient Iron Age spring, originally named after Anu, the Celtic Goddess of the Countryside. It was lost for many years until restored in 1908. The statue of Our Lady of Caversham may have later moved within the walls of St Peter's Church before the shrine was finally suppressed in 1538. Having lost its major attraction, the building was compensated soon afterwards by the gift of a decorative roof for its north aisle. This was brought from Reading Abbey which was then in the process of being demolished. A new Roman Catholic chapel and shrine, featuring a 15th century statue of the Virgin Mary, was re-established in South View Avenue in 1958.

The original shrine chapel and priory complex is generally thought to have stood on the site of Caversham Court, right next to the parish church, as a considerable quantity of medieval carving has been discovered there. Some remains were incorporated into the griffin head gate piers in the gardens, while a small Norman font or stoup dug up there can be seen in the church. The large post-Dissolution Tudor house on the site was called the Old Rectory, but commonly referred to as the 'Striped House' because of its beautiful vertical timber-framing around two courtyards. The house had a 1638 staircase, with bullet holes from a Civil War attack, and an elaborate heraldic decorated plaster ceiling. Both survived an extensive rebuilding programme by the great Gothic revivalist, Augustus Pugin, for the Simonds brewing family of Reading in 1840. Pugin gave the house a castellated façade and a Norman-style porch surmounted by the figure of Cardinal Wolsey; but the house only lasted about a hundred years more and the area is now a public park.

Before the Simonds family's residence, the house had been the home to many interesting characters. These include the Elizabethan Catholic, William Alexander (alias Milward), and his son, Richard. They still exemplify why English legal submissions should be kept clear and concise. For, during a dispute over monies arranged for a marriage that never happened, Richard's submission to the court covered some 120 pages that the judge felt could easily be covered by 16. As a result, Alexander was imprisoned and obliged to parade himself in Westminster Hall with his head stuck through a hole in his own paperwork. A member of the same household, Robert Newport, was also later suspected of being a Gunpowder Plotter. For most of its life, however, the house was owned by the Loveday family. Most famous was the 18th century antiquarian, John Loveday, who travelled the country writing about the places he visited. His private library from Caversham held 2,500 volumes and is now owned by Penn State University in America.

During the Civil War Siege of Reading, King Charles I made attempts to relieve the royalist garrison in the town and briefly had his headquarters at Caversham Park. His troops are said to have stationed a cannon on top of the church tower, but the parliamentarians quickly blew both it and the steeple to smithereens. When the royalist relief army finally tried to enter Reading, there was a bloody battle on Caversham Bridge. The King's men ultimately failed to cross and the town surrendered to Parliament soon afterwards. The besieged royalist troops were then allowed to leave for Oxford via Caversham.

Before 1898, Caversham Heights was pure farmland, covering the fields of Toot's, Ashcroft and Blagrave Farms. By 1911, when the south of old Caversham parish transferred its administration from Oxfordshire to Berkshire County Council (leaving Kidmore End behind), all the land west of Kidmore Road had been built upon. Blagrave Farm was originally in Mapledurham parish but this area was transferred to Caversham in 1977. It was named after its owner, Jonathan Blagrave, who in 1723 was robbed and murdered by three ruffians near Toot's Farm. He had earlier been heard in the Griffin Inn boasting about the profits he had made at Reading Market. The perpetrators were caught and hanged locally and their bodies are believed to be those dug up at the Great Galley (or Gallows) Common Field, at the junction of Shepherds Lane and Woodcote Way in 1888. Unusually, one of them was a woman.

For Caversham Park, see Caversham Park Village; *For Caversham Castle, see* Lower Caversham

Caversham Park Village

Queen Elizabeth I's treasurer, Sir Francis Knollys bought Caversham manor in 1542 but was not able to take possession until over forty years later. By this time, the estate had then been without a residence for about a hundred years, since the old castle (or fortified manor house) at Lower Caversham had been demolished in 1493. Knollys built the first great mansion, on the higher ground where it is likely the park keeper's lodge had previously stood. Sir Francis' nearby homes in Reading and at Rotherfield Greys (Oxfordshire) were his main residences, but, in his later years, he seems to have favoured Caversham and is described as of that place in his will. His son, William Knollys, the Earl of Banbury, entertained both Queen Elizabeth I and James I's queen, Anne of Denmark, there.

Figure 33: Captured Charles I led to Caversham Park

The house later became the home of the Earl of Craven, the great friend of Charles I's sister, the Queen of Bohemia. During the

Civil War, King Charles used the house as his headquarters during his attempt to relieve the Siege of Reading, whilst Craven bankrolled the royalist troops from his base in Europe. After the end of the siege, an epidemic of some kind struck the victorious parliamentary troops and the Earl of Essex was briefly obliged to retreat to Caversham Park while his soldiers camped on Caversham Hill. The Park was eventually confiscated and was used, for a time, as a luxurious prison for the King after he was finally captured. It was from there that he wrote the letter asking to be re-united with his children. He was allowed to see them for a short time only in Maidenhead, but Lord Fairfax found the meeting so touching that he allowed the young Royals to return to Caversham with their father. After the War, however, the house was in such a bad state of repair that it was pulled down.

Figure 34: Major Marsack's Caversham Park before the 1850 Fire

There have been a number of subsequent mansions on the site but, unfortunately, they have been susceptible to frequent fire damage. In 1718, Lord Cadogan started to rebuild the house. He was a good friend of the Duke of Marlborough, with whom he served in the War of the Spanish Succession, and tried to make Caversham's gardens rival those belonging to his friend at Blenheim Palace. The house was surrounded by courtyards, terraces, a kitchen garden and fashionable Dutch-style parterre gardens "with statues, vases and two fountains" as well as two 900ft long ornamental canals. There was even a (steam) engine house to pump them full of water. Just inside the main gates, the keeper's lodge was surrounded by a quail yard and there was also a pheasantry. These were probably both to supply the Earl's dining table, but the pheasants may also have been quite exotic and would have been complemented by the Earl's menagerie.

Cadogan's large winged house was burnt down in the late 18th century and replaced with a smaller one. Major Marsack much enlarged this in the 1780s until it became a fine Greek Temple style mansion. He was reputedly an illegitimate brother of King George III. The present Italian Baroque building was erected after the great fire of 1850. Not long afterwards the park lost the deer that had lived there since the 13th century. The estate's Welsh iron baron owner, William Crawshay II, gave the new house a metal frame, but this did not prevent another fire in 1926. The house was then a school but, in 1943, became the BBC World monitoring station and eventually the home of BBC Radio Berkshire. Caversham Park Village was built over the north and eastern part of the estate in the 1960s. In 1977, it transferred from Oxfordshire to the administration of Berkshire County Council and subsequently to Reading Borough Council. The rest of southern Caversham had already joined Berkshire back in 1911. The BBC moved out of Caversham Park in 2018 and the future of the house and land is uncertain.

Charvil

Charvil was historically the north-eastern portion of Sonning parish. The name may mean Charcoal Burners' Field or possibly Peasants' Field. If the latter, it could be related to the local administrative Hundred (a bit like a small district council) of Charlton which means Peasants' Hill. Perhaps the hundred court met on Charvil Hill. There were not many buildings in Charvil until the First World War. It was all open farmland belonging to Charvil Farm, a 16th century building in Gingalls Farm Road, and East Park Farm which stood where the pavilion is at the East Park Farm playing fields.

Figure 35: The Wee Waif at Charvil, named after a London charity

Charvil Farm was formerly called Hazel Park. In the late Tudor period when the present farm house was built, it was the home of the Burdets, a prominent family of recusant Roman Catholics who were heavily fined for their beliefs. Clement Burdet and his younger brother, Humphrey, came down south from Warwickshire in the late 1530s when Clement was appointed Rector of South Moreton and then of Englefield by their cousin, Sir Francis Englefield of Englefield House. Humphrey married Sir Francis' sister and the two had a large family at Hazel Park.

Clement even came to join them after he was ousted from Englefield Rectory for his Catholic beliefs. He brought with him a large collection of 28 medieval religious manuscripts from the dissolved Reading Abbey. It is not clear how he acquired them – possibly from Sir Francis via his friend Thomas Vachell who was overseer of the abbey's former lands. Humphrey's son, William, appears to have been less inclined to Catholicism and, just before he died in 1608, he gave the manuscripts to the Bodleian Library in Oxford where they are still housed today.

The Maidenhead to Reading section of the Bath Road was turnpiked in 1718. To fund its regular maintenance, a gate and tollhouse were erected immediately east of the junction of Gingells Farm Road and the Old Bath Road in Charvil. Gingells Farm Road led to Charvil Farm House, with Edward Road leading down from the outbuildings. It is suggested that this arrangement allowed the farmer to bypass the tollgate and avoid paying the tolls. The toll-keepers seem to have been rather enterprising and in the 1780s opened a pub called the Gate for travellers stopping to pay their tolls. The 1754 iron pump at the entrance to Park Lane was used to water the coach horses, as well as to provide running water for a handful of cottages in the area. This was the beginning of Charvil Village and four of these two hundred year old cottages survive today.

In the 1920s, houses began to be built between what is now the Wee Waif Roundabout and Charvil Farm. The first roads were Milestone Avenue, Park View Drive and Charvil Farm Road, now Gingells Farm Road – Duncan Gingell farmed there in the 1940s and 50s. The Wee Waif Hotel started life as a grocery and tea shop. Ernest Temple turned this into a licensed roadhouse to serve travellers on the Bath Road in 1928. It is said to have had many famous visitors, including Royalty. The name derives from the children helped by a London charity set up by Mr Temple's brother. The building was completely rebuilt in 1979.

Coley

Coley is the area of Reading east of the Kennet and south of Castle Hill. It is an Anglo-Saxon word meaning Charcoal Clearing. It perhaps started life as a small hamlet for charcoal burners in the woods south-west of Reading. The trees were later swept away in order to turn the land over to agriculture and, in 1309, John Vachell from Tilehurst began buying property in the area which he consolidated into Coley Park. The family maxim, "'Tis better to Suffer than to Revenge," is said to come from an incident involving this man. He was in dispute with the Abbot of Reading over rights of way across his estate. The Abbot sent a monk with a cartload of corn to test Vachell's resolve. In a fit of rage, he killed the Abbot's man but escaped with only excommunication and a heavy fine.

The Elizabethan house (and probably its predecessor) at Coley stood down by the Holy Brook between the Brookmill and the Lesford Road Allotments. It is known from an old engraving and the original old dovecote (1553) and barns (1619), depicted there as part of the Home Farm, can still be seen just to the east. Lady Hampden (formerly Lady Vachell), the widow of the famous parliamentarian John Hampden, is said to have watched the Siege of Reading from its roof. Afterwards, her nephew, Tanfield Vachell, entertained King Charles I there and the royalist army camped in the park. In the reign of William and Mary, Tanfield's cousin, Thomas, laid out the gardens in the fashionable Dutch Baroque style with tree-lined avenues, arch-covered walkways, topiary, 'parterres' of low box hedges in beautiful geometric shapes, water features fed by the Holy Brook and even a maze. It is difficult to imagine it there today. The old mansion was converted into a Palladian style house for Lieutenant-Colonel Richard Thompson, owner of a Jamaican sugar plantation manned by slaves, in the late 1720s. This was replaced, about 80 years later, by the present house on the hill above. It was the home of the civically-active Monck family for many years. They were cousins of the man who restored the Monarchy in 1660 and the family name was long commemorated by the massive gate piers on the Bath Road, at the end of Coley Avenue, featuring their wyvern (two-legged dragon) crest. Sadly, these were demolished in 1967 in order to widen the road. However, after many years in a ruinous state, the house is now a private hospital.

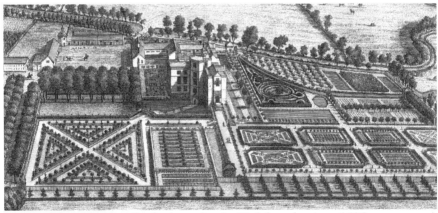

Figure 36: Old Coley Park, down by the Holybrook, circa 1695

From the 1830s, poor and overcrowded housing, called 'courts', began to be built at Coley Hill, in the north-east corner of Coley between Castle Hill and the Holy Brook. These Victorian slums had no running water and shared toilet and washing facilities between four houses. They were largely located between Coley Place and Coley Street. The latter street, now under the A329

Inner Distribution Road, was historically called Pigney Lane. It was named after the island where the Anglo-Saxons kept their pigs between the Holy Brook and the Kennet. These two streets were joined by Coley Passage, commonly called Coley Steps because it was on a steep hill with steps all the way down to the brook. It was a well-known feature of Reading until the adjoining slums were demolished in the 1930s and the steps themselves were removed thirty years later. The Monck family had sold up and moved away from Coley Park in 1906, after the heir to the property accidentally shot his father while crossing a stile on the estate. Subsequent owners sold off the land for further housing development in the 1950s.

Figure 37: Coley Steps circa 1911

Coley was the original home of S and E Collier's, the famous Tilehurst brickmakers. The family began their business in the Coley Hill area, under Samuel Collier (the father of S and E) in 1848. He had started out selling china and flowerpots in Minster Street in Reading. The firm moved to the Avenue Works, between Coley Avenue and Berkeley Avenue, and added the Coley Kilns, on the site of Coley Recreation Ground, in 1861 before being partially transferred to Tilehurst in 1870 and moving there completely in 1885. Samuel Wheeler, who founded Tilehurst Potteries, was also previously operating at Coley Pottery, where St Saviour's Church now stands, before closing the site in 1883. This works may have dated back to 1770. Like Emmer Green, Coley has deep chalk mine caves used in the brick industry. They were long forgotten until 2000 when houses in Field Road began to collapse into them.

During the First World War, the No 1 Schools of Military Aeronautics and Technical Training were formed in Coley in order to prepare pilots for service in the Royal Flying Corps. The Coley Park Aerodrome was built for them in 1915 and the following year they took over the new Co-operative Wholesale Society (CWS – now the Co-Op Group) Jam Factory nearby as it was unable to open due to a shortage of fruit and sugar. It was used for building AVRO 504 biplanes. After the aerodrome closed, jam production finally started in 1919 and continued until 1968. The site is now the automotive retail park in Rose Kiln Lane. The Co-Op also had a printworks in Elgar Road to provide the jam jar labels.

Dowlesgreen, Norreys and Keep Hatch

Dowlesgreen, the Norreys' Estate and Keep Hatch form the northern part of Wokingham's eastern suburbs. The Dowle family lived in Wokingham from at least the late 17th century. Dowle's Green was an area of Wokingham common land where the locals could graze their sheep and cattle. It spread along the eastern side of Keep Hatch Road and was enclosed and divided amongst local landowners in 1817. The small hamlet of

Dowlesgreen then developed at its northern end. The attractive mid-16th century timber-framed 'Keeper's Lodge' may still be seen in this area near the Mulberry Grove Roundabout. Dowles Green Farm House, dating from a similar period, stands hidden away between the modern houses in the appropriately named road called Dowles Green, a little to the south-east. It was earlier called Budge's Farm, as reflected in the names of Budge's Road, Budge's Gardens and Budges Cottages.

Keep Hatch was the name of the farm at the southern end of the old Dowle's Green. It was sometimes called May's Farm after the family who lived there for three generations from the mid-18th century. The ancient farmhouse survives as an unexpected sight at the end of modern Clover Close. It is a fine timber-framed building dating from the mid-16th century. Keep Hatch included Kiln Green whose name reminds us that the farmland was an early source of brickmaking in Wokingham, supplementing the Mays' income from at least 1800. Keep Hatch House was erected slightly further east of the old farmhouse, at the end of Montague Close, in 1871 for the retired Reverend George Edward Denis de Vitré, a former Curate of Cookham Dean and Vicar of Weston in Hertfordshire. He gave Wokingham the granite dolphin-bedecked drinking fountain now used as a plant-holder outside the town hall. His house was a rather attractive building but, having been unoccupied for several years, was demolished in 1997 and a large modern replacement now occupies the site.

The Norreys' Estate covers the old manor of Norreys and is named after the prominent Norreys family from Ockwells House at Cox Green and Yattendon Castle. There may also have been a small manor house at Norreys. Sir John Norreys – who, being Master of the Wardrobe, was a close friend of King Henry VI –

may have occasionally visited. In 1443, he set up a chantry chapel in Wokingham Church, with a chaplain to pray for his soul. So he clearly had some interest in the area. However, by the time Lord Norreys' sons were dominating the jousting tilt-yards at Queen Elizabeth I's royal court, there was probably only a farm in the Norreys area of Wokingham. Norris Barn long survived half way up the western arm of Norreys Avenue and its name was later transferred to the pub built alongside the shops in 1967. This has now become a small supermarket.

Figure 38: 16th Century Ashridge manor house at Ashridge Farm

Ashridge was officially a detached part of Wiltshire until local government reforms in 1844. This explains the naming of Wiltshire Road and Wiltshire Drive in Wokingham. Opposite the latter stands the late 16th century Wiltshire Farm House. This county anomaly was due to Henry II's son, the powerful William Longespée, Earl of Salisbury, having transferred his Berkshire lands into the jurisdiction of his Wiltshire hundred (like a district council) court at Amesbury in the early 13th century. However, Mid-Berkshire was so far away that a sub-court had to be set up in the manor of Ashridge (formerly called Hertoke). The old manor house is now Ashridge Farm, at the very northern tip of

Wiltshire Road. The present building is late 16th century and features a fireplace dated 1575 and stained glass from the following year.

Earley and Earley Rise

In the past, Earley has been called a place "without a centre," as historically, it was made up of rural farms and country estates. Until 1854, Earley was a liberty in the south-western portion of the large parish of Sonning. The name probably means Eagle-Clearing, although Gravel-Clearing referring to the geology near the Thames is another possibility. This was where the common fields of Earley were located until enclosed in 1742. The manor in this northern region was called Erleigh Court, also known as Earley St Bartholomew. It was named after the dedication of an ancient chapel which was established there sometime in the early 13th century. The old house, which stood on the site of Sidmouth Grange Close, is believed to have had a Tudor core. From 1708, it was owned by Sir Owen Buckingham, the Lord Mayor of London who made a fortune establishing a sail-cloth factory in the remains of the old royal palace in Reading. His son and namesake was killed in a London duel against his friend, Captain William Aldworth of Windsor, after an argument at a birthday party in 1720. Later, poor blind Sir John Powell Pryce owned the property but was thrown into a debtors' prison and tricked into selling up to John Bagnall in 1766. Bagnall's daughter and heiress married the famous politician, Lord Stowell. His brother, Lord Eldon (of Reading Square, Road and Street fame) was Lord High Chancellor and often came to stay. Stowell eventually died at the Court in 1836 and was buried in Sonning Church. His daughter, Maria Anne, and her husband, former Prime Minister Viscount Sidmouth, inherited the estate. They had earlier lived at Woodley Lodge. By 1932, the Court stood empty. It was purchased by a property developer and demolished three years later.

Figure 39: Erleigh Court, demolished 1935

The more southerly manor was Whiteknights Park. It has been the home of the University of Reading since 1947 and is rarely considered part of Earley at all. In essence, however, it is all that remains of the pre-1276 deer park and manor of Earley Whiteknights, otherwise known as Earley Regis or Earley St Nicholas. Legend says that the eponymous White Knight was a Norman soldier who gave up his manor and travelled barefoot to the Holy Land after he had accidentally killed the brother of his Anglo-Saxon lover. He was eventually buried in St Nicholas' Chapel which stood near the Wokingham Road gate to the park. This was a twin to the chapel at Erleigh Court.

The real White Knight, however, was a man named John d'Earley IV. He was given the nickname after having seen much action in King Edward I's campaigns in Scotland, presumably in shining armour. The D'Earleys lived at the manor from which they took their name throughout the medieval period. They were minor barons, some of whom became highly embroiled in national events. The most famous of the family was Sir John d'Earley II, the foster-son of the Regent of England, William Marshal, Earl of Pembroke, who lived at nearby Caversham Castle. After Marshal's death, D'Earley commissioned a now-famous epic poem about his mentor's life from John the Troubadour. D'Earley fought for King Richard I in France and for Marshal in Wales and Ireland. He brought the news of King Richard's death back to England and was, at one time, Marshal of the Royal Household to King John, though their relationship was generally rather stormy. The D'Earley family were eventually forced to sell off their Earley lands in order to pay ransom demands from the Spanish King in the mid-14th century.

The Catholic Englefield family eventually took on the estate after Englefield House was confiscated from them during the religious persecutions of the 16th century. During the Siege of Reading, the Governor, Sir Arthur Aston, used to ride out to Whiteknights to dine with Anthony Englefield (died 1667). In early 1643, the parliamentarians discovered this and sent 200 horse and 600 foot soldiers from Windsor Castle to kidnap him. However, Aston was warned by his scouts and so stayed safe within the fortifications of Reading that night. In the late 17th century, the Englefields often entertained literary society there, with visitors like Alexander Pope (from Binfield) and John Gay. However, the last of their family line, the scientist and antiquarian, Sir Henry Charles Englefield, sold the estate because he couldn't stand his neighbours' anti-Catholic prejudices anymore. In the late 18th century, the manor was bought by the family of the flamboyant Marquess of Blandford (heir to the Duchy of Marlborough) who led a life of great revelry there. He laid out ornamental gardens that were the envy of Kings – some trees from which still survive – and collected paintings, by the likes of Rubens, Titian, Cuyp, Rembrandt, Tintoretto and Gainsborough, and a most astonishing library of rare books. Eventually the poor man went broke and was forced to retire to Blenheim Palace.

Figure 40: Whiteknights House, circa 1830

It has been suggested that the medieval village of Earley stood on the site of the lake in Whiteknights Park. When this water feature was created for the Englefields in the 1740s, the village would have been swept away. The inhabitants had to move slightly east to the Three Tuns Crossroads on the edge of the park. This settlement was sometimes called Upper Earley. The Three Tuns may have been established around the same time as the Wokingham Road was turned into a toll road by the Windsor Forest Turnpike Trust in 1759. It became the meeting place of the Woodley Cavalry in the very early 19th century. They were an early form of territorial army raised at the expense of Viscount Sidmouth during the Napoleonic Wars and their barracks were in Church Road. The Whiteknights manorial court also met there until 1840. The pub was joined by a pond, a forge, a pound for stray animals and, later, a post office. Just to the north was Earleyheath Farm, now called the Manor House, and in 1844 the church of St Peter was built across the road as a memorial to Maria Anne, Viscountess Sidmouth of Erleigh Court. Earley St Peter's School joined it four years later. The Three Tuns was rebuilt in the 1930s when the tree-lined road was also straightened.

There was also a small hamlet, of fewer than five cottages, called Little Hungerford in the area of Earley Station from at least 1747 and probably much earlier. The station was opened by the South Eastern Railway in 1863 and Ginger Terrace built nearby was supposedly named after the hair of the Irish railway labourers who lived there. Most of the buildings there were purchased by James Wheble Junior of Woodley Lodge in the early 19th century and turned into estate workers cottages. Wheble retired to the adjoining Hungerford Lodge (formerly Earley Cottage), a large 1803/4 house that stood on the site of Stanton Close until the 1950s.

The housing estates of Earley began to appear in the late 19th century. Eastern Avenue and Hamilton Road were developed in 1853. Crescent Road originally led to Mock Beggar Farm which initially became a brickworks after the farm house was demolished. The Wokingham Road shops and the roads behind were laid out in the 1890s, giving birth to Earley Rise. Earley Common to the east was built on after the Second World War.

Eastheath

Eastheath is the southern suburb of Wokingham on the west side of the Finchampstead Road, below Molly Millar's Lane. Who Molly Millar was is something of a mystery. One theory says the lane was named by the Welsh drovers who passed this way with their sheep in the late 18th century and got to know Molly, an old woman who lived by the wayside. Local legend says more: she was not just any old lady but the town witch. This area covers the old manor of Evendons. This name probably means Geoff's Hill. The old manor house, which was demolished in 1837 and replaced by a farm house, stood where the club-house for Sand Martins' Golf Course is today.

Figure 41: The Two Poplars, formerly The Engineer

The North Downs Railway had been constructed through this area and into Wokingham in 1847-9 and an old house (perhaps then 40 years old) was converted into the Engineer pub – now called the Two Poplars – to serve those building it. This was the beginning of Eastheath as a settlement, for a small hamlet soon began to develop around the pub. Later, the nearby brickworks also had its own railway to take the bricks onto the main line. The Eastheath Brickworks of Thomas Lawrence and Sons, south of Molly Millar's Lane and west of Eastheath Avenue, joined their Warfield, Swinley and Easthampstead sites in about 1895. It eventually became their largest works, covering 58 acres and producing 10 million bricks a year, including those for the building of Westminster Cathedral. Production was reduced after a chimney collapsed during the Second World War and flooding finally forced its closure in 1960.

Around the turn of the 20th century, large villas for rich businessmen were built along the western side of the Finchampstead Road. The first, Eastheath Lodge (or the White House), was put up somewhat earlier, around 1853 for Robert Garrard II, ten years after he and his brothers had been appointed the first official jewellers to the Crown. Amongst their many commissions, they recut the famous Koh-i-Noor Diamond and created the Small Diamond Crown of Queen Victoria. In more recent years the Lodge became the centre of the White House Preparatory School, now Evendons Primary School.

Emmbrook and Matthewsgreen

A large hoard of 1,800 bronze Roman coins from the 4th century was found at Matthewsgreen in a broken pot in 1970. They were no doubt hidden during times of trouble when the Roman army were leaving our shores and Anglo-Saxon raiders were rampaging across the country but the owner may not have lived in the local area.

Beaches Manor stood on the Reading Road, on the edge of Matthewsgreen. Both the manor and Peach Street in the centre of Wokingham were named after its 14th century owners, the De la Beche family, heirs to the original Palmers. They do not, however, appear to have been related to the better-known family of 'giants' called De la Beche from Aldworth. The heirs of the Wokingham family were the Whitelockes. Edmund Whitelocke, a suspected Gunpowder Plotter, lived at Beaches Manor in the

1580s. He was uncle of the Keeper of the Great Seal, Sir Bulstrode Whitelocke of Chilton Lodge. His cousin, William Whitelocke, built himself a beautiful old brick manor house in 1624. This eventually became an hotel but burnt down in 1953. Next door, the Holt School was originally its dower house and has one old wing dating back to 1589, although it was mostly built for the Heelas family, owners of local department stores, in 1886. St Paul's Church was erected across the Reading Road by architect Henry Woodyer as a gift from John Walter III of Bearwood, proprietor of the Times Newspaper, during a decade of such expressions of Wokingham civic pride in the 1860s.

Figure 42: Beaches Manor. Did the Keeper of the Great Seal visit?

Other later country houses in the area include the neo-Elizabethan Glebelands of 1897, which has been the Cinema and Television Benevolent Fund's Care Home since 1936, and Cantley House (formerly Matthews Green House) of 1880, which is now an hotel. The earlier house on the Cantley House site dated back to at least 1680 and was the country estate of the Basnett family, who made their money as salt brokers in the City of

London in the days when salt was an expensive commodity. They sold up in 1795 but continued to be buried in the family vault under All Saints' Church until the 1860s.

Emmbrook has obviously adopted its name from the stream that flows through it. The name itself probably records the land of a local Anglo-Saxon man and means Eadhelme's Brook. The settlement began life as a small hamlet in the area around the Rifle Volunteer pub and down Emmbrook Road to the Dog and Duck. There was a mill on the Emm Brook on the site beside the Rifle Volunteer from at least the mid-18th century and for some time the two businesses were run from the same premises. The pub was known as the Little Mill and, later, the Horse and Groom, until the present building was built in 1859. This was at the time when Emmbrook was beginning to expand and thus the pub's prosperity was assured. The Westcott family turned the corn mill into a paper mill in 1868 but it had reverted to flour by 1895. During the Second World War, a company called Metalair made metal aircraft components for the De Havilland Mosquito there.

Unfortunately, Emmbrook became infamous in 1856 for the horrible and tragic murder of a bright little boy of five, resulting from mental health issues. Charles Forester from the London City Mission had been invited to the area with his wife and son by Mrs Saltmarsh of Bill Hill House who wanted to provide the villagers with some Christian teaching. However, she soon found him an incompetent preacher and sent for a replacement. Mrs Forester instead opened a shop in one of a row of houses near the present entrance to the Emmbrook School. Showing signs of tuberculosis, Mr Forester was sent up to a specialist hospital in London. However, he returned in a deep depression and, while his wife was serving a customer in the shop, he used a razor to sever his poor son's head while he slept, before walking out and giving himself up at Wokingham Police Station.

Figure 43: The Rifle Volunteer at Emmbrook

West of Emmbrook was Toutley Common (the northern part of Bearwood Common). In the late 19th century, there was a brickworks near the present play barn, at the junction of Toutley Road and Forest Road. In 1935 this became the Toutley Brick Works Ltd, with Warfield's prominent Thomas Lawrence Brickworks holding a fifty percent stake. Eventually, in the 1960s, Emmbrook began to expand over this area. Nearby stands Toutley Hall, the core of which is supposed to be late 17th century, although it was mostly rebuilt in the early 1800s. In the 1890s, it became the home to Elma Stuart, the friend and correspondent of George Eliot (aka Mary Anne Evans), the author of the Mill on the Floss. Stuart rose to prominence as the main promoter of the beef and hot water diet of the American Doctor Salisbury – inventor of the Salisbury Steak – in which vegetables and starchy staple foods were considered poisonous. She published a popular book on the subject, called 'What must I do to get well? And how can I keep so?' that ran to some 32 editions.

Emmer Green

Emmer Green developed around the dogleg crossroads on the western edge of the Caversham Estate. The place may be named after a person, Embe's Marsh, or it could mean Duck Marsh. The marsh was presumably in the area of the present pond that was created around 1800.

Figure 44: Chalk Caverns beneath Emmer Green

The brick kilns, on Rose Hill just to the north, are first recorded in 1654. They were owned by the Dormer family perhaps as early as 1759 and Brewerton and Stevens between 1891 and 1928, followed by the Caversham Brick and Tile Works until 1947. At its height, 12,000 bricks a day were produced there. There are extensive deep chalk caves hidden beneath the ground in the Kiln Road area and elsewhere. The chalk was almost certainly used for lining the brick kilns, but secondary uses included agriculture and construction. Today, the entrances are kept locked and inaccessible but graffiti inside indicates the caves were in regular use from at least 1722 and they are probably as old as the kiln site, if not considerably older. One local story, of uncertain age, records how King Charles I supposedly once hid in a 100-foot-deep chalk cave near Surley Row. Presumably this would have been around the time of the Battle of Caversham Bridge.

In the late 18th century, the outer reaches of Caversham parish became a popular area, within easy reach of Reading, for the gentry to build themselves fine country villas. Rosehill House (now flats), in Peppard Road, in northern Emmer Green, was built on the site of an old farm in 1791. A hundred years later, it was the home to Martin John Sutton of Sutton Seeds in Reading who liked to call it Kidmore Grange. He was followed by the military family of Makgill-Crichton-Maitland whose son once landed a hot air balloon on the lawn. Hill House (now divided in two) at the very bottom end of Surley Row, has Adam fireplaces installed by a Regency buck called Captain William Montague (died 1843). The nearby house called Springfield St Luke (now flats) was once the home of Lieutenant-General Sir Rufane Shaw Donkin (died 1841) who founded Port Elizabeth in South Africa and named it after his wife. He previously lived at Caversham House in Church Street. Caversham Grove (now part of Highdown School), further up Surley Row, is a Queen Anne revival house with a labyrinth of cellars below it. Its residents have included Commodore Arthur Forrest (died 1770), the commander-in-chief of the British fleet in Jamaica where he was also the rich owner of a sugar plantation manned by slaves, and Frederick George Saunders (died 1901), the chairman of the Great Western Railway.

Surley Row was once a separate hamlet and still retains a number of old cottages, some of which date back to the 1540s. Old Grove

House (aka Plaister's Grove) is an old Tudor farmhouse, at the Surley Row/St Barnabas Road junction, with a fine brick and flint frontage and a floor surface which may be medieval. There is a bizarre old legend that the grounds once sported an apple tree in which Oliver Cromwell hid from some royalists who were on his trail. Surley Row once had its own 'chalybeate' well, the water from which was apparently good for all sorts of ailments.

St Barnabas' Church was built as an iron church in 1897. This building became the church hall when the present church was put up by W, N and E Fisher in 1924. However, there was an older chapel built on Caversham Hill in 1827 as an offshoot of St Mary's Castle Street in Reading. The Fisher family had lived at Little End in Caversham in the 1830s but moved to the Peppard Road/Kidmore End Road junction at Emmer Green in 1872. William Fisher set up a wheelwright's and timber merchant's, before adding a forge when he joined forces with his sons, [William] Noah and Edwin. They later diversified into general carpentry and, through making coffins, undertaking, as well as owning the Belle Vue Hand Laundry. They turned to building with the arrival of the motor-car and the death of wheelwrighting in the 1920s. The firm built many houses in Emmer Green and Caversham and the family only finally sold up in 1981. Fisher's Court now stands on the site of their old builders' yard.

Historically part of Oxfordshire, Emmer Green has fallen within the region administered by Berkshire County Council and its successor, Reading Borough Council, since 1911. The area only really began to expand after the First World War and there have been many housing developments since. Rotherfield Way forms an interesting estate which was built in the 1950s by volunteer members of the Reading Family Housing Association, tired of waiting for council houses that never appeared.

Englefield

Figure 45: Elizabethan Englefield House

The parish apparently derives its name from the battle fought there between the Anglo-Saxons and Vikings in AD 870. It either means Englishmen's [Battle] Field or Warning Beacon Field. The invading Vikings had set up camp in Reading, from where a raiding party set out to attack Aldermaston. Aethelwulf, the Ealdorman of Berkshire who lived there, engaged them at Englefield and the Vikings were thoroughly defeated. They were, however, not finally expelled from the county until after King Alfred's victory at Edington in Wiltshire, some eight years later. Almost two hundred years on, William the Conqueror may have brought his army through Englefield, avoiding the narrow Thameside route to cross the Thames at Norman-friendly Wallingford, after the Battle of Hastings.

The Englefield family supposedly owned the manor from the time of King Edgar the Peacemaker in the mid-10th century until it was confiscated from Sir Francis Englefield, an infamous 16th century Roman Catholic who worked for 'Bloody' Queen Mary Tudor. He would not bow to the power of Elizabeth I's English Church and tried all sorts of ploys to stop the Crown getting its hands on his lands, including settling it on his nephew. But eventually he lost out and had to flee overseas. The Englefields later bought Whiteknights Park in Earley and continued to be buried in the Englefield Chapel in Englefield Church until the last of them died in 1822. They still have impressive monuments there, although seven fine brasses have disappeared, including one from the elaborate 1514 tomb-chest memorial to Sir Thomas Englefield, Speaker of the House of Commons. Arches under the south wall shelter a stone knight (shield missing) and a wooden lady: probably Sir Roger Englefield (died 1317) and his wife Joan (died 1340).

Sir Edward Norreys, Governor of Ostend, also lived in the parish and entertained Queen Elizabeth I at his house on the site of the old rectory. He was buried in the Englefield Chapel, but his body was later removed to Rycote Palace near Thame in Oxfordshire. Englefield House is basically an Elizabethan E-plan building, believed to have been built for the Queen's favourite, the 2nd Earl of Essex, after he bought the estate in 1589. His mother was a Reading girl, the notorious Lettice Knollys. A strong local tradition suggests that the old house had previously been rented to the royal spymaster general, Sir Francis Walsingham, although this is far from certain.

In 1623, the estate was purchased by Sir John Davies, the Attorney-General for Ireland. His wife, Lady Eleanor, was a somewhat eccentric lady who claimed to hear the voice of Daniel (of Lion's Den fame). She kept a young dumb lad in their household who later learned to talk and interpret her dreams. She wrote many prophecies which her husband burnt, but was severely punished by the Court of High Commission when she continued in a similar vein after his death.

Figure 46: Marquess of Winchester (centre) at the Taking of Basing House

After the Civil War, the house became the retreat of the 5th Marquess of Winchester when he returned from exile abroad. He had held his old home, the palace of Basing House (Hampshire), against a three-year siege by parliamentary troops, until Cromwell himself arrived to finish it off. Basing was then raised to the ground. Winchester's third wife was the granddaughter of Sir Francis Walsingham and they may have purchased the Englefield estate because of this family connection. They have a fine monument in the north aisle of the parish church but are buried in the south aisle under austere black slabs with long Latin inscriptions. These were only uncovered in the 19th century. The house was inherited by the Marquess' youngest son, Francis, who is said to have married his kitchen maid, a young girl from Tidmarsh. Male heirs in the family twice died without children, so the estate was inherited by the Wrightes and then, in a sideways move, by the Benyons. Rumour says that one heir was lost at sea and, when he eventually returned home, no-one recognised him and he was sent away.

The last of the Wrightes lived in Tidmarsh and the Benyons owned other large estates in Essex, so Englefield was sometimes rented out to tenants. One of these was the widow of Lord Clive of India who was looking for a suitable husband for her youngest daughter amongst the gentry of Berkshire in the 1780s. The county was then known as the English Hindustan because of the large numbers of Indian nabobs who had retired there.

Although the family have changed their name twice, the Benyons have been in residence at Englefield House since 1802. The artist, John Constable, produced a painting of it for them thirty years later. At the end of the 19th century, Richard Fellowes Benyon restored and embellished Englefield House and he did the same for the village whose community thrived under his influence. He created a model estate village, modernizing cottages and farm buildings and providing a bathing pool for boys and a penny soup kitchen, not to mention a new school and the modernization of the church, using Gilbert Scott as his architect. In the context of this obvious prosperity, it is not surprising to learn that there was a fine fire brigade in the village and that a shoemaker, a policeman and a nurse all lived in The Street or that the Rector had a curate to help him with his parish work. Benyon even moved the Bradfield Road from where it ran through the archway at the back of the house to its present route on the other side of the estate wall. As well as Englefield, the Benyons still own much of the London borough of Hackney and the current owner, Richard Benyon, was reputed to be the richest of our members of Parliament until he recently stepped down.

Farley Hill

The Devil's Highway Roman road, running between Roman London and Silchester, passes through the southern edge of Farley Hill, just above Joulding's Ford and the River Blackwater. When the Anglo-Saxons arrived, they called the place Fern Clearing Hill. It stands in the eastern portion of Swallowfield parish that was largely a detached region of Wiltshire until 1844. It is the location of a number of fine country houses: Farley Castle (formerly Wragg Castle), Farley Hall (formerly Farley Hill Place) and Farley Court (formerly Farleyhill Court).

Figure 47: Farley Castle at Farley Hill

Farley Hall was built in the late 1720s, probably for Charles Lannoy (thought to be an ancestral cousin of the Lannoy Hunters from Beech Hill) whose widow sold it to Alexander Walker in 1750. Walker was the owner of a large sugar plantation in Barbados, manned by many slaves, but he wanted an English estate on which to spend his retirement. His only daughter and heiress, Newton, married John Walter from a similarly prominent Barbadian family. His cousin had retired to nearby Newland in Arborfield. A mistaken understanding of the nature of the Barony of Bergavenny led to a bizarre and complicated situation by which John was legally the 5th Baron Bergavenny, although he almost certainly never knew it. He died without issue but is believed to have also been a cousin of the later Walters of Bearwood House at Sindlesham. Farley Hall has the most magnificent entrance hall with a flat ceiling painted by Gerard Lanscroon in 1729 to give the illusion of three-dimensions and featuring Roman gods representing the four elements of earth, air, fire and water. Further rural scenes were added by Joseph Francis Nollekens in 1748.

Farley Court also dates from the 1720s, but has later Victorian extensions. A circular domed room with Adamesque plasterwork on the garden front features in Mary Russell Mitford's 'Our Village'. Farley Castle was built as a mock castle, complete with semi-circular bastion, in 1809-10 for Edward Stephenson, a banker, who also owned the medieval Scaleby Castle in Cumberland. There were subsequently a number of other notable residents: Sir Benjamin Collins Brodie, a physiologist and pioneering surgeon in bone and joint disease, in the 1820s; Walter Mortimer Allfrey from Wokefield Park in the 1910s; and the amateur archaeologist, Frederick Mitchell-Hedges, who discovered one of the controversial South American rock-crystal skulls, in the 1950s. Before the 1980s, it was the Hephaistos School for special educational needs. Both these houses are now divided into apartments.

Finchampstead

Finchampstead's fine parish church is largely of the 12th century, with an unusual apse. Inside, there is a beautiful ball-chain decorated Anglo-Saxon font but the site is older still. The building stands on a prominent hill within what is usually considered to be a Roman earthwork of some kind. It is probably the enclosure of a Roman temple which was later taken over for Christian use, a principle encouraged by St Augustine of Canterbury in the very late 6th century. It stands in an ideal position, just off the Devil's Highway running between Roman London and Silchester. Small stretches of this old Roman road survive as modern highways, notably along Roman Ride.

Figure 48: The uniquely named Queen's Oak in Finchampstead

Alongside the church is the Queen's Oak, the only inn of this name in the country. It was changed from the White Horse, a name preserved in the lane alongside it, at the time of Queen Victoria's golden jubilee when a commemorative oak tree was planted nearby. Stories of Roman remains beneath its floors have led to a claim of being the oldest pub in the country. It could well stand on the site of a Roman hostelry set up to service pagan pilgrims. Roman aisled buildings are known from aerial photographs along the old Roman road between Park Lane and White Horse Lane, west of the church, and may also have been associated with the temple complex. One bizarre story, probably of recent origin, says that the Emperor Magnus Maximus stopped in Finchampstead on his way to London and thus to the Continent to claim the Imperial Throne in AD 383. He was a Spaniard by birth but became commander of the Roman army in Britain where he married a local girl and settled down, prior to being elected Emperor by his troops.

Figure 49: St Oswald & reminders of his Holy Well at Finchampstead

The old spring known as Dodwell's (or Dozell's) Well on Fleet Hill was named after the mid-7th century St Oswald, King of Northumbria. He also apparently travelled through this village on his way to meet King Cynegils of Wessex at Easthampstead. Feeling thirsty, he prayed for water and this holy well instantaneously sprang up at his feet. It is recorded in the Anglo-Saxon Chronicle that this spring flowed with blood (or at least with particularly iron-rich water) in 1098 and 1102. Its fame for such occurrences happening at times of national disaster continued throughout the early Middle Ages. It was generally said to have marvellous curative powers and was visited by pilgrims for eye complaints. The well was accidentally destroyed in 1872 by deepening of the adjoining ditch, but there is still sometimes a trickle of water from the spot and a plaque opposite the entrance to Constant Spring Cottage records its past importance.

From the late 13th century, the parish contained two manors, after the lands of the local lord, William Banister, were divided between his two daughters. Constance took East Court, which stood at the centre of the old medieval village near the church, where the Victorian 'Manor House' now stands. Only a 17th century wall with an attractive doorway remains from the older building. Agatha had West Court at Finchampstead Leas.

In 1452, East Court was purchased by the Pakenhams. Hugh Pakenham was granted the prestigious and lucrative right to hold an annual fair in Finchampstead for three days in Whitsun Week (May/June). It presumably met on Fair Green which is at the top end of the present village between the Village Road and Longwater Lane. Regular fairs only lasted for about a century, but a small hamlet later grew up on the green. A pub, eventually called the Greyhound, was built on its edge in the 17th century and, by the late 19th century, this had been joined by a school, Baptist Chapel and village pound for rounding up stray animals. An earlier pound was kept on Pound Green near Warren Lodge on the way to California. The largest local green was Moor Green, lying along Lower Sandhurst Road. Most of these were used as common grazing land until enclosed in 1818.

An old story about East Court during the Tudor era probably refers to the two daughters of Hugh's grandson, Sir Edmund Pakenham. Their names were Constance and Elizabeth. It is said that King Henry VIII was a frequent visitor to the manor house as he had amorous designs on one of two sisters who lived there. This lady's elder sister, however, was madly in love with the King herself and, in a fit of jealous rage, threw herself off the balcony in front of him in order to prevent her rival becoming Queen of England. Of course, neither Pakenham sister actually committed suicide and both went on to marry 'unroyal' husbands. Constance, the elder, married Sir Geoffrey Pole, son of the last of the Plantagenets, the Countess of Salisbury from Bisham Abbey; and Elizabeth, the younger, married Justice Sir Edmund Marvyn, an uncle-in-law of the notorious widowed Lady Marvyn who rebuilt Ufton Court in Ufton Nervet. The Palmers of Wokingham purchased East Court in 1661, but the manor house soon became a simple farmhouse and over the next 150 years fell into disrepair. When Charles Fyshe-Palmer of Luckley Hall inherited the manor in 1807, he decided to transfer the lord's residence to another property, called Coudrays, which is now the present house called East Court, between the War Memorial and the Greyhound.

Prince Arthur is supposed to have been hunting on the Ridges at Finchampstead with his father, King Henry VII, when he heard of the arrival in England of his fiancée, Princess Catherine of Aragon. They immediately rode out to meet her, but found their way barred by a party of Spanish cavaliers who insisted that, according to Spanish tradition, the Prince could not look upon his bride until after they were married. The King, who would have none of this, rode on to Dogmersfield Park (Hampshire), where the lady was staying, and arranged for her coach to ride along the Ridges, where Catherine raised her veil for her waiting groom. The marriage was thus cursed for breaking this sacred convention and Arthur died not long after exchanging vows. A plaque in Longwater Lane now commemorates these events.

Figure 50: Prince Arthur met his bride for the first time on the Ridges

Today the most famous feature of Finchampstead Ridges is the Wellingtonia Avenue, leading to Wellington College in Crowthorne. This superb double row of Wellingtonia trees was planted by John Walter III of Bearwood (and the Times Newspaper) as a monument to the 1st Duke of Wellington in 1869. They rival the Duke's column at Heckfield (Hampshire) and his equestrian statue at Aldershot (Hampshire) as his most spectacular memorial.

Grazeley

Historically, the Grazeley area has been a region of complicated borders and boundary changes. The villages of Grazeley and Poundgreen have always been part of Shinfield parish. Grazeley Green and Goddard's Green are now in Wokefield parish. However, before the end of the 19th century, they were in a detached part of Sulhamstead Bannister parish called Sulhamstead Bannister Lower End. There was also a detached section of Sulhamstead Abbots parish around Grazeley Manor Farm and Burnt House Farm, the north-west portion of which had half of the Royal Ordnance Factory built on it. Despite having few inhabitants, this became the independent parish of Grazeley for a while. It is now also incorporated into Wokefield parish.

Figure 51: Diddenham Manor at Grazeley

The name Grazeley was previously Graeg-Sol which is Anglo-Saxon for Badgers' Wallowing Place. In the 18th century, core

Grazeley was considered to stand between Burnthouse Bridge and Grazeley Green. The houses there had disappeared within a hundred years and the area is now under the site of AWE Burghfield. Modern Grazeley was then called Lambwood Hill. The little village church was built there in 1850 but was converted into a domestic home in 2017. It had a crucifixion window designed by the great Victorian Gothic revival architect, Augustus Pugin.

The manors of Diddenham and Moor Place are at Grazeley. The former was first established as a small Anglo-Saxon settlement at Dydda's Water Meadow. Dydda was the name of the father of St Frideswide, the patron saint of Oxford. He was a minor king in the Oxfordshire/Berkshire area in the 7th century, but whether this was the same man is unknown. The manor was owned by the De Diddenham family in the 13th century, and later passed to the Woodcocks who also owned Moor Place at Poundgreen. The 13th century deer park of Moregarston may also have been somewhere in this area. The name means Morcar's Town.

Poundgreen is named after the brick pound built there to house stray animals found around the region. The manor house at Moor Place stood just east of the hamlet. Its successor was called Grazeley Court. This house was purchased, with the winnings from an Irish lottery ticket, by Doctor George Mitford for himself and his family, which included his daughter, the authoress Mary Russell Mitford. He totally rebuilt the house, renaming it Bertram House, but he had a serious gambling habit and Mary had to turn to writing to support the family. At Bertram, she wrote:

- Miscellaneous Verses (1810)
- Christine (1811) and
- Blanche (1813)

Eventually, the Mitfords were forced to sell up and move to lesser accommodation at Three Mile Cross. The family fortunes only had a slight up-turn with the weekly publication of Mary's most famous work, 'Our Village', after 1822.

During the Second World War, a Royal Ordnance explosives filling factory was built on the border between Grazeley Green and Burghfield. Production began in 1942. After the War, in 1953, the factory was converted for the production of nuclear missiles. Accommodation, called a 'Residential Club', for 1000 mostly Irish female munitions workers was built between James's and Chandlers Farms. This has now gone and since 1987 the factory has been attached to the Atomic Weapons Establishment at Aldermaston and is known as AWE Burghfield.

Heathlands, Gardeners Green and Holme Green

These are the hamlets of Wokingham Without parish, beyond Northern Crowthorne. Anciently part of Wokingham, this rural area of the parish was split off in 1894. Heathlands is the main settlement, standing on the northern side of the Nine Mile Ride and named after an old house there. The road began life in the reign of King George III as a track for the royal huntsmen leading out from the kennels at Swinley Lodge. The whole area was once wild heath, moorland and woodland in Windsor Forest. On the edge of one surviving wood, the Gorrick Plantation, sits the Gorrick Well: once famous for its healing powers, but now capped off. Queen Elizabeth I once visited it.

The area is recorded to have been rather uncivilised well into the Victorian era. The locals lived in peat-built huts, partly let into the ground, like early Anglo-Saxon grub-huts, and were semi-pagan, worshipping broken figured crockery on little peat altars.

None of the couples were married, though they often had children. The men made their living making brooms and were known as broom-dashers or broom-squires. Twenty or so of them would club together and send their wares to market in Reading or even Bristol. Despite a lack of religion, Sunday was still their day off, when they participated in heavy drinking and bareknuckle boxing. Everything changed when the little church of St Sebastian at Heathlands was built in 1864. The old pub nearby (pulled down in the 1990s) is said to have gained its name around the same time from the Duke of Wellington who, feeling thirsty whilst hunting in the forest, was most surprised to find a watering hole there in the middle of nowhere and exclaimed, "Who'd 'a' thought it?" – which became the name of the pub. Unfortunately, the tale seems a little unlikely as there were alternative and earlier pubs not far away on the Ride, at the St Sebastian's Roundabout (the Dog and Partridge) and by the railway bridge (The Forester).

Figure 52: Was the Crooked Billet moved to the other side of the road?

The pub at Gardeners' Green is still there. The Crooked Billet is an attractive weather-boarded building dating from the mid-19th century. It stands near a ford over the Emm Brook and there is an unlikely old story that it was moved from the other side of the road to avoid flooding. Both greens, which developed as settlements around Wokingham common land used for grazing livestock, are probably named after local families. Holme Green (formerly Hones' Green) surrounds Norman Shaw's neo-Tudor Holme Grange, built in 1883 as a weekend house for the stockbroker, Bartle Goldsmid. It is now a school. To the east is Ludgrove School, famous because it was attended by Princes William and Harry of Wales in recent years. On this site was originally a house called Tangley (hence Tangley Drive in Luckley), the home of Captain Sir Edward Walter, son of John Walter II, proprietor of the Times Newspaper from Bearwood. Sir Edward founded the Corps of Commissionaires with the aim of finding employment for discharged soldiers and sailors who had served in the Crimean War. It still operates today as Corps Security, the oldest security company in the World. The house was rebuilt in Arts-and-Crafts style in 1889, two years after Wixenford School moved there from Eversley (Hampshire). The building was taken over by Ludgrove School in 1937.

The Johnson and Johnson buildings and the adjoining Pinewood Activities complex, further towards Bracknell, cover the site of the old London Open Air Sanatorium. This was established in 1898-1901 as a hospital for 46 male tuberculosis patients in the healthy surroundings of pine woodland. The buildings had large windows providing good light and ventilation and patients could stay for up to six months. It was expanded to accommodate 160 patients and renamed the Pinewood Sanatorium in 1919. It closed in 1966.

Hurst

The parish is officially called St Nicholas Hurst, but is always simply called Hurst locally. The original settlement was at Whistley Green. However, in about 1080, the Abbot of Abingdon, who was lord of the manor, had a small wooden church built for the local people. The site chosen was a small previously wooded hill, just to the south, known as a Hurst: and the name stuck. The church was dedicated to St Nicholas by St Osmund, the Bishop of Salisbury. It was not a parish church, however, but a chapel-of-ease to the mother church at Sonning, out of whose region Hurst parish was later carved. So, while the Abbot was able to appoint the priest at Hurst, he was obliged to have all the revenues sent to the Rector of Sonning.

Figure 53: Hurst House, built in 1545 & reduced in size in 1847

The present church seems to have been built in stone in the 12th century, but mostly dates from the following two hundred years. In 1220, the Dean of Salisbury made one of his regular visitations to Sonning and insisted on interviewing the curates from the surrounding chapels. The credentials of Richard of Hurst were found to be highly suspect when he refused to answer questions about his knowledge of scripture. He, furthermore, persuaded the other curates to do the same and thus found himself suspended for "ignorance and insubordination".

After plague decimated the local population in the 1340s, supplies between Abingdon Abbey and Hurst began to dry up. The villagers who were left ceased to be supplied with their two free meals a week from the Abbey's grange at Whistley Green and went on strike, refusing to tend to the manor crops. However, they were ultimately unsuccessful in their actions.

Because it was forestland, most of the manors in the parish were small, created as a result of forest clearance. Broad Hinton was the northern manor (including Twyford): a detached part of Wiltshire until 1844. In the 13th century it was split into three. The two new manors were Hinton Pipard, based on Stanlake Park (mostly in Ruscombe), and Hinton Hatch, based around Hinton House. Built about 1610 by William Hyde (one of the widespread Hyde family from Denchworth near Wantage), Hinton House is nationally important as a very early form of what is called a 'triple-pile' house. This basically means it has a corridor through the middle: a major innovation at the time. It is now part of the Dolphin School.

Hogmoor Lane leads south from Hinton to Hurst, crossing Broadwater Lane before it continues on down Tape Lane. This is supposedly named after Molly Tape, a local girl who hanged herself there after attempts at witchcraft failed to stop her lover – Dick Darvell from Darvell's Farm – from leaving her. Her scantily clad spirit is said to haunt the lane still. The junction with Broadwater Lane is known as Warde's Cross. This reminds us of Richard Warde (originally from Winkfield), Henry VIII's sub-treasurer who was given the main Hurst manor at the Reformation. The Abbot's steward had only ever had a small house in Whistley, but Warde built himself Hurst House, near the church, in about 1545. It was a huge Tudor mansion with large chimneys, at least twice the size of all other houses in the area. Unfortunately, it was totally reconstructed in 1847, although the builders did reuse the old materials. It therefore retains some original doorways, panelling and fireplaces. Richard managed to retain office throughout the political changes of the Tudor period and his beautiful enamelled gold ring in Reading Museum demonstrates the great wealth he amassed.

Figure 54: Monument to Bible translator Sir Henry & Lady Savile

Richard Warde has a fine family monument and brass (1577) in Hurst Church. Alongside him lie many other local dignitaries, commemorated by a wide array of elegant monuments. His daughter, Alice Harrison, has a brass depicting her in childbirth during which she died in 1558 (although the brass dates from around 1622). Lady Savile, the mother-in-law of Alice's grandson, Richard Harrison, who retired to Hurst, has a vast draped monument with kneeling figures of various family members (1631) including her last husband, Sir Henry Savile. He was the Warden of Merton College, Oxford, and Provost of Eton, who helped translate the King James Bible. There is a chunky wall monument (1683) to Richard's son (and namesake) and his wife. Then there is Henry Barker of Hurst Lodge, just east of the village ponds, who has a recumbent effigy with a finely carved figure of skeletal death kneeling at his feet (1651). The Barkers were patrons of the almshouses built opposite the church in 1664. The plainer heraldic monument to Richard Bigg of Haines Hill looks like a table because it was used to stack up the bread that he left to be distributed to the poor every Sunday. Other treasures in this building include a 1636 hour-glass with oak foliated stand, to monitor sermon length, and the late 15th century rood screen, the rood cross being replaced with royal motifs. The Berkshire brick tower is dated 1612.

Figure 55: William Barker's Almshouses near Hurst Church

Next to the church is the Castle Inn, once called the Bunch of Grapes. The so-called Coffin Room within was where bodies would be laid out while awaiting burial and possibly autopsies carried out too. This relationship to the churchyard burials shows the inn's original use as a 'church-house' where the clergy sold ale to raise ecclesiastical funds. It also had the only bread ovens in the village, which can still be seen. The bowling green adjoining the pub is the oldest in the county. King Charles I is said to have played on it. He may have been visiting his Secretary of State, Sir Francis Windebank, at Haines Hill on the northern edge of Broad Common. When Windebank worked from home, he had a special stage coach to take state papers to the King. His high position at court had been obtained for him through the influence of his great friend and the King's right-hand man, Reading-born Archbishop Laud. His Grace often visited both Haines Hill and Hurst House and sometimes preached in the parish church. As a Royalist, Sir Francis escaped to France during the Civil War and his lands were confiscated.

The Harrisons were also Royalists during the Civil War and spent most of their fortune raising three troops of horse for the King. However, as they were away fighting most of the time, a small party of parliamentarians was able to station itself in the village. In 1643, there was an armed skirmish when some of the royalist garrison at Reading rode out to attack them, but the Roundheads were eventually triumphant.

Katesgrove

Katesgrove is an extension of the medieval settlement of Reading St Giles, south of the River Kennet. It sits on the west side of Southampton Street and originally developed as an industrial area of the town because the wharfs on the Kennet made it so easy to ship raw materials in and finished products out. The Katesgrove Tannery dated back to at least 1716, probably 1700 or earlier. From 1829 it was owned by George Higgs, who had been Mayor of Reading three years earlier. Around 1834, he seems to have retired to Elm Lodge in Battle and the business was purchased by the Philbrick brothers. The family owned it for just over a hundred years, living in Katesgrove House for much of that time. During their ownership, the business unfortunately suffered two serious fires, although it was rebuilt each time. The 1839 fire was at night and could be seen as far away as Woolhampton. The descriptions of people falling in the tanning pits while desperately trying to save stock and records would be comical if the event were not so tragic.

Figure 56: The Reading Ironworks in Katesgrove Lane

Next door stood Barrett, Exall and Andrewes' Ironworks, known from 1864 as the Reading Ironworks, one of the leading players in Britain's agricultural engineering industry. It started life in 1818 as Perry Brothers, a small plough manufacturer and general foundry on the corner of Southampton Street and Katesgrove Lane. Barrett joined later and the other partners followed after

Perry's death in 1830, the same year that the Swing Riots exploded against the machines they produced. The company soon moved into the national agricultural marketplace and worked with Isambard Kingdom Brunel to bring the railway to Reading. By 1848, they expanded into the production of steam engines and in the 1850s employed twice as many people as the next highest employer in the town, Huntley and Palmer's Biscuits. At their height, they were technically superb and full of innovation; but a recession, a lack of investment and poor management led to their demise by 1887.

During the Napoleonic Wars, the area was also well-known for its sailcloth industry and it was often said that the Battle of Trafalgar was won in Katesgrove Lane because Nelson's fleet was serviced by such a huge number of sails from the 140 looms at Musgrave Lamb's Sailcloth Manufactory there. Around the same time, the Leach family were making bricks just down the road at the Katesgrove Kilns (as well as in Caversham) along a lane that was to become Elgar Road. In 1815, they named their more southerly kiln, the Waterloo Kiln, after the Duke of Wellington's great victory. Upon John Leach's retirement, in 1867, this was sold to John Poulton who, like the more famous Collier of Coley and Tilehurst, had started out dealing in china and glass before moving into pottery and bricks. The firm, known as the Adamantine Brick and Terracotta Tile Works, produced silver-grey Reading bricks but was sold to S and E Collier's in 1908, when William Poulton decided to concentrate on his boiler engineering works instead. The site of the brickworks is now the Nimrod Industrial Estate. Slightly further south on the other side of the road, the Co-Op had a printworks, for the packaging and print needs of shops all over southern England, from the 1930s until 1981. The current Herald Printworks stands on an adjoining site. The Co-op also had a jam factory just across the Kennet in Coley

Lea Heath and Davis Street

Lea was a minor manor in the parish of St Nicholas Hurst, originally the northern part of the manor of Sindlesham. The old manor house stood at or near Lea Farm. From the 14th century, this was the southern home of the Restwold family of High Head Castle in Cumberland. They apparently found life up North rather remote and favoured Sindlesham Lea (or Lee) as their chief residence, enclosing a deer park there in 1346. It was particularly popular with Richard Restwold Junior (died 1475), a prominent Yorkist lawyer and Member of Parliament for Berkshire who worked for key movers and shakers in the Wars of the Roses, including the Earls of Suffolk (from Ewelme) and of Salisbury (from Bisham).

Figure 57: Hatchgate Farm with George Ford's dog on the wall

John Dalby purchased both Lea and Hurst manors in 1722. His son, Thomas Septimus Dalby, sold up in 1785 but retained an old house near Lea Farm which may have been the original Lea Manor House. He had it rebuilt on a square plan shortly afterwards and called it Hurst Grove. Dalby was a partner in the Morant Plantation in Jamaica with the Thompson sisters from Coley Park. Forty years later, Captain Henry George Boldero had two attractive angular bays added to the south-east front of the house. He was an MP for Chippenham who came to public attention in 1842 when he fought a bloodless duel with fellow parliamentarian, Craven Berkeley, after he had made inappropriate comments about Queen Victoria. Hurst Grove is now offices.

High Chimneys is a huge red brick country house with prominent chimneys that was built in 1661. The smaller farmhouse next door is now the café at Dinton Pastures Country Park. In the early 20th century, it was the home of George Ford Junior who ran the George Ford and Son's agricultural merchants that had shops at Lea Heath Stores in Davis Street and elsewhere in Eastern Berkshire. His father, George Ford Senior of Hatch Gate Farm, had founded the business when he discovered he could rent out threshing machines and be paid in grain. This would then be sold on at a premium when demand was high. The hamlet of Davis Street sits around the entrance to Dinton Pastures Country Park. The park was opened in 1979 after the area had been used extensively for gravel extraction. The landowner came from Dinton in Buckinghamshire, so the park was named after that village.

Lower Basildon

The earliest evidence of occupation at Basildon seems to have been down by the railway, surrounding the banks and ditches of an early Neolithic mortuary enclosure (*circa* 4,000 bc) for the exposure of bodies prior to dismemberment and partial burial. Bronze Age burial mounds (*circa* 2,000 bc) were later built up in the same area and it appears to have been at this very early period that the area first became a consolidated unit, as the Grim's Ditch still runs along part of the parish boundary today. Though the ditch dates from the Bronze Age, the name is Anglo-Saxon, indicating that these later settlers were so impressed with the size of this monument that they thought it could only have been built by the chief of their gods, Woden, nicknamed Grim.

While constructing the railway line in 1839, workmen found a relatively modest, though luxuriously decorated, Roman villa. The main discoveries were two mosaic floors, one in superb condition, which the navvies unfortunately smashed up soon afterwards. Luckily the greater of the two was first sketched by the antiquarian, Charles Roach-Smith. The villa itself has been completely lost beneath the railway, though stone-built outbuildings have more recently been excavated nearby; and the remains of a large series of ditched paddocks can be seen from the air. The place was built in a fine position overlooking a crossing of the Thames and was occupied from the 1st to the 4th centuries. In the early Anglo-Saxon period, the area was known as Basilford and it was there that the parish church and manor first developed. The name Basildon refers to the upland area at what is now called Upper Basildon.

The present Basildon Church is mostly 15th century in date. It is best known as the place of baptism and burial of the famous 18th century agriculturalist, Jethro Tull. Known as the 'Father of the Agricultural Revolution', he invented a seed-drill in 1701 and wrote 'Horse Husbandry', a famous pioneering work on farming methods. Though he died at Bagshot, near Hungerford, in 1741, he was buried in Basildon churchyard where a modern gravestone, showing his revolutionary drill, was erected in the late 20th century. Nearby is a touching monument to the Deverell brothers, showing two teenage boys who drowned in the Thames in 1886.

Figure 58: Basildon Park, a Palladian masterpiece saved from demolition

Basildon is, of course, best known for Basildon Park, the county's finest National Trust property. A previous house had been the home of the Viscounts Fane but the present building was erected by John Carr of York for Sir Francis Sykes between 1776 and 1783. It is a beautiful example of a Palladian villa. Sir Francis made his money working for the East India Company at the court of the Nawab of Bengal. Unfortunately, his son died of scarlet fever and his grandson was a spendthrift. The estate was sold to the millionaire, James Morrison MP, in 1838 and became home to his vast collection of paintings, including works by Constable, Da Vinci, Hogarth, Holbein, Poussin, Rembrandt, Reynolds, Rubens, Titian, Turner and VanDyck. Amongst his many famous visitors was JMW Turner. His work, 'Rain, Speed and Steam' – considered by many to be the first Impressionist painting – is sometimes said to depict Basildon Railway Bridge. However, it is recorded that Turner was inspired by the Maidenhead Railway Bridge and the picture does seem to show Maidenhead Bridge in the distance. Though the connection is unknown to many, Basildon Park is remembered through 'Basildon Bond' writing paper which was named in honour of the place after the head of the stationery firm stayed there with James' grandson, Major JA Morrison. Major Morrison was a great benefactor to Basildon and a patron of the architect, Sir Edwin Lutyens, who erected a number of cottages in Upper Basildon. The park was requisitioned by the territorial army and then a US battalion during the Second World War and was in a state of ruin by 1945. However, it was somewhat miraculously restored by the 2nd Lord Iliffe.

Figure 59: Basildon Grotto & its lost Chinese Wallpaper

Basildon Grotto is a second elegant mansion in the parish, with fine views over the Thames. It was built in the early 18th century by Mary, Viscountess Fane, who lived at Basildon Park. It was a garden folly covered in attractive shellwork, which she used as a riverside retreat. It was much expanded and altered over the centuries to include many fine rooms including a Chinese Room which was decorated with original 18th century Chinese wallpaper. Unfortunately, this has been totally destroyed through the house's neglect over the last few years. The ghost of Lady Fane's daughter-in-law is still said to haunt the house. She has been claimed as the famous 'Mistletoe-Bow Bride' who died, trapped in a blanket chest, on her wedding day (a story more usually associated with other houses in Hampshire or Norfolk). However, Lady Fane actually died an old lady and the more common story says she fell down a well.

Lower Caversham

The earliest evidence of Christianity in Berkshire comes from Lower Caversham. An ancient well, probably attached to a Roman villa, was examined at Dean's Farm and found to contain a crushed metal tank. It is decorated with the ancient Christian Chi-Rho symbol and would thus appear to be one of several examples of portable lead fonts that have been discovered around the country. These were used by the early Christians of Roman Britain to baptise the faithful and may indicate that the nearby villa was a local Christian meeting place.

It is possible that the area continued as a Christian centre right up until Tudor times, for there appears to have been a medieval chapel there, whose existence was reflected in the name of a field next to Dean's Farm recorded as Capull (a corruption of Chapel) alias Rayley in 1633. This still exists as the Ray Meadow at the northern end of Reading Bridge. The word Ray is a corruption of the Anglo-Saxon phrase Atter Eye which means 'At the Isle', probably referring to the adjoining View Island. This is joined by a footpath over the weir at the 'clappers' to De Bohun Island (named after the patrons of Caversham 'Priory') and Caversham Lock. The lock was historically in Reading (rather than Caversham) and was first recorded in 1493. There had presumably always been a flash lock associated with the nearby mill, and the name 'clappers' suggests a medieval crossing point along the weir crest that may have been the dangerous ford mentioned in early records as pre-dating Caversham Bridge. The current pound lock was only created in 1778.

Caversham Mill stood east of View Island spanning the mill stream on the Thames and crossing over to Heron Island. It was first mentioned in the Domesday Survey of 1086. It seems to have been both a corn and a cloth fulling mill, sometimes at the same time as it had up to four mill wheels. The beautiful old Victorian mill was converted and extended to become a cork factory in 1952. The present housing estate was built on the site in 1986.

Figure 60: Old Caversham Mill, once part of the castle complex

Lower Caversham was historically called East Throp, meaning the village east of the main settlement at Caversham. Throp or thorp is generally a Viking place-name only found in the north and so may have been coined when the Viking army made Reading their southern headquarters in the 9th century. It is likely that the medieval amenities there were all part of a single complex centred on the important castle (or fortified manor house) of Caversham. It probably stood somewhere near the farm house at Dean's Farm itself (previously called Caversham Farm). It was the favourite home of William Marshal, Earl of Pembroke, the eighty-year-old Regent of England during the minority of King Henry III. He died there in 1218. The castle later passed to the Earls of Warwick, who also favoured it. Anne daughter and eventual sole heiress of Richard Beauchamp, 13th Earl of Warwick, was born at Caversham in September 1426. The Earl later made his will there in August 1437. Richard Neville, son of the 8th Earl of Salisbury (from Bisham 'Abbey' Manor) is supposed to have proposed to the Lady Anne on Caversham Bridge, although the two had been betrothed since before she was thirteen. They married and Richard eventually inherited the title of Earl of Warwick upon the death of Anne's young niece. He became so powerful that it was his support that determined who was king during the Wars of the Roses: Henry VI or Edward IV. He has been remembered by History as 'Warwick the Kingmaker'. The castle at Lower Caversham was pulled down in 1493 and the moat filled in.

Although historically in Oxfordshire, since 1911 Caversham and its associated hamlets in the south of the old parish have fallen within the region administered by Berkshire County Council and subsequently Reading Borough Council.

Lower Finchampstead and the Leas

Neither of these names are much used today. Lower Finchampstead is the area around the Tally Ho! pub at the northern end of Eversley Bridge. The community had its own shop and forge in the Victorian era. To the west, it runs up the Reading Road and into Finchampstead Leas where one of the twin manor houses of the parish stands. The wider manor was divided in two after the death of William Banister in the 1270s. His daughter, Constance, was given East Court near the parish church, while his daughter, Agatha, had West Court at Finchampstead Leas. The Roman road from Silchester to London runs up the drive and a Roman milestone, discovered in 1841, is preserved at nearby Banisters House.

West Court is a fine 17th century building which, before changes were made in 1835, still had a moat and a drawbridge. It was owned by the descendants of Agatha Banister for over three hundred years. Latterly it came into the hands of Lady Marvyn, the builder of Ufton Court in Ufton Nervet, and her heirs, the Catholic Perkins family. The family sometimes lived at Ufton Court but regularly had to rent it out in order to pay the heavy fines imposed on them for not attending the local Anglican church. During these periods, they lived at Bathampton House, north-west of Salisbury, where they were neighbours to fellow Catholics, the Tattershall family of Stapleford. In 1584, Francis Perkins sold West Court to his brother-in-law, George Tattershall Junior, and the family moved to Berkshire. The Tattershalls frequently travelled to Ufton to attend secret masses held there by under-cover priests. George was almost certainly among those who lost large sums of money seized when Ufton was raided by the authorities in 1599.

The old house at West Court was totally rebuilt about 1685 by the Honourable Charles Howard, a well-known horticulturalist and alchemist of his day who had married the last of the Tattershalls. They were grandparents of the 10th Duke of Norfolk. However, despite the couple mostly having lived at Deepdene near Dorking in Surrey, they are remembered in the heraldry inserted into one of a number of superb Jacobean carved fireplaccs at the Court, with allegorical figures of Wisdom, Justice and the Arts. These were brought from the old house when it was demolished. In 1704, the Court was sold to James Goodyer and later passed to his sister's family, a branch of the St Johns from Dogmersfield Park (Hampshire) who provided four generations of rectors to Finchampstead. The place was requisitioned by the Army in 1941 and used for training Special Operations. They purchased it in 1950 and until recent years the house was the officers' mess for the REME at Arborfield Garrison.

Figure 61: The New Inn (now the Tally Ho!) at Lower Finchampstead

Reverend Henry Ellis St John and his brother were keen huntsmen and the rector purchased the Duke of Bridgewater's hounds in 1810 so that he could hunt whenever he liked. His kennels were at Barkham and he took over the hunting region on the west side of the River Loddon. His hounds were later merged with the Garth Hunt. Huntsmen and their dogs were often seen in Finchampstead in the past, including the Royal Hunt from North Ascot. It is therefore not surprising that the local pub is named the Tally Ho! which was a popular hunting cry. Before 1969, it was called the New Inn and may have been a popular watering hole since at least the mid-18th century.

The St Johns also owned the manor house of Banisters on the lower slopes of Fleet Hill, which they purchased upon the death of their cousin, John Banister, the last of the Banister family, in 1821. These Banisters had been descendants of the original Banister line of Finchampstead manor, who were supposedly given this sub-manor as a reward for betraying the Duke of Buckingham to King Richard III in 1483. Unfortunately, this story appears to relate to one of their distant Staffordshire relatives. The family had in fact held the manor from the reign of King Edward II and built the present beautiful brick house in 1683. The place was originally called Hatch Farm because it owned the parish mill between the Leas and Lower Common at Eversley. This would have once had an attached fish hatchery. By 1563 the mill belonged instead to West Court but, in that year, Thomas Harrison of East Court was renting the building and controversially rebuilt the mill a few hundred yards upstream from the old one, which was then demolished. Thus the 'New Mill' which stands today was born, though it has been much changed and extended since. It was operating as a corn mill until the 1950s but is now a restaurant.

Lower Padworth

The whole of Padworth parish north of the River Kennet is really Lower Padworth. The settlement so named developed in the early

20th century along the Bath Road. This Reading to Speenhamland section had been turnpiked and thus improved and tolled in 1728. The first residence in the area was the Hare and Hounds pub which was actually in Beenham parish and the Beenham Manor Courts were sometimes held there. The parish boundary crosses the road to divert around it, suggesting an early origin. The pub took its name from the fact that it was a regular meeting place for the South Berkshire Hunt and records for the place date back to at least 1773. It was also popularly known as the Halfway House as it was a convenient stopping point for coach travellers half-way between Reading and Newbury. In deep snows in winter, travellers out of Reading thought themselves lucky to reach as far as Halfway.

Figure 62: The old Fox & Hounds at Lower Padworth

While the turnpike roads made long distance travel quicker and easier, travel could still be precarious. In August 1781, it is recorded that three young weavers from Trowbridge had rashly run away from their friends and family in order to find higher paid work in London. While travelling on a waggon near Lower Padworth, one of them lost his hat. Slipping down to catch it, he fell under their transport which ran over his legs. He was taken to the Hare and Hounds in a terrible state and died an hour later. His poor dejected friends gave up their journey to London and returned home. In 1846, towards the end of the great coaching era, the horses pulling a 'White Horse Company' coach set off on their own while the ostler was not paying attention. The coachman ran after them, but tripped whilst trying to halt the animals, and his head and legs were thrown under the wheels. He died instantly. The pub was demolished in 1990 and the site is now an hotel.

A fine 4th century Roman bathhouse was discovered near Lower Padworth, just over the border in the south-east of Beenham parish. It was probably associated with a Roman villa, just to the west, that remained unnoticed while gravel extraction destroyed it. Imported building materials indicate a complex of some ambition. The bath suite was certainly a luxury: a large rectangular building with an underground heating system (hypocaust). It was probably divided by a wooden partition into a warm room (tepidarium) and sauna-like hot room (caldarium). A narrow unheated annex was probably the cold room (frigidarium) and may have contained a portable plunge bath. An adjoining building was probably a changing room and water was drawn from a nearby well.

Luckley and Woodcray

Luckley is on the eastern side of the Finchampstead Road in southern Wokingham, built on the land of Luckley Hall, south of Luckley Road. The first country house at the centre of this estate was called Crutwell's and stood about halfway between the present Luckley and Ludgrove Schools. It was built in the late 16th century for John Crutwell III in an area then known as Simonds' Green. It was later the home of Charles Fyshe-Palmer, the Reading Member of Parliament in the 1820s and 1830s. Despite being brother-in-law to three dukes and a marquess, he commanded little respect from the author Mary Russell Mitford from Three Mile Cross who described him as "vastly like a mop-stick, or, rather, a tall hop-pole, or an extremely long fishing-rod, or anything that is all length and no substance". The 1723 Palmer School (now All Saints') was named after the family.

Figure 63: The 17th century Lucas Hospital at Chapel Green

The old house at Luckley was demolished in 1840. The present building is an interesting neo-Carolingian country house built in 1906 for Edward Mansfield, the retired headmaster of Lambrook School in Winkfield Row. It became a girls' school twelve years later and has recently started to admit boys as well. It was, no doubt, built in a style sympathetic to the nearby Lucas Hospital almshouses at Chapel Green. These were put up by the estate of Henry Lucas, secretary to the Earl of Holland, in 1665-7. He had no specific connection with Wokingham but *was* interested in the welfare of the people of Windsor Forest. They are the town's finest building and have been attributed to a young Sir Christopher Wren – although evidence is lacking. Sadly, the Charity Commission gave permission for them to be sold in 2002 and they are now private apartments. At the same time, the Henry Lucas Charity merged with the Whiteley Homes Trust at Walton-on-Thames.

Woodcray is slightly further south on the edge of what was Hagfield Heath, towards the Throat on the Finchampstead parish boundary. In the 14th century, Woodcray manor was the earliest known home of the Simonds family who went on to become well-known brewers and bankers in Reading: hence the naming of Simonds' Green at Luckley. Three generations before the founding of these businesses, John Simonds was operating the old Marlowe Tannery on the Emm Brook from 1690 to 1710. It is now the site of the Bridge Retail Park at the northern end of the Finchampstead Road.

Maiden Erlegh and Lower Earley

Maiden Erlegh covers the estate of Maiden Erlegh House which stood where the loop of Crawford Close is today. This had been the centre of the new or maiden manor of Earley since 1362 when John d'Earley VI split off 19 acres of his Whiteknights estate (now the campus of the University of Reading) to become the home for a younger branch of his family. The core of the last house on the site is believed to have been built in the early 1780s for Edward Golding, an East India Company nabob who became Lord of the Treasury during the premiership of his neighbour, Viscount Sidmouth of Woodley Lodge. However, it was largely rebuilt by the Master of the South Berkshire Hunt, John Hargreaves, in 1878. He established a racecourse in the Hillside Road/Sutcliffe Avenue/Mill Lane area with the grandstand opposite the site of Loddon Primary School. It was mostly used for steeple chases and remained in use up until the First World War.

Figure 64: Maiden Erlegh House, home of Solly Joel

In 1903, Maiden Erlegh House became the home of Solly Joel, the extravagant, mining, brewing and railway magnate. He spent a small fortune making the house one of the most beautiful in the county, expanding it to over seventy rooms, fifty of them bedrooms, perhaps with the help of the local architect Alfred Waterhouse. Most opulent were his Italian marble winter gardens and 'Pompeiian' swimming pool with colonnade surround and nude frescos. The latter was built at a cost of £12,000 (about £700,000 today) and finally sold for just £350, with the intention of shipping it to Barbados. Stories of mysterious visitors and extraordinary parties featuring skinny-dipping chorus girls have passed into local folklore. Alas, after Solly's death in 1931, the building's life as a Boys' School and Training College were short-lived and Berkshire County Council decided against its purchase for council offices. It was demolished in 1960 to be replaced by the housing estate. Only the old lake and the two approach roads (Betchworth Avenue/Silverdale Road and Maiden Erlegh Drive/The Parade) still survive.

Lower Earley is the low-lying part of Earley along the River Loddon. It may have been the site of the manor mills, although only two fisheries are mentioned in the Domesday Survey of 1086. Most of the region was historically the site of Earley Upper Common and Lower Wood Common. These were common grazing land south of Maiden Erlegh Park, enclosed in 1820 and added to the existing farms in the area. Two of these survive today. Radstock Farmhouse (now Radstock Cottage) in Radstock Lane dates back to the early 17th century. Rushey Mead, hidden away at the bottom of the drive between Red House Close and Turnhouse Close, was built about fifty years earlier as the farmhouse of Lower Earley Farm (aka Lowerwood Farm).

New Farm, in the Measham Way area, was built just prior to the enclosures about 1815. Solly Joel later renamed it Home Farm and turned it into a horse stud, home to up to 70 horses at a time. Joel was a highly successful racehorse owner and the stud became one of the most famous in the country. It continued in operation until the 1980s. A very small hamlet, called Home Farm Cottages, was built at the same time as the farm, along the section of Beech Lane that runs parallel with Rushey Way. This included a short-lived Primitive Methodist Chapel. Only one of the houses still stands. The housing estate at Lower Earley was developed from 1975. At one time, it was the largest private housing development in Europe.

Newtown and Cemetery Junction

The eastern half of Newtown and the old cemetery itself were historically in the Earley part of Sonning parish and were only transferred to Reading in 1887. Reading Old Cemetery was created at what became Cemetery Junction after this was allowed by a special act of Parliament in 1842. It once had two chapels, one for the Church of England and one for other denominations, but these have long been demolished. It has many fine monuments to the great and the good of Reading, but the best known is that to the young motorcycle racing driver, Bernard Hieatt, who stands in full racing attire:

To the proud and beautiful memory of Air Pilot Bernard Laurence, the beloved eldest son of BL and L Hieatt, who was suddenly called away in his hour of victory on May 3rd 1930, after creating two world records in the two hundred miles motor cycle and sidecar race at Brooklands, aged 21 years

Figure 65: Bernard Hieatt's Monument & St Bartholomew's Church

Cemetery Junction is now known worldwide from the 2010 Ricky Gervais comedy film named after it. The author grew up in the Newtown area just to the north. This estate was built from the mid-1870s for the workers at Huntley and Palmer's biscuit factory just across the Kennet. The firm mostly built their employees terrace houses, with their size and facilities reflecting the status of the occupier within the company. There are no pubs on the estate because the Palmers were teetotal Quakers. Palmer Park, to the east of the cemetery, was gifted to the people of Reading by the factory's owner, George Palmer. It was originally supposed to cover only 21 acres but Palmer decided to increase this to 49 acres on the strict condition that no alcohol should ever be sold there. It was opened in 1891 and in 1930 Palmer's statue by George Blackall Simonds, a local brewer as well as a sculptor, was moved there from Broad Street.

Figure 66: The old Marquis of Granby at Cemetery Junction

Another great Reading company, Sutton Seeds, had their trial grounds in the triangle between London Road and the two railway lines. In 1962, they moved their main business premises there from the Market Place in the centre of town. Sutton's eventually relocated to Torquay in 1976, after 170 years in Reading, but we are still reminded of their patronage by the name of the business park now on that site.

Immediately opposite the entrance to the old cemetery is the bizarrely named Hope and Bear pub, squeezed between King's Road and London Road. Before changing names three times in recent years, it was appropriately called the Jack of Both Sides for over 150 years. It was last called the Abbot Cook after Hugh Cook (of Faringdon), the last Abbot of Reading who was hanged outside the Abbey Gateway in 1539. Until 2012, the ice-cream parlour across the road was the Granby, originally the Marquis of Granby, pub. The first pub on the site was presumably one of the many so named and opened by soldiers who had served under this popular British general in the Seven Years' War of the 1760s. It would then have stood in open countryside some way to the east of Reading. However, it must have taken a while for the name to be chosen, as it was called the New Inn in 1790. There is a strong local tradition that it was previously known as the Gallows Tavern because the condemned would have a last drink with their executioner there on the way to the 'Old Gallows' on the parish boundary at what became Cemetery Junction. Sadly, evidence is lacking and a similar story is told of the old Oxford Arms in Silver Street. In 1828, three young men were executed at Reading Prison for having shot a gamekeeper in the hip in Sunninghill Park. The corpse of one of their number, Thomas Field of Old Windsor, was returned to his friends who apparently took the coffin to the Granby, opened it, sat Thomas up and offered him a drink. In 1786, the landlady had set up a theatre on the premises to entertain coach travellers heading into Reading.

She put on Shakespeare and Restoration Comedy but it did not last long as the inn was broken into and all the scenery, props and costumes stolen. Other prominent buildings in the area include William Ravenscroft's fine red and grey brick Wycliffe Baptist Chapel of 1880-1 and WGA Hambling's elegant Co-Op supermarket of 1901 which originally sported a fine clocktower.

Reading Technical College was built on the old tennis grounds adjoining Victoria Square, off the King's Road, which it purchased in 1950 and opened five years later. Across the road, between Victoria and Montague Streets, CityBlock Student Accommodation stands on an interesting site of early industrial activity outside the town centre. In 1867, the Berkshire Brewery was established there, followed by Salmon's Tea Warehouse which moved up from the western end of King's Road in 1884. This was the wholesale storehouse and printing and packaging department of a popular national brand of tea in late Victorian England. Salmon's was purchased by the Brooke Bond Tea Company in 1902 and the premises continued to handle tea packing and label printing as the Berkshire Printing Company, named after the old brewery. The firm moved to the Oxford Road in 1932.

Padworth

There are a number of ancient, and now disjointed, banks and ditches around Padworth, locally known as Grim's Ditch. The name indicates that the Anglo-Saxon settlers in the area thought they were so impressive that they must have been built by the chief of their pagan gods, Woden, who was nicknamed Grim. In fact, the position of the ditches indicate that they encircle the northern boundaries of Calleva, the Roman town of Silchester, just over the border in Hampshire. It is generally accepted that they were constructed for a post-Roman king who had set himself up as the protector of the Romano-Britons still living at Silchester after the Roman army had left the country and the central administration had collapsed. At that time, Berkshire was a fast-growing Anglo-Saxon colony and, when things got tough, the new-comers would attack the British urban populace. In response, the banks and ditches were built to protect the old northern route-ways into Silchester and were, no doubt, constantly guarded by the local Romano-British militia.

Figure 67: Grim's Banks & Ditches around Calleva (Roman Silchester)

The Anglo-Saxon leader who settled in this precise area with his family was probably called Padda. Hence the place became Padda's Farm or Padworth. However, it may possibly mean Toad Farm and there are other personal names, including the Celtic Pedrog or Padrig, which could also give rise to such a place-name. After the Norman Conquest, the manor was owned by the prominent Coudray family who appear to originally have been called De Padworth. They were resident throughout the 13th and 14th centuries but later inherited, through the female line, Sherborne Coudray (now Sherborne St John) and Herriard in

North Hampshire, which they seem to have preferred. They sold their residence in Padworth in 1586.

A secondary manor called Hussey's lay near the border with Ufton and was owned by the wide-ranging Fettiplace family from North Denchworth near Wantage. By Tudor times, however, it was run by the Perkins family of Ufton Robert Manor (and later Ufton Court). Mr Richard Perkins let his brother, Francis, live at Pam Hall, the manor house of Hussey's, but a serious dispute concerning the manor's overlordship arose with their neighbour, Sir Humphrey Forster of Aldermaston House. Forster was the son-in-law of King Henry VIII's Lord Chamberlain, Lord Sandys of the Vyne (at Sherborne St John in Hampshire). He spent much time at the Royal Court and clearly thought himself socially above other Berkshire gentry. To match his inflated ego, he also had a very bad temper. It is not known what eventually brought the argument to a head but one day in 1534 Sir Humphrey armed his servants with bows, arrows, swords, shields, daggers and spears and at half past five in the morning they marched on Pam Hall. Finding Francis Perkins in his nightshirt in the hall, Sir Humphrey immediately began to assault him. He was only prevented from killing the man by the pleas of his poor wife who came running downstairs in her nightdress. Instead, he was tied up and escorted to Ufton Robert where he was thrown at the feet of his brother, Richard Perkins, who was taking breakfast with a number of guests. Sir Humphrey then started on Richard, taking him by the hair and insisting that he keep his hands off the Forster lands in Padworth. One guest tried to intervene but was quickly punched in the stomach. Sir Humphrey drew his sword and was about to do still worse damage to Richard, when his wife held back Sir Humphrey's arms. Forster decided to leave but took Francis Perkins with him and threw him in his local Aldermaston lock-up for the night. The Perkins brothers took Sir Humphrey to the local court in Wokingham but he bribed and threatened the jury. The outcome of a later case at the London-based Court of the Star Chamber is not known. It was Richard Perkins' intervening wife, Elizabeth, who later, as Lady Marvyn, instigated the famous dole of bread and cloth for the parishioners of Ufton and Padworth. It is supposed to have been set up in thanks to the villagers for having helped her find her way home after getting lost in the woods in 1581.

Figure 68: Sir Humphrey Forster leads an attack on Pam Hall

In September 1643, during the Civil War, roundhead troops passed through the parish when they continued their march towards London after having defeated the Royalists at the First Battle of Newbury. In Padworth Gulley, however, Prince Rupert's cavalry managed to surprise them one last time. Three hundred men are said to have been killed. They were buried in large pits in the parish churchyard. A memorial in the church porch tells their story. Just over a year later, more parliamentary troops, from Aldermaston, crossed the Kennet at Padworth whilst on their way to the Second Battle of Newbury.

Figure 69: Padworth House & Archbishop Chichele's Saltcellar

Padworth parish church is one of the smallest in the county. A fine Norman apsed building with decorative doorways, it was almost completely constructed in about 1130. The interior features a medieval wall painting of St Nicholas and grand monuments to the Brightwell family and their heirs who built the present Padworth House alongside. This is the main manor house of the parish and was in their hands from 1655. When Loftus Brightwell died in 1738, his grandson, Christopher Griffith, inherited the place. He married Catherine, daughter of Sir William St Quinton. Both were painted by Gainsborough and his portrait of Christopher is now in the collection at Reading Museum. Having no children or other family, Christopher left his estates to his wife's nephew, Matthew Chitty Darby, who subsequently took the name of Griffith as well. He was a general in the grenadier guards, served with distinction in the Peninsula War and was wounded at the Battle of Corunna. His descendants owned Padworth House well into the 20th century. As collateral descendants of Archbishop Chichele, the family once kept many fine relics associated with him at the house. The chief of these was his extraordinary mid-15th century saltcellar in the shape of a fork-bearded huntsman which can now be seen in the Ashmolean Museum in Oxford.

In the late 1820s, Padworth House was rented by Thomas Bushby Bacon, the son of the great Welsh ironmaster, Anthony Bacon. He sold up his ironworks in Merthyr Tydfil to move to Padworth. There he is believed to have raised a black and white Newfoundland dog which was later owned by his daughter, Mary Ann, the wife of Mr Newman Smith of Croydon Lodge in Surrey. Smith was a great friend of Sir Edwin Landseer who admired the dog so much that he painted him in his iconic work, 'A Distinguished Member of the Humane Society', which is now part of the Tate Collection. However, the dog, called Paul Pry from his habit of investigating every place he came across, was there portrayed in the role of a famous life-saving sea-going dog called Bob and Mr Newman was not best pleased that his pet thereby lost his identity. It is because of this painting that black and white Newfoundlands are now known as Landseers.

The two Mortimer murderers, Abraham Tull and William Hawkins, were born and baptised in Padworth. Their parents were humble, honest and respected folk and the families both lived in Ufton. In 1787, at the ages of nineteen and seventeen respectively, they waylaid an old labourer and bludgeoned him to death for the sake of eleven shillings, which they then failed to find on his body. They were hanged on Mortimer Common, on a piece of land just within Ufton parish, now called Gibbet Piece.

Pangbourne

The Roman road from Silchester to Dorchester-on-Thames runs through Pangbourne parish somewhere – traditionally on or near the line of the A340. Signs of Roman occupation have been uncovered on Shooters' Hill, including many gold and silver coins and a number of skeletons. Pangbourne means Paega's People's Stream, showing that it was the home of an early Anglo-Saxon chieftain of that name and his retinue. The place is first recorded in a grant of land there from the Bishop of Leicester to Bertwulf, the King of Mercia (the Midlands) in AD 844. The monarch is prominently depicted on the village sign near the village hall.

Figure 70: Bere Court, where the last Abbot of Reading was captured

Pangbourne manor was given to Reading Abbey by King Henry I and the abbots often used the manor house of Bere Court, below Bowden Green, as a summer get-away. The last of their line, Hugh Cook Faringdon, was hiding in the mass of underground tunnels there when he was captured and sent to Reading for execution in 1539. His 15th century illuminated copy of John Wycliffe's English translation of the Bible was found in the house and now belongs to the University of Manchester Library. Bere Court later came into the hands of Sir John Davis, who had made his fortune capturing Cadiz with the Earl of Essex in 1596. His large effigial monument can be seen in the parish church. This also houses the largest array of hatchments (heraldic funerary boards) in the county, all to the Breedon family who were subsequent lords of the manor. The first of this old Bedfordshire family to live in Pangbourne was John Breedon, a London alderman who bought the manor in 1671. He was later Sheriff of Berkshire, while his brother was the Governor of Nova Scotia. In the churchyard is buried a more lowly but perhaps more notable individual: Lord Nelson's favourite bo'sun, Tom Carter.

Not far from Bere Court is Pangbourne College, founded in 1917 by Sir Thomas Lane Devitt and his son, Philip, on the site of an old towered folly connected with Bere Court. It was used by the extravagant Marquess of Blandford as an apiary when he briefly rented the manor house in the 1790s. The two Devitts wished to train boys for the Royal and Merchant Navies but always made sure they received a rounded education in case any lad decided a life at Sea was not for him. Today, it incorporates the Falkland Islands Memorial Chapel, the national memorial to those who fell in the 1982 Falklands War. Former pupils include the film director Ken Russell. Beyond Bowden Green, just over the border in Ashampstead parish, is another well-known school, St Andrew's. It was converted in 1934 from Buckhold House, designed by local architect, Alfred Waterhouse, in 1885. Former pupils include the author John Le Carré, the television historian Adam Hart-Davis, the Admiral of the Fleet Benjamin Bathurst and HRH the Duchess of Cambridge.

Pangbourne has always prospered as a centre of communications, with major roads, the river, a ferry and, from 1893, a bridge named after the village of Whitchurch on the Oxfordshire bank of the Thames. The present iron structure was put up in 1901. Pangbourne has always therefore had its fair share of hostelries to serve local travellers. The George is an old coaching inn, a version of which is believed to have stood on the same spot since the 13th century. Four hundred years later, a local woman called Betty Price was apparently forced to hide in the cellars of the old inn after she was hounded by the people of Pangbourne as a witch. The cellars were prone to flooding and the poor woman almost drowned. She was, however, eventually hunted down and, whilst being dragged from the place, she cursed the parson and her other captors. It is not recorded what happened to these men but Betty was executed for her supposed crimes and her ghost has haunted the pub ever since, despite rebuilding. Historically, the Swan, by the weir, was the only part of Whitchurch parish south of the Thames. It is thought to have a 16th century core but reached its height of popularity during the Edwardian boating age and is immortalized in Jerome K Jerome's 'Three Men in a Boat'. Kenneth Grahame, the author of 'The Wind in the Willows', is also said to have been a regular visitor.

Figure 71: The George Inn, where the Pangbourne Witch hid

Grahame retired to Church Cottage (originally the old smithy – see cover) in 1924 and died there eight years later. His funeral was conducted in the adjoining church, though he is buried in Oxford. The old village lock-up can be easily seen from the road in Grahame's garden. He wrote 'Wind in the Willows' in Cookham Dean, but the rolling River Thames at Pangbourne is said to have been the inspiration for many of EH Shepard's beautiful illustrations. However, although there is something of Mapledurham House to his Toad Hall, this drawing is known to have been based on Foxwarren Park near Cobham in Surrey.

Further upriver from the Swan, the steep sides of Shooters' Hill rise up from the road named after it. The hill is supposed to have been named in the 17th century. One story tells of locals who were pursuing a dangerous highwayman but, unable to follow their prey over the border into Oxfordshire, shot at him from the top of the hill instead. Alternatively, an artillery station may have been positioned there during the Civil War to guard the Thames crossing. Cannon balls were dug up nearby when the Great Western Railway was laid.

Pingewood, Burghfield Bridge and Sheffield Bottom

Pingewood was a pre-Roman Celtic settlement. There are several ancient earthworks in the area and the name preserves the old Celtic word 'pen' meaning head, peak, tip or end. The 'ge' is a contraction of 'coed', Celtic for wood. When the Anglo-Saxons moved into the area, they did not understand the meaning and added their own descriptive word 'wood' on the end. The name of the parish, Burghfield, is Anglo-Saxon and may mean Barrow Field, perhaps in reference to the burial mound excavated on the site of Burghfield Golf Course, just off the Burghfield Road north of the motorway. It was considered so important that the early

7th century Anglo-Saxon settlers in the area made it the focus for a small cemetery, with the chief members of the community buried in the barrow itself.

Figure 72: Burghfield Mill, now residential apartments

Historically, Burghfield parish was divided into three manors: Burghfield Regis, Burghfield Abbas and Sheffield. Sheffield was the smallest. Originally called Schewell, the name means Shelter-covered Well (or Spring). The old manor house may be the 'Old Manor' at Whitehouse Green that was built in 1685. Amners Farm was erroneously said to have been the centre of another manor, but it is really part of Burghfield Abbas and was named after the almoner of Reading Abbey who ran it. The almoner was in charge of distributing alms (or charity) to the poor. Old Moatlands Farm was probably also attached to this manor, as the old manor house had a medieval moat. In the mid-18th century, Moatlands was the home of William May, the joint-founder of May's Brewery in Basingstoke. He also owned and ran the nearby mill, although the present building only dates from 1884. It closed its doors in the 1960s and was converted into apartments in 1986. On the north-western edge of the motorway services once stood Field Farm. It was for many years home to the Burges family and Colonel Elizeus Burges grew up there. He was a famous late 17th century drunk, womaniser, duellist, murderer and gaol-breaker. His military record, however, allowed him to become the Governor of New England and Ambassador to Venice.

Burghfield Abbas and Regis were largely in the more southern portion of Burghfield parish but they shared responsibility for Burghfield Bridge. Matthew de Burghfield, the tenant of Burghfield Abbas manor in the early 13th century, was the first to have a bridge built at Burghfield. The villagers had previously had to wade through the marshes and ford the deep River Kennet, and there had been many accidents. Matthew's landlord, Reading Abbey, would not pay for a proper crossing but he was so moved by his vassals' brave determination that he put his hand in his own pocket for a narrow wooden structure, which he later widened for the use of carts and horses. By the reign of King Edward I, this bridge had become an important river crossing but overuse had left it in a bad state. The King ordered its repair and the original builder's grandson, Peter de Burghfield, the tenant of Burghfield Abbas manor, found himself presented with a large bill by the King's agent, Theobald le Carpenter. He protested in the strongest terms and refused to pay because the bridge had only been erected through his grandfather's selfless generosity and he therefore considered himself under no obligation to keep it in working order. In the end, Peter's cousin, Sir Roger de Burghfield (Regis), stepped in and agreed to pay for repairs to the southern half of Burghfield Bridge, if Peter would pay for the northern half.

It was probably during the Abbas manor lordship of Lord Williams of Thame, whose mother came from the old Burghfield family of Moore, that Burghfield Bridge was first rebuilt in stone. It continued to be an important crossing over the Kennet and during the Civil War was the subject of a minor clash after the First Battle of Newbury (1643), when Prince Rupert's cavalry attacked a brigade of roundhead troops leaving that town. The outcome is unknown, but there probably wasn't much in it either way. By October of the following year, the bridge had been destroyed. Seven hundred royalist troops, returning to Oxford in disguise (and escorting one hundred prisoners) after briefly having relieved the Siege of Basing House in Hampshire, found there was no crossing available to them. The foot soldiers were obliged to mount up behind the cavalrymen in order for the horses to carry them across the river.

The name of the Cunning Man pub (previously the Swan Inn) at Burghfield Bridge was apparently transferred from another pub across the road, now a café at the Pingewood Road junction. A misguided story tells that the original pub was built by a local man who used his cunning by placing the bricks vertically in order to save on building materials. However, the bricks on the building are laid normally and its surface area would be the same whichever way it was built. Might the name be ironic and refer to an earlier building, now gone? Much more likely is the idea that the place was named after a local wizard, the so-called Cunning Man of Tadley, who lived in the late Georgian era. The villagers often travelled to Tadley, over the border in Hampshire, in order to consult this man on any number of issues, like thefts or would-be lovers. The churchwardens' accounts for the parish show that similar practices spread back to at least 1584 when payments were being made to a local witch or cunning woman for helping to recover missing church goods.

Purley

The name Purley is supposed to mean Pear Tree Clearing although this is not universally accepted. There used to be two villages in the parish, one for each manor. Westbury Farm stands on the site of the deserted medieval village of Purley Parva or Little Purley. Its manor house was Purley Hall which was not completely within the parish: the boundaries of Purley, Sulham and Pangbourne once met in the dining room. For many years, the hall was rented out to Warren Hastings, the disgraced Governor of India, while he awaited his trial around 1788. This unhappy time there was brightened by the Indian menagerie that he kept about him. His ghost is still said to haunt the house.

Figure 73: Purley Hall, formerly called Hyde Hall

The place was originally called Hyde Hall after the Hyde family from Denchworth near Wantage, who built it in 1609, although many of the internal features date from 1719 as shown by the coat-of-arms of the Hawes family displayed on the ceilings and in the glass. The place was the childhood home of the well-known 18th century socialite and party animal, Frances, Viscountess Vane. She was the daughter of Francis Hawes, one of the directors of the South Sea Company, who lost the Hall when the company's infamous financial bubble burst.

Purley Village was originally Purley Magna or Great Purley and sits nearer the parish church with its own manor house, Purley Park. This manor was anciently held by the Huscarle family, who were probably descended from one of King Canute's personal bodyguards, who were known as 'Huscarles'. The first of the family, Roland, certainly had a good Scandinavian name. After the death of Sir Thomas Huscarle in the 1350s, the manor passed to his widow, Lucy, and her new husband, Nicholas Carew. The couple liked Purley but their descendants preferred Beddington Manor in Surrey, Lucy's paternal inheritance. Eventually Purley became the home to a younger branch of the family and upon the death of another Nicholas Carew in 1485, the property passed to his sister, Sanchea, and her husband, Sir John Iwardby from Farley Chamberlayne in Hampshire. Their eldest daughter and coheiress, Jane, married Sir John St John, the Chamberlain to King Henry VII's mother, Margaret, Countess of Richmond. Jane has a textual memorial (1553) in the parish church at Purley. The main St John estate was at Lydiard Tregoze near Swindon in Wiltshire but, being convenient for both London and Windsor, Purley became a favoured second home. Indeed, the couple's grandson, Nicholas St John, seems to have preferred Purley to his other houses, probably because his wife was a Blount from Mapledurham House, just across the River. Their son, Viscount Grandison, a rather over-enthusiastic Lord Deputy of Ireland, grew up at Purley during the 1560s and is believed to have financed the rebuilding, in 1626, of the church tower, which bears his coat-of-arms. The Viscount's nephew, John, the first St John baronet, was lord of the manor at the time and seems to have lived at Purley Park from time to time. He married Anne Leighton, a granddaughter of Sir Francis Knollys from Reading, and they later became the great grandparents of the 1st Viscount Bolingbroke of Bucklebury House. They were staunch royalists and three of their sons were killed during the Civil War, one at the Second Battle of Newbury.

Figure 74: Anne, wife of Edward Hyde, later Earl of Clarendon

It is Sir John's residence at the Park which explains the existence of the mural monument in the parish church to Anne, the first wife of Edward Hyde, later 1st Earl of Clarendon. By his second wife, he became father to Anne Hyde (who was born at Cranbourne Lodge), the first wife of King James II, when he was Duke of York, and mother of both Queen Mary II and Queen Anne. An erroneous old story, often repeated, tells how this second Anne Hyde was a member of the family of that name who lived at Purley Hall. The monument to her father's earlier wife being cited as proof. However, her family were from Wiltshire and had little to do with the Berkshire family of Hyde. Anne, wife of Edward Hyde, was only buried at Purley because she was the niece of Sir John St John. She was apparently taken ill with small pox at Reading, while travelling from London to Wiltshire, and was removed to her uncle's house at Purley Park. There she died and she was subsequently buried in the parish church. Although standing on an ancient site, the entire church, apart from the tower, was rebuilt in Victorian times. Extensive enlargements in 1983 include a multi-purpose hall and other facilities which cleverly open out directly from the nave arcading yet remain unobtrusive both inside and out. The building's great treasure is its superbly carved Norman font.

Reading

Traditionally Reading is accepted as being Anglo-Saxon for [Place of] Readda's People, a local chieftain; although the prefix could also refer to Hreda, the Anglo-Saxon Goddess of Victory. Alternatively, the name could be Celtic Rhydd-Inge or Ford through the Water Meadows which fits the town's topography rather well. The river would, of course, be the Kennet, not the Thames. Tradition, or wishful thinking, says that St Birinus, the Anglo-Saxon evangelist from Italy, founded a small chapel on the site of St Mary's Church in the 7th century. In AD 979, Queen Aelfthrith transformed this into a royal nunnery, supposedly in repentance for murdering her step-son, St Edward, king and martyr. It was destroyed by the Vikings in 1016 but a small, controversially dated, doorway could possibly survive in the present structure. With four of her nuns, this wicked queen appears today on Reading's coat-of-arms (despite her depiction originally having been of a king). At some point, St Mary's became an Anglo-Saxon minster, as echoed in nearby Minster

Street and the title adopted by the church in recent years. The top of this street was once called Tothill, indicating an Anglo-Saxon lookout point. Another interesting street-name close by is the Butts where the medieval townsfolk would have practiced their archery, particularly after an act of King Edward III's reign forcing them to do so on holy days. The town had a minor Anglo-Saxon mint during Edward the Confessor's reign, when Corff and Brihtric the Moneyers lived there. Royal Reading mints later re-emerged in the reigns of the Norman and early medieval kings.

Figure 75: Reading Abbey dominating the extant Abbey Gateway

In 1121, King Henry I founded Reading Abbey in this small town as a private mausoleum for his family. It was built on the site of the Viking stronghold set up in AD 870, during the Viking wars of King Aethelred's reign. The Vikings used it as their countrywide invasion headquarters and the King and his brother, Alfred (later King Alfred), besieged them there unsuccessfully. At the time of the 'Anarchy' civil war between King Henry's daughter, the Empress Matilda, and her cousin, King Stephen, the Abbey was still being built. Stephen apparently constructed a wooden motte and bailey castle in its grounds, possibly to harass Wallingford, although this is a fair distance away. The castle was destroyed by the Empress' son, later King Henry II, in 1153 but its exact site is unknown. The low mound that can still be seen in the Forbury Gardens is not the old motte, but part of the Civil War defences of the town. The Abbey was finally completed in 1164, forty-three years after construction began. It was consecrated by the Archbishop of Canterbury and later saint, Thomas Becket.

Figure 76: King Henry I's Funeral at Reading Abbey

It was at Reading Abbey, in 1185, that the Patriarch of Jerusalem offered King Henry II the Crown of his city if he would defend it against Muslim invaders. The King, however, declined. On three occasions, the Papal Legate summoned ecclesiastical councils at the Abbey and Parliament also met there several times, particularly in the 15th century when plague forced the Members of Parliament to flee Westminster. Arrangements varied but the House of Commons often gathered in the Chapter House while the Lords were installed in the Refectory. There were also royal occasions at the Abbey: weddings and funerals, jousts and tournaments, all of which brought lords, ladies and knights with huge entourages to Reading, as well as the Royal Household who may have had a semi-permanent home there. The town's hostelries would be packed to overflowing and the trade that followed in their wake allowed Reading to prosper.

Several of the English Royal Family were married at Reading Abbey:

- Prince Lionel of Antwerp, Duke of Clarence, son of King Edward III married 9th September 1342 to Elizabeth daughter and heiress of William De Burgh, Earl of Ulster. They had been officially and very hurriedly married in the Tower of London a month earlier. He was three and she was ten.
- Prince John of Gaunt, Earl of Richmond, later Duke of Lancaster and claimant to the Throne of Castile and Leon, son of King Edward III married 19th May 1359 to Blanche daughter and heiress of Henry, Duke of Lancaster.
- Princess Margaret, daughter of King Edward III married 19th May 1359 to John Hastings, Earl of Pembroke
- Princess Philippa, daughter of Prince Lionel of Antwerp, Duke of Clarence and Earl of Ulster married February 1359 to Edmund Mortimer, Earl of March
- King Edward IV married 1st May 1464 in secret at Grafton Regis (Northamptonshire) to Elizabeth, widow of John Grey, Baron Grey of Groby and daughter of Richard Woodville, Earl Rivers. The marriage was publicly announced to the World at Reading Abbey on 29th September 1464.

Others were buried there:

- King Henry I of England, died 1135, (bowels, brains, heart, eyes and tongue at Rouen). He was buried (traditionally in a silver coffin) in the quire in front of the High Altar – probably under the children's day nursery next to St James' Roman Catholic Church. There is a small plaque in the abbey ruins and an early 20th century memorial cross in the Forbury Gardens.

- Prince William, Count of Poitiers, died 1156, aged two, eldest son of King Henry II, lies at the feet of King Henry I.
- Princess Constance of York, died 1416, wife of Thomas Le Despenser, Earl of Gloucester and daughter of Prince Edmund Langley, Duke of York. She lies in front of the High Altar.
- Prince John of Cornwall, died 1233, son of Prince Richard, Earl of Cornwall and Holy Roman Emperor
- Princess Isabella of Cornwall, died 1234, daughter of Prince Richard, Earl of Cornwall and Holy Roman Emperor

Today, Reading Abbey is well known as the place where the song, *Sumer is icumen in*, was composed. It has been described as both "the oldest secular English music" and "the oldest known musical round with English words". The Abbey's major claim to fame in its heyday, however, was as one of the great pilgrimage centres of medieval England. It had been given the supposed hand of St James by King Henry I and the Head of St Philip by King John. The abbey also held a large collection of some 232 other relics. Like the royal events at the Abbey, these relics attracted huge numbers of people who made both the monastery and the town rich. The almoner (poor relief manager) had to open a large public cookshop (basically a medieval café) in Minster Street to help feed them all. St James' hand was found blocked up in the ruins 200 years ago and is now kept at Marlow Roman Catholic Church in Buckinghamshire, although the medieval pilgrims would be disappointed to know that it has recently been radio carbon dated to around AD 1000.

The Tudor monarchs were frequent visitors to Reading. There is an old story that King Henry VIII once locked up the Abbot in the Tower of London so he could win a bet made with him whilst in disguise. This is commemorated by a pair of ghosts who appear in the area: a stout mounted huntsman in Lincoln Green beckoning on a cloaked companion. They are supposedly the King's gaoler taking the Abbot to London. Despite their being good friends, at the Dissolution of the Monasteries, the King had the Abbot hanged outside the Abbey Gate.

Figure 77: The Abbey Hospitium Dormitory in St Laurence's Churchyard

The Abbey's Inner Gateway is one of the few remnants of this once great monastic complex still standing today. In the 18th century, it was part of the Reading Ladies' Boarding School attended by the author, Jane Austen. There are also some ruins of the Abbey's south transept, chapter house and associated features adjoining the Forbury Gardens, where the largest sculpted lion in the World stands as a memorial to the Royal Berkshire Regiment killed at the Battle of Maiwand (1880) during the Second Anglo-Afghan War. It was made by local artist and brewer, George Blackall Simonds, in 1886. Despite stories to the contrary, there is nothing wrong with the lion's stance and Simonds studied the live animals extensively in order to get it right. The other substantially intact Abbey building remaining today is the dormitory of the pilgrims' hospitium (or guesthouse), once part of the Hospital of St John the Baptist. This is now the children's nursery that stands back from the path through St Laurence's churchyard. The rest of the hospital lies beneath the town hall (designed by Alfred Waterhouse and Thomas Lainson). The hospitium later became the abode of the Royal Grammar School founded by King Henry VII (now Reading School in Erleigh Road), stables for Henry VIII's horses when the Abbot's House became his palace, the barracks of Civil War soldiers and, in 1892, the home of University College Reading (now the University of Reading: hence St James' scallops on its coat-of-arms). Nearby can also be seen window tracery removed from St Laurence's Church after Second World War bomb damage and a wooden memorial to a man killed in a whirlwind.

St Laurence's Church was built by the Abbey monks for the people of Eastern Reading to worship in. Its north chapel was the hospital's Chapel of St John, connected to the guesthouse by a private door and wooden cloister. The demolished south transept was known as the Knollys Chapel. The descendants of Queen Elizabeth I's treasurer, Sir Francis Knollys, were buried there, as they lived at Abbey House, the old royal palace converted from the abbey ruins. Their remains still lie under the road outside. Jocelyn Palmer, Reading's Protestant martyr burnt at Newbury, had been tutor to Knollys' children.

St Laurence's has a striking early 17th century wall monument inside to John Blagrave. He was a well-known mathematician in his day who lived at Southcote House. His family owned most of the town for many generations. The allegorical ladies around him represent various three-dimensional mathematical shapes. The bizarrely named Blagrave's Piazza was built with this man's money along the church's south side in 1520. It was a covered walkway (rather than a public square) that housed the borough stocks and ducking stool and had a small lock-up at one end until demolished in 1868. It was once attached to the Abbey's Compter Gate that served as a prison both before and after the Dissolution of the Monasteries. The borough pillory for further public humiliations was conveniently nearby in the centre of the Market Place.

Figure 78: The Norman Abbey Mill Arch over the Holy Brook

The Abbey's millstream, called the Holy Brook, once ran open through the streets of Reading but is now mostly covered over. It is a natural brook which splits from the Kennet at Theale, only to re-join it just behind the Reading Central Library (which stands on the site of the Abbey Stables) in King's Road. It is at this point that the Holy Brook emerges into the open air to be spanned by the original arch of the old Abbey Mill. You can find glimpses of it elsewhere in the town as well, notably flowing under the Minster Street entrance to the Oracle Shopping Centre.

The Grey Friars of St Francis of Assisi arrived in Reading in 1233 and, after a brief quarrel with the Abbot, established themselves in what is now called Friar Street in their memory. From there they went out into the community preaching the word of God, probably on the steps of several stone crosses which are known to have been scattered across the town. After the Dissolution of the Monasteries, their church was granted to the town as a Guild Hall. The Corporation's previous home, at the end of what became Yield Hall Lane, was small and rather noisy due to the cries of the washerwomen on the banks of the Kennet outside. The building survived until the mid-20th century as part of Wilder's Ironworks. The new hall at Greyfriars was also found to be unsuitable and the Corporation moved out after only twenty years. It then became a hospital-cum-workhouse and finally a prison, before falling into disrepair. It was eventually restored and reconsecrated as a church (minus its east end) in 1863. The Corporation, meantime, had moved to the old refectory of St John's Hospitium, which is why the town hall later developed on the land adjoining it to the west.

Near to the first Guild Hall stood Minster Mill down an alley off Minster Street, used for both grinding corn and cloth fulling (cleansing and thickening) in Queen Elizabeth I's time. It stood on the site of one of six mills recorded in the Domesday Survey of 1086. Its last incarnation as a mill was for spinning silk in the early 19th century, after which it became a paint works. Further down Minster Street was the Oracle, a workhouse for poor clothiers, established by the will of John Kendrick in 1624. Unlike the later Victorian workhouses, it genuinely helped people learn a trade and stay out of poverty. John had made his money in the cloth business established by his father. His brother, William, who has a monument in St Mary's Church, later converted their house for the institution's use. The site, with a central courtyard through which the Holy Brook ran, covered some two acres and had an imposing Dutch-gabled entrance. Above its archway was a niche which probably housed a statue of the oracle himself, John Kendrick, the infallible guide (like that of William Goddard at the Jesus Hospital in Bray). The massive wooden gates featured the founding date of 1628 and John's initials. They can still be seen in Reading Museum. Unfortunately, a corrupt administration sent the Oracle into rapid decline. It was used as troop barracks during the Civil War but was only finally demolished in the mid-19th century. It stood immediately opposite the back entrances to John Lewis in Minster Street, lining the entrance path to the Oracle Shopping Centre and facing down Gun Street. The Kendrick Schools were founded with what was left of the original bequest.

Figure 79: The Oracle, with Minster Street to the left

Another famous Reading cloth merchant family was that of the mid-17th century Archbishop of Canterbury, William Laud, advisor to King Charles I. He was born in 1573 at 47 Broad Street, where a popular chemist's chain store now stands, and attended Reading School. Slightly earlier, the great Francis Walsingham, Queen Elizabeth I's spymaster, apparently owned a handsome timber-framed town house in Reading, amongst his many properties across the country. It stood on the corner of Broad Street and Minster Street and was once famous for its plaque displayed over the entrance showing the Royal Coat-of-Arms. This indicated that Walsingham had entertained the Queen on the premises and she stayed overnight. The Earl of Essex later used the house as his headquarters after the Siege of Reading. Unfortunately, Walsingham House, or Hounslow's Corner as it was later known, was pulled down in January 1905.

Figure 80: The Civil War Siege of Reading, April 1643

Reading essentially supported Parliament during the Civil War and was originally garrisoned in 1642 by Henry Marten MP, a rather unsavoury character from Beckett House in Shrivenham. However, with reports of approaching cavaliers, he quickly abandoned the undefended town. The borough council had, in fact, been split and some welcomed the royalist army that arrived three days later. Reading became the largest royalist garrison outside Oxford, with three thousand soldiers to feed. The town was heavily taxed for this 'honour' and the council's finances were crippled. By the time the parliamentarians decided to besiege Reading though, it was highly fortified with large banks, ditches and bastions. The Earl of Essex laid siege to the town for some ten days in April 1643. The gunfire was fierce until the roundheads discovered plans for royalist reinforcements from Oxford and headed them off at Caversham Bridge. With no relief force the town's garrison was forced to surrender.

Forty-five years later, the Battle of Broad Street saw the only fighting of the Glorious Revolution of 1688. The people of England wished to rid themselves of the Roman Catholic King James II and had welcomed his Dutch Protestant son-in-law as William III instead. As William marched up from the West Country, James held London but sent out an advance guard of several hundred Irish troops to intercept his son-in-law at Reading. The Readingensians were terrified of the Catholic Irishmen, who they believed would massacre them in their beds rather than give up the town. They did however manage to send out messages to William at Hungerford warning of the Catholic strategy. When William's Dutch army arrived, they easily routed the Irish Catholics, pushing them back from their posts around the (Golden) Bear Inn in Castle Street and St Mary's Churchyard. The main body of men defending the Market Place fled in the confusion.

The town has had many historic pubs over the years, often associated with the coaching industry. A few still survive. The Sun Inn in Castle Street is perhaps the most fascinating. It has a supposed Norman archway, which once led to a large underground hall. The place certainly seems to have been a hostelry as far back as the 13th century. As a popular 18th century coaching inn, the undercroft could house up to fifty horses. At times, it was also used for prisoners awaiting entry to the gaol next door and for Napoleonic prisoners of war. Sadly, this underground room collapsed in 1947 after being damaged by circus elephants tethered down there two years previously. The now demolished Oxford Arms in Silver Street also had penal connections. The hangmen from Reading Gaol would stop there for a drink with their victims before they were led to Gallows Common in Shinfield Rise. A well-known, but unfortunate, resident at the Gaol was Oscar Wilde, who was sentenced to two years hard labour there in 1895 as a result of public outrage over his love affair with Lord Alfred Douglas. Apart from his 'Ballad of Reading Gaol', he never wrote again.

The 18th century saw the beginnings of Reading's growth as a huge industrial centre that became consolidated with the arrival of the railway in 1840. The boom lasted throughout the 19th and most of the 20th century. The town was always traditionally famous for its Three Bs: biscuits, bulbs and beer. Chronologically, beer arrived first. There were relatively large breweries in the town from about 1627, but it was the founding of the Simonds' Brewery by William Blackall Simonds in 1785 which was to make Reading famous worldwide for its beer. Banking should perhaps have been a fourth B, for he also launched the Simonds' Bank with his cousins not long afterwards. The brass plaque bearing the family name clung to the old Barclay's Bank building (now a restaurant), with its magnificent carved entrance in King Street, until it closed in 2009.

Figure 81: Simonds' Seven Bridges Brewery around Soane's House

The original brewery was at the top of Broad Street, but very quickly moved to Bridge Street, with Simonds' home standing at the centre. Both were designed by his friend, the Reading-educated architect of the Bank of England, Sir John Soane. He also designed the obelisk in the Market Place. The older name for Bridge Street was Seven Bridges, indicating how wide the Kennet Bridge once was and how many streams the river divided into. The Simonds' business pioneered pale ale, gained contracts to supply the Royal Military Academy in Sandhurst, the British Army in Aldershot and in India and many railways in Southern England. In the early 20th century, they expanded enormously and by the time the Second World War broke out they were producing just over one percent of all the beer brewed in England. They were famous for their red hop leaf logo, but unfortunately merged with Courage and Barclay in 1960 and the Simonds name was dropped ten years later. In 1985, they moved to a vast new brewery, the largest in Europe, down by the M4 motorway. The old brewery was pulled down to make way for the Oracle

Shopping Centre, while the new one was also demolished in 2010. The business was wound up and the brands are now owned by Marston's Brewery of Wolverhampton.

Reading's bulbs were produced by Sutton Seeds, who started as a corn merchant's in King Street in 1807, later specialising in seeds under Martin Hope Sutton. Their fine building in the Market Place – more spectacular still than the surviving bank a few doors down – was pulled down in the 1960s. There was a vast complex behind all the shops that went right through to a grand entrance arch in the Forbury. The company moved out of the town to Torquay in 1976 but is still prominent in the seed world.

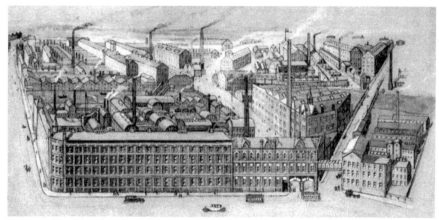

Figure 82: Huntley & Palmer's Biscuit Factory

The biscuits came from Thomas Huntley's bakery, opened in London Street by his father in 1822. It gained a new partner in 1841: George Palmer, who was to become a famous Reading benefactor with a statue in Broad Street (now in Palmer Park). The company became Huntley and Palmer's, long World famous for their "superior Reading biscuits". The factory, off the King's

Road, was built on the site of an old silk mill five years later. Over the years, it grew to cover a vast area and dominated the town for over a hundred years. It closed in 1976 and has been all but swept away. Only the old social club survives still proudly sporting the company logo. The name is still used however. The firm, having undergone a number of changes in ownership, now operates on a much smaller scale out of Suffolk.

It has occasionally been suggested that Reading has had other major industries that should be added to the list of Bs: Bricks (from Coley and Tilehurst), Bacon (from Reading St Giles) and Bikes from Warrick Cycles in the Butts. Then there are Boxes (from Huntley, Boorne and Stevens in Reading St Giles), Books (i.e. printing in Battle, Katesgrove and Thameside) and Brown Sauce. In the Victorian era, the town was well known for Cocks' Reading Sauce, manufactured just past the current library in the King's Road. Very like Worcester Sauce, it was even more popular in its day. Sadly, demand gradually declined in the 20th century and the company eventually went into liquidation. Today, of course, Reading industry is dominated by bytes.

The industrial expansion of the town was naturally followed by a retail boom managed by many other prominent local families. The oldest retail business still operating on its original site in the town is Heelas' Department Store, a branch of the John Lewis Partnership since 1953, which sadly lost its individual name in 2001. It was founded as a small draper's shop in Minster Street by the brothers Heelas in 1854. Their father had a similar shop in Wokingham. With the purchase of premises around them, by 1870 the Reading business had expanded through to Broad Street and the range of goods available there broadened into a full department store within the next ten years. Other once well-known department stores have now gone. Bull's, across the road in Broad Street, was also part of John Lewis but closed when they bought Heelas. Wellsteed's was the oldest, founded in Middle Row in the centre of Broad Street in 1842, although it quickly moved across the road to where its 1920s Art Deco façade remains as the Broad Street entrance to the Oracle Shopping Centre. Wellsteed's was eventually taken over by Debenham's, whose branch in the Oracle has recently announced its closure.

Figure 83: The Oracle at Wellsteed's. Walsingham House inset.

McIlroy's Department Store had the finest building. It still stands in Broad Street West but has sadly lost its striking turret. It was known as Reading's Crystal Palace because of its huge glass frontage. It is now given over to individual shops and the upper floors are flats. Hickies Music Shop (founded 1864) is believed to be the oldest shop in Reading that still retains its original name.

Other old businesses include Hill's Rubber (incorporated in 1899) which once stood on the corner of the High Street and the Market Place but is now in Cardiff Road; and Haslam's Estate Agency (founded 1838) originally in Broad Street but now on the corner of Friar Street and Cross Street. It was owned by a well-known family of local architects who designed many Reading buildings including Queen Anne's School in Caversham. The oldest firm in the town, however, is C & G Ayres' Removals (founded 1816). They started out as coal merchants on the Kennet in Bridge Street but, from 1883, were in Friar Street for almost a hundred years. They are currently based in Ross Road.

See also Reading St Giles, Reading Thameside *and other suburbs.*

Reading St Giles

The building of the great abbey at Reading for King Henry I in 1121 brought a huge boost to the town's trade and development. By about 1190 there was a sizeable village on the south side of the River Kennet which needed its own church as floods often prevented the residents from journeying to St Mary's. So St Giles' Church was built on the lowest slopes of Southern Hill.

St Giles' stood on the medieval pilgrimage route into town from Winchester and Southampton and housed a popular statue of St Christopher, patron saint of travellers. Alongside the churchyard, on the south side of Crown Street, was a sanctuary where criminals could escape from justice for forty days and forty nights. They then had to decide whether to give themselves up or admit their guilt and go into self-imposed exile abroad. This may have replaced the Abbey's old leper hospital. During the Reformation, the Abbot's advisor, John Einion, was the vicar. He got into trouble for distributing the demands of the Pilgrimage of Grace rebels who wanted a return to the Roman Catholic Church and was eventually hanged, along with the Abbot, in front of the Abbey Gateway in 1539.

Figure 84: Old St Giles' Church & the first Huntley & Palmer's Bakery

During the Civil War Siege of Reading, tradition says the Royalists mounted a cannon on the church tower which led to the Roundheads bombarding it to such an extent that the old spire was totally destroyed. In the late 17th century, St Giles' churchyard was where many of the dead from the Battle of Broad Street were buried. This was when Reading saw the only fighting of the Glorious Revolution which placed King William III on the Throne in 1688. Later, in the 18th century, the vicar was the Honourable William Bromley Cadogan from Caversham Park, a charismatic and highly popular evangelical preacher. When his successor took office, he was such a disappointment that a large part of the congregation walked out and established a new church dedicated to St Mary in Castle Street instead (not to be confused with St Mary's Church in the Butts). St Giles' was almost entirely rebuilt in 1871-3.

The Crown Inn, on the corner of Crown Street and London Street, was one of the town's major coaching inns and regularly hosted political meetings and dinners for Reading Members of

Parliament. After 1822, their clientele benefitted considerably from the freshly baked biscuits sent over from Joseph Huntley's bakery on the other side of the road (now the offices of a charity for older people). His son, Thomas, later entered into partnership with his wife's cousin, George Palmer, to open a factory in King's Road and Huntley and Palmer's Biscuits were born. Joseph Huntley Junior also set up an ironmongery and whitesmith's shop in London Street which later became Huntley, Boorne and Stevens. Its factory totally surrounded the Crown. They became famous for the exotic tin biscuit boxes which they made for Huntley and Palmer's, their eventual sister-company. Huntley, Boorne and Stevens' beautiful triple-oriel window offices at the top end of London Street were unfortunately pulled down in the 1970s. There had also been workers' entrances in both Crown Street and Southampton Street.

The site now occupied by the Deep Blue City Gate Apartments on the corner of Southampton Street and Upper Crown Street was, for many years, the home of Messrs Venner and Sons' Bacon Factory. The firm started by accident when Mrs Martha Venner's specially-blended butter became so popular that she and her husband turned their home into a grocer's shop in 1856. In 1888, however, their sons demolished several dwellings to build a large bacon factory, which included bacon and ham curing, lard refining, sausage making, brawn packing, butter and cheese making, egg packing and meat canning. It had a high chimney with 'Venner' written up the side and the buildings were so extensive that there was a bridge joining them together across the northern arm of Upper Crown Street (now demolished). The business survived into the 1970s.

Lower Southampton Street was originally called Horn Street because it was the home of the town's workers in animal horn. This smelly industry used the "plastic of the Middle Ages" to make many everyday items such as spoons and even window 'glass'. Parallel to this is London Street, the finest Georgian street in Reading: an amazing survival for a town beset with modern developments. The best house in the street is Addington House at Number 73, built for Doctor Anthony Addington in 1748-9 (there is a blue plaque). He was father of the Prime Minister, Viscount Sidmouth from Woodley, who is commemorated elsewhere in the town, and attended the aftermath of the infamous murder, in Henley, of Francis Blandy (second cousin of the first Reading solicitor's father) by his daughter, Mary, after she was tricked by her lover into poisoning him for her inheritance. Later, his place in history was assured through his early specialisation in mental health conditions. Through his friendship with the Pitts, he was appointed physician to mad King George III, who recovered for a while under his watchful eye. Number 75, next door, was added for the accommodation of such patients in 1754.

The Reading International Solidarity Centre's World Shop in London Street was, for many years – until bought out by Blackwell's of Oxford in 1987 – William Smith's well-known 'London Street Bookshop'. The southern end started life in 1832 as George Lovejoy's General Subscription Circulating Library (aka the Southern Counties' Library). Lovejoy was a keen correspondent with many popular authors of his day including Mary Russell Mitford, Elizabeth Barrett Browning, Thomas Hughes, Charles Kingsley, Charlotte Brontë and Charles Dickens. Several of them became firm friends and advised him on purchases for his stock which, by the time of his death in 1883, was in excess of 80,000 volumes – the biggest library outside

London. In the 17th century, the building had been a Quaker meeting house attended by William Penn, founder of Pennsylvania, who lived at Ruscombe. His ghost is said to haunt the premises despite the many changes made to its fabric over the years.

Figure 85: The Literary, Scientific & Mechanics' Institution Hall (1843)

A couple of doors down stands the imposing ionic-columned portico of the Great Expectations pub and hotel. It was built as the 'New Hall' of the Reading Literary, Scientific and Mechanics' Institution in 1843 and later became a Methodist Church, local newspaper offices and a theatre twice over the course of its history. It may have been Lovejoy who persuaded Charles Dickens to visit the first theatre, where on two separate occasions he read extracts from his books to a delighted audience populated by many workers from the Huntley and Palmer Biscuit Factory – hence the name of the hotel (although Great Expectations was not one of the readings). Dickens was later asked to stand as Reading's Member of Parliament but declined the offer.

Figure 86: St Giles' Mill & Water Tower in Mill Lane

Mill Lane at the bottom end of London Street, now part of the Inner Distribution Road, was once well known for its brewery and its mill. The former was apparently first begun in 1627 and, for many years was owned by the Stephens family from the Aldermaston Wharf Brewery and then the Blandy family, now best known for their firm of solicitors in Friar Street. In 1855, when the well-known Reading Brewery of Blandy and Hawkins was born, they moved to Castle Street. St Giles' Mill was probably one of those mentioned at Reading in the Domesday Survey of 1086 and was certainly given to Reading Abbey as part of its endowment. Through most of the Middle Ages, it was a fulling mill for the town's extensive cloth industry but, by the time of the Dissolution of the Monasteries, it also had a wheel grinding corn. In 1799, Thomas May the miller of Brimpton purchased the lease of, what was by then, purely a corn mill for his two sons, John and William. Nineteen years later, they gave over part of the estate for the building of a huge water tower and associated pump works for the town. The tower dominated the skyline until demolished, along with the mill, in 1900. The bricks were used to raise the level of Mill Lane. The following year, the Corporation's Central Tramways Depot was built on the site. It housed garages, repair shops and power generating facilities for their new state-of-the-art electrically powered trams. This later became the bus depot before being demolished in 1995 to make way for the Riverside shops and car park of the Oracle Shopping Centre. These still retain the old name plaque for the Tramways Power Station.

Reading Thameside

The 'vastern' of Vastern Road is an old word for defensive earthworks and is believed to be named after those put up by the Vikings to prevent attack from the River Thames when they made Reading their headquarters from which to conquer Southern England in the AD 870s. They were besieged there by King Aethelred and his brother, Prince (later King) Alfred, in AD 871. This area of water-meadows was very wet and, though drained by ditches in medieval times, these were not very effective and the area was always difficult to cross. A causeway was built across it in 1631 but even this was not high enough to avoid the floods and it was another hundred years before it was properly traversable.

It was while staying at Reading Abbey, in 1163, that King Henry II witnessed the trial by combat of Henry d'Essex and Robert de Montfort on De Monfort Island (aka Fry's Island) in the Thames. De Montfort was an ancestral uncle of the De Montforts of Remenham and Yattendon (but unrelated to the founder of Parliament, Simon de Montfort). Essex was married to De Montfort's second cousin and the two were involved in a long-standing land dispute. Things came to a head when De Montfort accused Essex of treachery and cowardice during the Welsh

Wars. In order to discover the truth, the two fought a long hard battle on the island until De Montfort was victorious and Essex therefore found guilty. The latter was thought to be dead and was taken to Reading Abbey where he subsequently recovered, revealing that his defeat had been due to his being blinded by a vision of St Edmund. He remained a Reading monk for the rest of his life.

The Grey Friars of St Francis of Assisi arrived in Reading in 1233, hoping to minister to the town's poor. The Abbot of Reading was not best pleased at having a rival religious order on his doorstep but, being under royal patronage, he was obliged to give them a small parcel of land. This was on the edge of town, on the way to Caversham Bridge, possibly in the area of the Station Shopping Park where the Portman Brook used to run. The land was too marshy though and, despite much building work, it was only fifty years before the friars complained to the Archbishop who, being a Greyfriar himself, quickly intervened. The friars were soon relocated to what later became known as Friar Street.

There has been a bridge between Reading and Caversham since at least the 1220s and Reading was always historically responsible for the upkeep of the southern half. Hence, before 1869 when an iron lattice structure was erected, the Caversham half was a strong stone and brick structure, while the Reading half was a rather ramshackle wooden affair. It used to have a drawbridge to allow for some control over travellers or hostile forces approaching from the North. The present bridge was built of concrete in 1926. On the west side of the southern end of the old bridge stood the White Hart Inn, which was owned by a branch of the boat-building Freebody family from 1748 until

1855. It was replaced by the Caversham Bridge Hotel in 1901 and the Holiday Inn in 1986.

Figure 87: Great Western Motors in Vastern Road

The area around Vastern Road and (the lower end of) Caversham Road was still open fields until the late 1880s. Development began to the south-west of the junction of the two roads and then, in the early 1890s, spread down the north side of Caversham Road from the bridge area. De Monfort Road is, of course, named after the medieval combatant from the nearby island. Brigham Road is so-called because this area was historically called Brigham Mead. It is named after Anthony Brigham, one of King Henry VIII's cofferers (i.e. treasurers), and his family. At the Dissolution of the Monasteries, Anthony had purchased the lands of Notley Abbey in Caversham and settled at Cane End House.

However, while the roads around Caversham Road were residential, Vastern Road was mostly industrial. Most of the southern side, including the area of the Station Shopping Park, was taken up by the Great Western Ironworks, which made signals, signal boxes, locking gear, junctions and similar railway metalwork. To the west, on the other side of the Caversham Road stood Messrs J and J Mackie's Berkshire Ironworks founded in 1879 which specialised in wrought iron spring drums or pulleys. Cardiff Road was the home to one of Reading's many printers. Wyman's moved there in 1901 and built the Great Western Printing Works, later becoming Cox and Wyman's before closing in 2015. On the north side of Vastern Road, around the present Norman Place, was the Thames Bank Ironworks founded by Henry Lewis in 1891. This was later replaced by Allen and Simmonds motor body builders and then Great Western Motors. To the east were boat houses all along the Thames, where the southern end of Reading Bridge now stands, towards King's Meadow. Reading Bridge was built in 1923 to improve links to Caversham which had been amalgamated into Reading Borough only twelve years earlier. When complete, its strength was tested by a large convoy of steam and traction engines from local farms and businesses.

Historically called the Abbot's Meadow or East Meadow, King's Meadow was cattle grazing pasture belonging to Reading Abbey until taken into royal hands at the Dissolution of the Monasteries. It is thought that this was probably the site of a number of medieval jousts that are known to have taken place in Reading. The chief of these was the tournament held after the weddings, at the Abbey, of King Edward III's children, Prince John [of Gaunt] and Princess Margaret and their respective spouses in May 1359. The King, his four eldest sons and nineteen knights took part in a three-day event in King's Meadow, followed by three further days in London.

Figure 88: Royal jousts were held at King's Meadow

Between 1843 and 1874, the meadow was the home of Reading's racecourse, encouraged by Tompkins the Friar Street/Station Road horse-dealer who owned the site. However, when it came into the hands of the biscuit-baking Palmer family, their Quaker beliefs obliged them to cancel these events. The council purchased a large portion of the meadow in 1869 for use as a recreation ground. The Thames Lido or King's Meadow Swimming Pool was added in 1903, starting life as the Reading Ladies' Swimming Baths, built alongside the men's pool of 1879, which has since been removed. After closing in 1974, the place was neglected and vandalised until local campaigners worked together with developers to achieve a sympathetic restoration. The building now houses a popular spa and restaurant around a fully heated open-air pool. It is thought to be the oldest surviving outdoor municipal pool of the early Edwardian era.

Redlands

The Redlands area is sandwiched between the two University sites, the Whiteknights and London Road Campuses, in Reading. The name is a corruption of Red Lane, perhaps named from the ironstone found in this area beneath the brown London clay. An earlier name for the area was Spitalfields: arable land and pasture that had been given as an endowment to support the leper hospital attached to Reading Abbey (although the hospital's actual location is unknown, possibly it was near St Giles' Church).

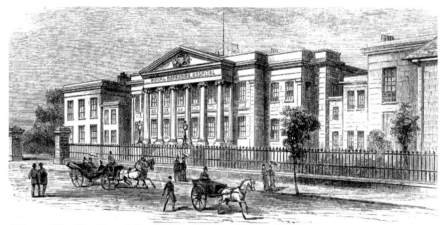

Figure 89: The Royal Berkshire Hospital, founded 1837-9

Redlands House is now almost forgotten but it was once one of Reading's finest gentlemen's villas. It seems to have been erected in the 18th century as an early coachman serving there used to keep the road outside neat and tidy around the time that the Reading and Hatfield Turnpike was introduced in 1768. The turnpike road which ran down Silver Street was kept in good order but was a toll road. When word got round that Redlands Road was just as good but free to access, travellers quickly switched route – that is until a gate was built to stop them. In the

1840s, Redlands House was the home of Thomas Bacon. He had become one of the richest men in the country when, with his brother, he inherited the vast fortune of their father, the great Welsh ironmaster Anthony Bacon, the man who industrialised Merthyr Tydfil. The extension to Wantage Hall now stands on the same site. Wantage Hall was the first new hall of residence built for the University of Reading. It was donated by Lady Wantage from East Lockinge and built in 1906-8. It is a superb neo-Tudor brick building with gatehouse and courtyard just like a mansion from the time of King Henry VIII. Many smaller villas of the gentry once lined the road and some still survive.

It was the erection of the Royal Berkshire Hospital which first stimulated the widespread development of housing south of the London Road in Redlands. Easily recognised by its huge classical Ionic portico, the hospital was founded in 1837-9 in the fields along the London Road, at the corner of Redlands Road. Its main patrons were the former Prime Minister, Henry Addington, Viscount Sidmouth from Woodley, Richard Benyon De Beauvoir from Englefield and the late King William IV. It has been much expanded since. One of its most famous patients was the well-known aviator, Douglas Bader, who was brought to the hospital after his infamous flying accident at Woodley Aerodrome. Unfortunately, the doctors were forced to amputate both his legs, yet he went on to become a Second World War flying ace, as recorded in the 1956 film, 'Reach for the Sky'.

Just the other side of the Redlands Road junction, on the London Road, is the University of Reading's London Road Campus. The University Extension College (part of Christ Church, Oxford), as it then was, moved there from the old Abbey Hospitium when the site was given to them by Alfred Palmer, of Huntley and Palmer's

Biscuits in 1904. At the time, Acacias, the house of his father, the more famous George Palmer, was also given to the University and now houses the Senior Common Room. The institution gained a Royal Charter and became the University of Reading in 1926. The complex includes the magnificent Great Hall, where graduations take place, and the striking War Memorial Tower. It is currently the University's Institute of Education. Just around the corner is the Museum of English Rural Life in a house called East Thorpe (formerly St Andrew's Hall), which was originally built for Alfred Palmer by Reading architect Alfred Waterhouse, well known for designing the Natural History Museum in South Kensington.

Riseley

The ancient Roman road from London to Silchester, called the Devil's Highway, passes along the county and Swallowfield parish boundary immediately south of Riseley. On certain October nights it is said you can still hear the thunder of ghostly chariot wheels racing along it. The line of the Roman road crosses the Basingstoke Road at its junction with Sun Lane and the wood just to the south of the lane is called Coldharbour Wood (in Heckfield parish). The place-name Coldharbour is quite common and, being usually associated with an ancient road, it is thought to refer to a Cold-Sheltering Arbour where Romans and early Anglo-Saxons could stop to keep out of the extremes of British weather. A possible Roman enclosure has been identified on the east side of the Basingstoke Road from aerial photographs and this may indicate the site of the actual arbour.

A double ditched enclosure at Riseley Farm is believed to be a Roman ironworking site, built near the road for ease of transportation for both raw materials and the finished product.

Though a low-grade ore, bog iron was plentiful around Arborfield and Finchampstead. To the west, the old road crossed the River Loddon at what is now Stanfordend Bridge but, in those days was the original Stone Ford after which the area is now named. The old mill at Stanford End is quite picturesque. Riseley means Brushwood Clearing, an area on the edge of Windsor Forest cleared of woodland and so named by the Anglo-Saxons. St Leger's Copse on the west side of the village is named after Henri Le Coq St Leger of Trunkwell House at Beech Hill and his daughter, Jane, who married John Dodd of Swallowfield Park.

Figure 90: The Bull at Riseley, a pub since the 18th century

In times past, the village of Riseley was sometimes known as West Swallowfield, the name Riseley only being used for the common grazing land east of the Odiham Road. Riseley is barely west of Swallowfield village. South Swallowfield might have been a more appropriate name. However, until 1844, all of the parish west of Swallowfield Park, including Riseley, was a detached part of Wiltshire and to highlight this was known as West Swallowfield. Confusingly, there was another detached part of West Swallowfield, around Farley Hill, that was in the east of the parish.

Today, the village still boasts a number of old 16th century cottages, including the very early Tudor Farm and Pound House near the place where stray farm animals were once impounded. The 17th century timber-framed smithy is now a private house but the Bull Inn, which has been a pub since at least the late 18th century, survives to this day as a local amenity. Even older is a possible medieval moated site at Springalls Farm where there were once two L-shaped ponds.

Ruscombe

The suffix of the name is Celto-Latin 'camp' which appears to have been taken into the Germanic language as meaning an early Anglo-Saxon settlement on the edge of a Roman one. There may perhaps have been a Roman village at the Twyford river crossing. There are certainly archaeological indications of a possible Roman villa in the Castle End Farm area of Ruscombe.

Figure 91: Ruscombe Church dates from the 13th century

The parish church was anciently a chapel-of-ease to its mother-church at Sonning, owned by Salisbury Cathedral. When the Dean made a visitation in 1220, he found the chapel and chaplain's house almost ruinous and, in 1301, there were reported to be broken windows there. In the 14th century, Windsor Forest spread as far as Ruscombe and its bounties were a great temptation to the locals. On one occasion, Oliver the Rector was charged at the Forest Court with having shot a large stag with bow and arrow. Parts of the church where he preached survive in the present building, dating from around 1200. The attractive brick tower and nave were, however, put up in 1638-9. Inside, there are colourful 15th century wall paintings of saints on the window jambs and some nice mural tablets, mostly to the occupants of Stanlake Park but also of Ruscombe manor.

The manor house, Ruscombe House, stood where the railway now runs just south of the church. The last house was mostly built in 1787 for the judge, Sir James Eyre, but retained some 16th century parts. William Penn, founder of Pennsylvania, had lived and died there between 1710 and 1718, but this did not prevent it being torn down in 1829. Nearby Stanlake Park is the manor house of Hinton Pipard in Hurst. The medieval house stood within the moat in Botany Bay Copse, part of Ruscombe, but the present building is just in the adjoining parish of St Nicholas Hurst. This beautiful gabled brick H-plan house was built by Richard Aldworth (died 1623), the son of a rich Reading burgess, in 1610. He was descended from the well-known tanning family of Aldworth from Wantage and his cousin's son and namesake (died 1654) founded the Reading Blue Coat School. The 'King's Bedroom' at Stanlake contains stained glass depicting the Royal Coat-of-Arms dated 1626, reputedly given by King Charles I after one of his visits. The Aldworths were supporters of Charles' younger son, the Roman Catholic King James II, early in his reign. However, after a brief skirmish near the house during the Glorious Revolution of 1688, they came to accept the inevitable change of regime.

Earlier, there was also supposed to have been a Civil War skirmish in Ruscombe at which Lieutenant George Mynd of Sonning was killed. The parish register records his and twelve other soldiers' burials in the first three months of 1642, so there must have been wounded housed in the village for some time. The villagers were apparently so scared, that they deserted their homes and hid in Ruscombe Lake. It was still full of water then and was not drained until the 18th century. The mysterious tunnels reported in the area may have been used as their escape route.

Figure 92: William Penn and the house that replaced his at Ruscombe

The Maidenhead Turnpike, which improved the local stretch of the Bath Road, was laid through the parish in 1718 as an important highway to the West Country. Thirty years later, in 1748, this was the scene of a major highway robbery scam designed to cheat the local Hundred (like a district council) of Sonning out of almost £1,000 (that's over £100,000 today). Thomas Chandler, a legal clerk in London, had studied highway law and knew that the hundred was liable for any losses incurred from robberies on the roads within their boundaries. So he contrived to borrow £900 from his father and his employer, then rode off down the Bath Road, supposedly to see a client in Wiltshire. Instead, however, he stopped at Ruscombe, abandoned his horse and hid in a chalk pit where he somehow managed to tie himself up before hopping back to the road to be rescued by a local shepherd. He told the authorities that he had been robbed of all his money by three ruffians and described three poor innocent men he had seen on Maidenhead Thicket. Sometime later, he had to return to Berkshire to give evidence to a local Justice of the Peace but, despite hiring an enthusiastic Wokingham barrister, the hundred were unable to stop Chandler claiming the money he had supposedly lost. Luckily, however, their lawyer continued to collect evidence against the man over the next two years and, when he had gathered enough, tracked him down in Coventry. The scoundrel was arrested, thrown in Reading Gaol, was tried and sentenced to transportation – although he was excused being pilloried in Reading Market Place first, for fear that the people of Sonning Hundred might murder him.

St John's Village

The St John's Village region, around Queen's Road in Reading, began to develop as a residential area in the early 1830s. However, a few buildings are earlier. Watlington Street was originally called Abbey Lane and then Orts Lane because it led to Reading Abbey's east gate, where the monks distributed orts (or left-overs) to the poor. The Orts name had earlier been applied to the western end of London Road and has now been transferred to the present Orts Road behind Reading College. The Watlingtons were a well-known Reading cloth-making family who first moved to the town in the early 16th century. In 1688, Samuel Watlington built himself a fine brick house in the rural lane soon to be named Watlington Lane (now Street) after the house – which he had modestly called Watlington House. From 1794, it was the home of Captain Edward Purvis, who had fought in the Peninsular War against France. He used to train the Berkshire Militia in Orts Meadow on the Watlington Street/Kennet Side corner. After his death, his red military jacketed ghost was often seen smoking a pipe in a certain window at the house. From 1877 to 1927, it housed Kendrick Girls' School and is now home to the Mills Archive.

Figure 93: Watlington House, built in 1688

The Georgian Gothic Revival Anglican Church of St John was built in a then leafy Watlington Lane in 1837. It was, however, completely flattened and rebuilt in 13th century French Gothic style with a 150ft spire in 1872-6, when its parish united with St Stephen's (in Rupert Street, long demolished). Since 1981, it has been the Polish Roman Catholic Church of the Sacred Heart: a fortunate transfer of denomination, as the Church of England had wanted to demolish it. The Wesleyan Methodist Chapel on the corner of Queens Road, was built at the same time, 1872-3. The Trinity Congregational Church, in a similar position at the end of

Sidmouth Street, was built in 1848 for a break-away group from the Broad Street Independent Chapel. It was sold to the University and pulled down in the 1980s.

Opposite Trinity Church stood the Kendrick Boys' School. The Kendrick Girls' School moved to its present site in London Road in 1927, taking in Sidmouth House, the old home of Doctor George May, one of the founding staff at the Royal Berkshire Hospital. After the failure of the 17th century cloth-merchant John Kendrick's Oracle Workhouse in Minster Street, what was left of his charitable legacy had been used, in 1877, to found both these schools. However, in 1916, Reading Corporation decided to merge the Boys' School (whose buildings subsequently became a health centre) with Reading School. This latter school, in Addington Road, has fine Gothic revival buildings, built in 1868-72 by local architect, Alfred Waterhouse, when the school moved there from beneath the old Abbey Hospitium, then being used as the Town Hall.

Most of the old shops in the area have now gone but there are still numerous offices and there has always been industry alongside the grand houses. The Queen's Road Multi-Storey Car Park site was Clark's Lead and Colour Works (paint and lead pipe manufacturers) from 1832, but they moved to Elgar Road in 1963. Opposite was the Royal Albert Brewery (which included the Queen's Hotel), at the junction of Queen's Road and East Street, founded by James Dymore Brown in 1864. It was taken over by Morland's of Abingdon in 1943 and used as a bottling plant until 1970. At the end of the 19th century, Dymore Brown had briefly gone into partnership with Meaby's Bakery to produce more easily digestible malted-grain based 'Triticumina Biscuits' next to the Lyndhurst pub. They were a rival to Hovis, but the endeavour did not last long. In 1894, Meaby's also opened a biscuit factory in South Street but this was quickly bought by Serpell's Biscuits who were located there from 1899 until 1959, despite a devastating fire in 1904. Meaby's had first started out as a simple bakery in Albert Road (now Avon Place) in Newtown in 1871, before opening more shops, the chief of which had been 82 Queen's Road, on the corner of St John's Street. They would bake privately made cakes in their ovens there for a penny. The shop remained a baker's, under different management, well into the 1970s and the old sign of A Lee Bakery can still be seen above the current letting agency there.

Figure 94: Queen's Road showing Kendrick Boys' School

There were also two mineral water bottling factories, producing ginger beer and lemonade: Cheadle's (previously Weaver's) in Eldon Square from the very late 19th century and Humphries and Holt in St John's Hill. Mr Holt was a former Reading Football Club player and Mr Humphries ran the adjoining Lodge Hotel, a temperance hotel (with no alcohol allowed on the premises), built, under the sponsorship of the Quaker George Palmer of

Huntley and Palmer Biscuits, for commercial travellers to his factory.

Addington Road and Sidmouth Street are both named after the Prime Minister, Henry Addington, Viscount Sidmouth, who grew up in London Street. Eldon Square is named after his wife's uncle, the Earl of Eldon. The gardens there have a statue of the Reading Member of Parliament (1904-13), Rufus Isaacs, Marquess of Reading, of Foxhill in Earley, who was later Viceroy of India. The statue used to stand in central New Delhi but was ejected after independence and brought to Reading.

Before she moved to Grazeley in 1806, Mary Russell Mitford lived with her parents in the London Road, in the fine mansion opposite the end of Kendrick Road: a plaque on the wall records her residence. Mary was an author, famous, not only in Berkshire but throughout England and America, for writing such works as 'Our Village' and 'Belford Regis'. Her father was a hopeless gambler and poor Mary was obliged to write to keep the family together. The Reading house was even bought with the £20,000 winnings of an Irish lottery ticket which Doctor Mitford had bought for his daughter. Belford Regis was, in fact, a thinly disguised view of Reading itself, which has also featured elsewhere in great literature. Thomas Hardy called it Aldbrickham in 'Life's Little Ironies'. Sam of 'The Son's Veto' had a fruiterer's shop in the town. Later, in 'Jude the Obscure', Reading (or Aldbrickham) appeared again as the home of Jude and Sue, with their monumental masonry business.

Shinfield

Shinfield is a controversial Anglo-Saxon place-name, said by some to mean the Selingas' Field, the Selingas being an Anglo-

Saxon tribe named after Chief Sela. However, this explanation is derived from a single, admittedly the earliest (1086), spelling of the name. All other versions are variations of Shinningfield. It may be the Scieningas' Field, named after a different chieftain called Sciene. However, popular local etymology suggests the name derives from the Shining Fields where the River Loddon still floods today on the Arborfield border.

The village's entry in the Domesday Book (1086) is rather interesting. There were 8 villeins (tenant farmers), 5 bordars (cottage dwellers), 2 serfs and their families living in the village. There was a mill and an extraordinary 5 fisheries producing 550 eels per year, 16 acres of meadow (presumably down by the Loddon) and woodland to support some 90 pigs in winter; but the number of hides available for agriculture had been reduced from five to nothing. This suggests that all the residents were engaged in animal husbandry and at the fisheries. These rich pickings had all been taken directly for the new king from an Anglo-Saxon with the wonderful name of Sexi.

The parish covers a number of outlying hamlets: Shinfield Rise, Spencers Wood, Three Mile Cross, Poundgreen, Ryeish Green, Grazeley, Diddenham and the Hartleys. However, Shinfield proper was the area around the parish church. The rector lived on the site of the house immediately next door that was known both as the Rectory and the Manor House. Church Farm, opposite, provided his income. The present farmhouse was built in 1604. The church itself was built in 1069 by order of William FitzOsbern, Earl of Hereford, who subsequently gave it to his foundation, Lire Abbey in Normandy. Whilst hunting in the woods at Shinfield with King Edward I in 1275, it is said that Bishop (later Saint) Thomas Cantilupe, the Chancellor of

England, who sometimes resided in Earley, took the opportunity to bemoan the sorrowful state of his Hereford Diocese which was burdened with the building of a new cathedral. The King suggested that he take the tithes from Shinfield Church to help. However, the church does not appear to have passed to this bishopric until twenty years afterwards. Later, during the Civil War, the tower of the church was badly damaged by cannon fire when a group of royalist soldiers, retreating from the Siege of Reading, took refuge in it. The parliamentarians surrounded the church and blasted the men out of the sky. Luckily, the theatrical 1580 monument to Henry Beke of Hartley Court was spared the destruction. It was called "the most original of the early Renaissance tombs in Berkshire" by poet and church lover, Sir John Betjeman.

Figure 95: Henry Beke & Family in Shinfield Church

Settlement gradually expanded southwards from the parish church, with a concentration of housing at School Green, the southern part of the village, after the handsome infants' school was built there in 1707 by Richard Piggot, a local boy made good. He had become a rich cutler (cutlery maker and vendor, particularly knifes and other blades) in Westminster, but never forgot his Berkshire home. The attractive gabled bellcote is dated 1860.

Figure 96: Richard Piggot's School (1707)

Cut Bush Lane, to the north, is named after an old thorn tree that a local farmer trimmed into the shape of the Prince of Wales Feathers some two hundred and fifty years ago. However, the man had a rival who took to spoiling the bush and a long feud ensued. The area retains a number of 16th century farmhouses. Queen Elizabeth I's chief physician, Robert Huick, and his grandson, Sir Simeon Steward, the poet, lived in the parish at this time, although the exact location of their home is unknown.

The old moated Tudor manor house stood north of the motorway in Shinfield Rise, then called Shinfield Green. In 1786, however, Shinfield manor was purchased by Alexander Cobham, a judge in India and sometime Sheriff of Berkshire. In 1802, he pulled down the old house and moved to the old Rectory next to the church, which became known as Shinfield Manor. When he died from a fall from his horse in 1810, this passed to his grand-nephew, Alexander Cobham Martyr, who subsequently changed his name to Cobham. He lived there before moving to a 1655 house in Cutbush Lane which he called Shinfield House. He lived to the great age of ninety-three but changed the house's name to Shinfield Grange when he greatly enlarged it in 1866. Upon his death in 1902, his eldest son moved back the old Rectory or Manor House beside the church and his younger brother took on the Grange. In 1920, the Cobhams sold up and, until 1985, the Manor House was the home of the National Institute for Research in Dairying (NIRD), who had close links with Reading University and farmed much land in the parish. It later fell into ruin and was pulled down a few years ago.

Shinfield features twice in the works of Thomas Hardy, who called it Gaymead. Its principal appearance was as the setting for 'The Son's Veto' from 'Life's Little Ironies'. Sophy, the chief character, even married the local rector in the church there. Later, Hardy wrote of Jude the Obscure working as a decorator in a church near Gaymead, though its exact location is uncertain, perhaps Arborfield. In Shinfield Church are buried the parents of another author, Mary Russell Mitford, who lived at Poundgreen and Three Mile Cross.

Shinfield Rise

The old moated Tudor manor house of Shinfield used to stand on the eastern side of the Shinfield Road, under the slip road leading off the Black Boy Roundabout towards Reading. Although Henry VIII's queen, Catherine of Aragon, does not appear to have owned it as sometimes suggested, there is a strong local tradition that she stayed there and planted a cedar tree in its grounds, thence known as Catherine's Tree. Perhaps she dropped by when staying at Reading Abbey. In the late Tudor period, a younger branch of the Martin family from Wokingham lived there and Edward Martin's kneeling effigial wall monument can be seen in the Martin Chapel in Shinfield Church. Through Edward's only daughter, the manor passed to her husband, Willam Wollascott III. His family, from Woolhampton House, were well known for retaining their Roman Catholic beliefs after the Reformation. They used their Shinfield house when visiting Reading. Around 1786, whilst repairing a chimney, a workman discovered a number of important 13th century Roman Catholic manuscripts carefully concealed within a bricked-up cupboard, including a Sarum Psalter and the Wolloscott Manuscript, a cartulary of charters now in the British Library. Some family member must have taken them away from Reading Abbey at the Dissolution of the Monasteries and kept them safe. The house was pulled down about fifteen years later.

On the northern edge of Shinfield parish is Crosfields School, once Leighton Park's Junior School but independent since 1957. It incorporates what is left of an old house called Goodrest Lodge. This was built about 1630 as Shinfield Park and was an estate favoured by the ancient Englefield family after they had been ousted from Englefield House but before they had settled at Whiteknights, down the road in Earley. It is said that, during the Civil War, Sir Anthony Englefield (died 1667) gave shelter there to King Charles I on his retreat from the First Battle of Newbury in 1643. The King was able to relax there and, upon leaving, declared that he had had a very "Good Rest". The name was therefore adopted for the house. In the Victorian era, this building was joined, on the west side of Shinfield Road, by the Grove (under the road heading to the old Shire Hall from the Black Boy Roundabout) and Shinfield Lodge (now part of the European

Centre for Medium-Range Weather Forecasts). The houses on the east side were built after the First World War and the settlement, at that time, was known as Shinfield Green.

Figure 97: The Gallows Tree at Shinfield Rise

Over the Reading border, the northern part of Shinfield Rise, around the Shinfield Road shops, should more properly be called Gallows Common. Until 1793, when they were moved within the prison walls, the executions of felons from Reading Gaol took place there on the border of Earley, Shinfield and Reading. Its name stems from a natural gallows: a three-hundred-year-old elm tree known as the Hanging Elm or the Gallows Tree which stood near the Elm Road/Langdale Gardens junction until it was cut down in the 1930s. It must have been quite a deterrent to would-be highwaymen on the Reading and Basingstoke Turnpike Road (now Shinfield Road), created in 1718. The turnpike gate for toll-collection stood at what is now the junction of the road called Shinfield Rise. The last man to be hanged at the old gallows is said to have been most surprised at his demise. He had, for many years, made himself useful to the prison governor as a handyman and his execution was unofficially postponed. That is until a new governor was appointed and looked back through the records.

On the north side of the shops, past the Sportsman, stood a mansion called Cressingham Park, built in the 1860s for Charles Easton, a solicitor and property speculator from Park House at Whiteknights. He immediately sold it to Henry Adolphus Simonds, the director of the Simonds' Brewery in the centre of Reading. In about 1880, it was bought by Frederick Mousley Lonergan but in 1883, while he was away in London, plumbers mending lead pipes on the roof accidentally caught it alight and the place quickly burnt to the ground because of the high winds at the time. The replacement building was given a private Roman Catholic chapel served by Farnborough Abbey (Hampshire). It became Reckitt House, part of Leighton Park School, in 1928 but was demolished in 1997 and a housing estate built in its place. It is remembered in the name of Cressingham Road opposite. Leighton Park started out as Pepper Farm, built in 1763 on the site of the present School House which replaced it around 1830. This was given Italianate styling for Captain Cobham from Shinfield House in 1862. It became the Quakers' School in 1890 after which the local architect, Alfred Waterhouse, built more additions there. Former pupils have included Labour Party leader Michael Foot, film director Sir David Lean and actor Jim Broadbent.

Sindlesham and Newland

Sindlesham, often shortened to Sinsham in the 18th and 19th centuries, is an Anglo-Saxon word meaning Sunna's Water Meadow. Sunna was a local chieftain or king who lived at Sonning. It is known that the Anglo-Saxons used the Sindlesham area for charcoal burning, since the remains of several 8th century charcoal clamps – charcoal burners' pits on which to build the wood piles for slow burning – have been discovered beneath the Wokingham Cricket Club grounds in Sadlers End. Still earlier, this area was the site of a rare large-scale Middle Iron Age iron smelting complex.

Figure 98: Sindlesham Mill, run by the Simonds Banking Brothers

The village itself started out around the mill next to the Poacher's pub (the old mill-house) at what is now the Double Tree Hilton Hotel, with the locals harvesting coppiced willow rods for basket-making along the Loddon. This was probably one of the mills in the Sonning entry for the Domesday Survey of 1086. The sluice-gates of the current mill building are dated 1887. It was the first business of the Simonds brothers who started the Simonds' Bank in Reading. Their family lived at Newland Lodge, built between Mole Road and Bearwood Park in 1816 after they had swept away the village of Newland (or Hughes' Green). However, a single Bearwood tenant remained in the middle of their estate. So, when he hit is wife, they encouraged the locals to perform a 'rough music' protest outside his house in order that he might leave. John Simonds II enjoyed the life of a country gentleman, while Charles Simonds II worked at the Reading bank. An old story tells how John and the Garth Hunt chased a deer right into the centre of Reading. So, he decided to visit his brother and ensure that profits were high. The bank staff were quite shocked when he turned up in full hunting pink. The family sold the estate in 1948 and the house unfortunately burnt down in the 1970s.

An old story tells how Devil's Island, in the River Loddon near the mill, got its name. The place was once joined to the riverbank and cultivated by a local farmer. However, one day he was busy haymaking when his wagon and horses completely disappeared. They had been drawn into the river by Old Nick himself. Just on the higher ground nearby stands Sindlesham Court, now the headquarters of the Berkshire Freemasons. It was built in the 1770s on the site of the old medieval manor house that had been home to the ancient De Sindlesham family.

Sindlesham, Bearwood and Newland were, until the 14th century, a southerly region of a very large parish of Sonning, which belonged to the Bishops of Salisbury. Robert de Sindlesham built a chapel-of-ease near his manor house in 1220, because he didn't think much of the muddy trip he had to take every Sunday to the mother-church at Sonning. The Vicar of Sonning protested since he then lost all the revenue from his Sindlesham parishioners. The matter was eventually settled when Robert agreed that the chapel should only be used by himself, his family and servants. The peasants would have to walk to Sonning. This building has long since disappeared and by the late medieval period, Sindlesham and Bearwood had become attached to Hurst parish and then Newland to Arborfield parish.

Anciently located in Sonning parish, the wood then called Bishop's Bearwood was always claimed by the Bishops of Salisbury as their personal hunting chase, where they rode with their guests when staying at Sonning Palace. However, by 1300, the King was trying to claim Bearwood as part of Windsor Forest. The dispute between the two continued until the bishops sold Sonning to Queen Elizabeth I in 1574. Soon afterwards, James I created Bearwood Walke as a division of Windsor Forest with its own hunting lodge. As stocks were low, the King had some deer transferred there. However, fearing they would wander off, he had the keepers, Sir Francis Knollys Junior (from Reading and Battle) and Richard Arrowsmith, fence them in. This did not go down well with the locals who, led by the Allwright family, rioted in the night and pulled down the enclosure. Finally, the royal servants lost control during the Civil War and the lodge was demolished in 1655.

Figure 99: Bearwood House, built for the Walter Newspaper Magnates

This old royal park was purchased by John Walter II, proprietor of the Times Newspaper, around 1830. He may have been attracted to the area because his relative, John Abel Walter, had previously lived at Newland in the 1780s. John Walter II built himself an elegant house there, as well as St Catherine's Church for his estate workers in 1846. The National Grid Control Centre stands on the site of the old parsonage next door. The church's dedication commemorates Walter's daughter who tragically drowned in the lake and there is a sad memorial to his grandson who did the same whilst saving his brother and cousin. It was this boy's father, John Walter III, who built the magnificent Jacobean-revival mansion, slightly to the south-east of the old house, at the height of his publishing reputation in 1864. The architect was Robert Kerr. Since 1921 it has been a school, originally for boys wishing to enter the Merchant Navy and now part of the Reddam House group.

Sonning

This well-known bridging point on the River Thames may well date back to Roman times, for there appear to be signs of a Roman road heading this way across Southern Oxfordshire from Wallingford. It may have then been a simple series of fords between the river islands. It was certainly well established during the Anglo-Saxon and then medieval periods when Sonning became an important crossing point for merchants and traders travelling from London to Oxford and the West Midlands. The bridge is not mentioned in extant records until the 1530s however. It had a toll, so there was also a cheaper ferry service up until 1835. During the Civil War, when royalist Reading was under siege from the parliamentarian army, relief sent from Oxford could not cross the Thames at Caversham and so was diverted to Sonning, from where 600 musketeers rowed upstream to bolster the town's defences. Tradition says they took much needed supplies of flour with them from Sonning Mill and this is why, when a parliamentary spy was captured in Reading, he was found carrying orders to burn the mill down. In later centuries, the millers ran barges to take their flour up to London.

Being on the island in the river, the mill complex was in the Oxfordshire section of the old parish of Sonning. Prior to 1866, Sonning was a cross-county parish incorporating parts of both Berkshire and Oxfordshire. These days, the area north of the river forms the Oxfordshire parish of Eye and Dunsden. The superb mill house is currently the English home of the Hollywood actor, George Clooney. Like the mill, it is of similar date to the present brick bridge of twenty-seven bays. This was built by John Treacher, the General Surveyor of the Thames, to replace its wooden medieval predecessor in 1773.

Figure 100: Sonning Bridge, built in 1773

Treacher was also in charge of all lock construction but had started out running the manor lord's large timber yard. Sonning had had a flash lock (only usable in the Summer) since at least the 1570s. The present pound lock was built in 1772 but there was never a wharf and labourers had to stand in the water to unload produce. In the 16th century, the roof of Henry VIII's chapel at Hampton Court had been made there from Sonning wood. Boat building was an established industry in the village from at least the 1750s and basket-making, using rods from the

Thameside osier beds, was another popular industry stemming from the River. Before this, there were also two large chalk pits on the edge of the village but the extraction was dangerous and many deaths are recorded. The pits were also used for local gatherings: theatrical performances and sports like cudgel-play and wrestling.

The name Sonning means [Place of] Sunna's People. Sunna is thought to have been an Anglo-Saxon chief whose people were widespread in Eastern Berkshire. Their other settlements included Sindlesham (near Wokingham), Sunninghill and Sunningdale (near Ascot), and also Sunningwell (near Abingdon). Sonning was the capital of Sunningum, an administrative province in the late 7th century which may have been the northern equivalent of the South-Regum (or Southern Kingdom) of Surrey. Sunningum was probably also connected with southern Buckinghamshire, where the Kings of Surrey had a palace at Quarrendon, near Aylesbury. Sonning's importance is shown by the fact that it was chosen as the site for an Anglo-Saxon minster from where priests would travel out into the surrounding countryside to preach to the locals. Sonning Minster's territory originally covered Wokingham, Hurst, Ruscombe, Sindlesham, Arborfield and Sandhurst, as well as Sonning itself, and these places did not gain their ecclesiastical independence until the 14th century.

In AD 909, Sonning Minster was converted into one of the twin cathedrals of the newly created Diocese of Ramsbury and Sonning. Sculpted fragments of the old cathedral can still be seen built into the present church tower. A bishop's palace was built alongside, where holy men such as St Bertwald, St Aelfstan, St Oda and two other future Archbishops of Canterbury often resided. The bishops seem to have made Sonning into something of a pilgrimage centre, for the church held a relic of St 'Sarik'. There was still a chapel dedicated to him in existence around 1600, which may have been on the site of the south chancel aisle or immediately behind the chancel. He should probably be identified with the Middle Eastern St Cyriacus, whose relics were also revered at nearby Abingdon Abbey. It is possible that Bishop Sigeric may have seen him as a namesake and patron and so acquired a relic for Sonning in the AD 990s.

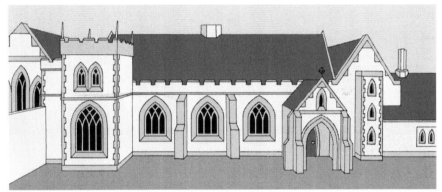

Figure 101: The medieval Bishop's Palace at Sonning

The Sonning Diocese was later united with Sherborne (Dorset) and then transferred to Salisbury (Wiltshire), but the bishops continued to live at Sonning on occasion and the complex was much expanded, particularly upon its crenellation in 1337. St Osmund owned the manor at the time of the Domesday Book (1086) and, as he is known to have dedicated a number of Berkshire churches, he must have resided there quite often. Bishop Roger of Salisbury is known to have stayed at the palace while attending the funeral of King Henry I at Reading Abbey in 1135. He arrived by state barge up the Thames. In 1216, Bishop Herbert Poor acted as custodian, at Sonning, for at least one of

King John's noble prisoners and the King himself arrived to receive his ransom money there. The Black Prince frequently rode over from Wallingford Castle and his daughter-in-law, the seven-year-old Princess Isabella of France, became a further prisoner at the Bishop's Palace upon her husband Richard II's deposition in 1396. She was visited in her splendid gaol by his supporters, hopeful of his restoration, but their 'Epiphany Rising' came to nothing. Isabella later returned home, across the Channel, though her ghost is said to still walk the fields over the palace ruins at Sonning. King Richard's personal symbol was the white hart (a pun from Rich-Hart) and was long reflected in the name of a local Sonning inn, now unfortunately renamed the Great House. This was probably the site of the house of Elias the Ferryman around 1100.

Figure 102: The Epiphany Rebels ask for Young Queen Isabella's Support

There is nothing to be seen of the old Bishop's Palace today but a Tudor wall and a low mound near Holme Park. However, the 16th century Bull Inn is thought to have been the bishops' guesthouse where St Sarik's pilgrims stayed. Its name stems from the bovine supporters and crest of Sir Henry Neville who was the steward to Queen Elizabeth I at Sonning after she bought the manor from the Bishops of Salisbury. Her Majesty visited the place at least twice.

The parish church was owned directly by Salisbury Cathedral. Its dean, as official rector, had an occasional residence, Parsonage House, at Sonning from about 1284 until the 1660s, although he was rarely in residence. Deanery Garden, a masterpiece of Arts-and-Crafts architecture by Sir Edwin Lutyens still stands on its site north of the church. It is currently the home of the Led Zeppelin musician, Jimmy Page. The Dean held regular visitations and, in 1220, found that the local curate did not understand the Latin services. Things must have improved, however, as Sonning Church was chosen as the scene of much pomp when William Scammel was consecrated Bishop of Salisbury there in 1284.

The present church at Sonning, though considerably restored in Victorian times, is largely 13th and 14th century in date. Building work may have been delayed by the Black Death, which apparently took the life of the vicar and many of his parishioners in 1348. The church houses a fine collection of monuments. There is a superb brass to Laurence Fyton (1434), the younger son of the lord of Gawsworth in Cheshire. He found his own way in life by becoming the Bishop of Salisbury's bailiff, running the Sonning estate on a day-to-day basis between intermittent episcopal visits. Further 16th century brasses and later monuments are to the Barker family, royal under-stewards at Holme Park and later owners of the old Parsonage House. They show well the changing fashions of the age. They were a demanding family and one of their number, Sir Anthony Barker, is recorded, in 1618, as having pulled seven guns on a certain Thomas Ewen, Ewen's lawyer and other supporters. Armed with swords and daggers, they had pulled up the park's palings, presumably over some land dispute.

Only a small group of six kneeling figures remain of what must have originally been a fine Jacobean monument, to the Blagraves of Bulmershe Court in Woodley. They were found in the old family vault. The most striking monument, however, must be that to Sir Thomas Rich (1667). This extraordinary memorial features no effigy but four cherubs supporting a slab with two large urns, all in stark contrasting black and white. It has been described as "the vilest paganism imaginable" but would have been the height of fashion at the time. Rich was an Alderman of Gloucester who traded in wine in Turkey and lent the King large sums of money during the Civil War. He bought Sonning manor, by then called Holme Park, in 1654 and made it a home for dispossessed clergymen, including the Bishop of Exeter. He was made a baronet at the Restoration and became a great patron of the Reading Blue Coat School, now housed in the successor to his own home. His old ice-house survives in the grounds. A new house was built for Richard Palmer, the Duke of Bedford's lawyer, in 1797 and then more or less rebuilt in its present form for Henry Golding-Palmer by Henry Woodyer in 1880-2.

The church also had some interesting characters to tend to the spiritual needs of the locals. One medieval vicar was in the habit of wearing his sword in the pulpit. Another upset the churchwardens, in the 1570s, by erecting a new pew for his wife and letting his cattle run free in the churchyard, while the locals were not allowed to erect their annual maypole there. While staying with friends in Hurst in 1623, the Reading-born

Archbishop of Canterbury, William Laud, preached at Sonning with the vicar, Robert Wright, who had been newly appointed Bishop of Bristol. In the 19th century, the vicar was fond of entertaining eminent guests to dinner. Unfortunately, these included an unscrupulous doctor who would laugh and joke with his host while his associates robbed the graves in the churchyard for his dubious research. Another clergyman associated with Sonning is the poet rector of Byfleet in Surrey, Reverend Doctor Stephen Duck. He tragically committed suicide in 1756 by throwing himself into the river behind the Black Lion pub in Reading and was pulled from the Thames at Sonning, where he was subsequently buried.

Figure 103: Sonning High Street facing towards the Grove

During the Napoleonic Wars, Viscount Sidmouth's house on the High Street, The Grove, was the prison of Admiral Villeneuve, the French commander at the Battle of Trafalgar. The Prime Minister, William Pitt the Younger, visited him there. Towards the end of his life, Pre-Raphaelite artist, William Holman Hunt, came to live at The Acre in Sonning, where he painted his second version of 'The Light of the World' for St Paul's Cathedral. A less salubrious residence, a cottage at the end of Sonning Lane called Turpins, is said to have been the home of Dick Turpin's aunt. Being frequently engaged on the Bath Road, Dick would flee the Berkshire authorities by galloping to his aunt's house, then on foot through the churchyard to Oxfordshire and safety. Black Bess would casually stroll down to a loose-box hidden below the cottage. Turpin was said to have drunk at the Dog pub in the High Street. His aunt's cottage also later became a pub called the Rich Arms after the lords of the manor. The gallant French highwayman, Claude Duval, is also sometimes said to have owned a house in the village.

Southcote

Southcote was historically the rural western part of the parish of Reading St Mary. It was the Southern Cottage opposing the Northern Cottage at Norcot in Tilehurst. Until the early 20th century, the area was almost entirely agricultural fields. From at least the late Anglo-Saxon period, there was only a manor house and a mill there. The small hamlet of 5 villeins (tenant farmers) and 8 bordars (cottage dwellers) and their families disappeared sometime in the medieval period but two farms were established in its place. The manor house, Southcote House, was given a large moat fed by the Holy Brook in the 13th century. This still survives today, if now dry, in Hatford Road around the flats opposite the end of Glenmon Close. The house that once stood within the moat is well-recorded in old photographs, engravings and descriptions.

The oldest parts of Southcote House were probably built by Walter Sambourne in the mid-15th century and included an arch-braced wing behind the later house and a prominent corner brick guard-tower. Other parts, including a large gatehouse-cum-stables, were added in the 1590s by John Blagrave, a member of the famous Reading family who were landlords for most of the town. He was a well-known mathematician and map-maker who studied the heavens from his Solar Tower and wrote several important books at Southcote. His demi-effigy can be seen on the wall of St Laurence's Church in the town.

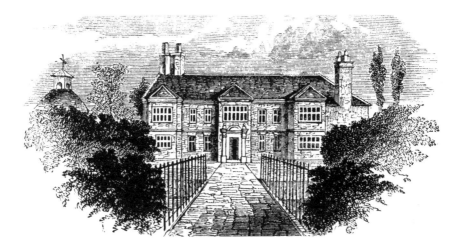

After Blagrave's death, his nephew and namesake illegally took possession of the house but is said to have been frightened off by his uncle's angry ghost. The true heir, the second John's younger brother Daniel Blagrave MP, then moved in and, in the 1620s, built the main short-winged house within the moat. He was a determined anti-royalist who, during the Civil War Siege of Reading in 1643, allowed the parliamentary commander, the Earl of Essex, to use Southcote House as his headquarters. He later became one of the signatories to the King's death warrant and therefore had to flee to Jamaica when the Monarchy was restored. The Blagraves moved to Calcot Park in the early 1760s and

Southcote was rented out to tenants for years. These included Charles and Frances Lutyens, the grandparents of the famous Arts-and-Crafts architect, Sir Edwin Lutyens, and an eccentric recluse, Wastel Brisco, who died whilst restoring the house. Sadly, it subsequently fell into disrepair and, despite much local opposition, was demolished in 1921. The gatehouse remained until 1960.

John Blagrave the Mathematician also built a second new house in Southcote, possibly for his nephew, Daniel. This was Southcote Lodge on the site of the current house of that name on the Burghfield Road. An old story tells how, during their incarceration after the Civil War, King Charles I's younger children were sent to the Lodge for protection from an outbreak of smallpox. The present house was probably put up in the late 1740s by George Noyes, with the large bow-fronted wing being added by his son, Thomas Buckeridge Noyes. Both were the rich heirs to a number of important Berkshire families, including the Buckeridges of Basildon and the Noake brewers of Reading. The house was later rented to a succession of high-ranking army officers, including the 18th Baron Saye and Sele. It is now retirement apartments.

To the west, over the old Tilehurst border, stands Prospect Park. The mansion house there was constructed around Dirle's Farm in the mid-18th century by Benjamin Child, the former lord of the manor of Tilehurst in right of his wife, Frances Kendrick. He had retained this piece of land when he sold Calcot House to the Blagraves, because it was the place where he had agreed to marry his notorious spouse. Having fallen head over heels in love with him, Frances had appeared in disguise and, at sword-point, challenged him to fight or marry her. He sensibly decided to plump for the latter option and the two were very happy together for many years. The house is now a restaurant said to be haunted by Frances' ghost. Her statuette stands in the main dining area.

Figure 104: Prospect Park, where Benjamin Child chose to marry not fight

In the mid-19th century, Reading began to spread west across the railway line between the Bath Road and the Tilehurst Road. Southcote Road in particular became home to large villas for the town's rich businessmen. Lord Saye and Sele's father moved his family to Sunbury House there in 1894 after his gambling habit got him into serious debt and he was forced to rent out his ancestral home, Broughton Castle near Banbury in Oxfordshire. Further out on the Bath Road, in 1876, a country house called Oaklands was built for Edwin May, a prominent Reading solicitor and youngest son of one of the founding staff at the Royal Berkshire Hospital. It later became part of Presentation College but was scandalously torn down in 2010.

By the 1930s, Oaklands had been joined by other grand villas, but Southcote Lane, northern Circuit Lane and the Burghfield Road were also being developed with more standard housing.

The land for the development of Southcote itself was compulsorily purchased after the Second World War and building began on a planned community, with churches, a pub, a library and other facilities, in 1951.

Spencers Wood

Spencers Wood and Three Mile Cross formed the Wiltshire part of Shinfield parish until 1844. This was a hangover from the time when the land was owned by the Norman Earl of Salisbury. Spencers Wood is probably named after a wood "at Diddenham," near Grazeley, that was given to Geoffrey Le Despenser, from Beaumys Castle at Beech Hill, in the 13th century. The name is specifically first mentioned in 1500 and it was probably around this time that the area began to be deforested and turned into common grazing land for the peasants of the local manors. The area was gradually enclosed and sold to private owners throughout the 19th century until 1864, after which the village developed rather quickly.

Figure 105: Stanbury Park at Spencers Wood

The main Basingstoke Road through both villages became the Reading and Basingstoke Turnpike Road in 1718. In the following centuries, two fine country houses were built on its west side, although only one survives. The house called Highlands was built near Highlands Barn (dated 1756) in about 1819 by John Carter from Beenham, who unfortunately died very soon afterwards. It was rented out, in the 1820s to Admiral John Mackellar, who was known for his "scandalous, cruel and oppressive conduct". It was then purchased by Lord Palmerston's former secretary, William Merry. Merry supported Christian evangelism and wrote books on Christianity that were an inspiration to the authoress, Elizabeth Barrett Browning. His family lived at the house until 1911. It is now offices.

The other country house, Stanbury Park, was erected on the Hill House Farm estate in the late 1850s by Frederick William Allfrey, whose brother was already living at Wokefield Park. He later lived at Ashridgewood House. During the Second World War, it was requisitioned by the Royal Engineers. It was also used as a prisoner of war camp, with their Nissan huts lining the drive. In the 1950s, the 60ft orangery from Solly Joel's millionaire's mansion at Maiden Erlegh was purchased by the owner of Stanbury and re-erected there. Unfortunately, the house suffered from a fire when being converted into flats in 1960 and was subsequently demolished. The orangery was dismantled and moved to Cornwall in 1983.

Stratfield Mortimer and Mortimer Common

Stratfield Mortimer had occupants as far back as the Bronze Age, when there was a small farmstead in the Damson Drive area. Later, a 1st century Roman cremation cemetery was established there. The remains were buried in pots in wooden boxes and some included grave goods such as a rare silvered 'box' mirror. The home of the deceased is currently unlocated, but was no doubt a small settlement built near the Roman road from Silchester to Dorchester-on-Thames. The name of the present village partly stems from this road: Anglo-Saxon Strad-Feld, modern Street-Field, means the Roman road among open land. The Anglo-Saxons have left their mark on the parish church where an extremely rare tombstone of that date may be seen. It reads:

On 8th before Kalends of October,
Aegalward son Kypping was laid in this place.
Blessed be he who prays for his Soul.
Toki wrote this.

Aegalward is mentioned in the Anglo-Saxon Chronicle in AD 994. He was a historian, a translator of the chronicle and a man of influence. Kypping, his father, was the lord of Stratfield Mortimer. Toki was a wealthy courtier in King Canute's reign. No doubt, he took advantage of the lull in hostilities between Vikings and Anglo-Saxons to erect this monument to a learned man of the previous century.

The Mortimer part of the place-name stems from the lords of the manor, the Mortimer family, the Earls of March from Wigmore in Herefordshire. They were given the manor shortly after the Norman Conquest and held it throughout the Middle Ages. Hugh Mortimer probably spent some time there, as he was a great patron of Reading Abbey, where his heart was buried after his death in 1227. His brother, Ralph, established a rabbit warren at the manor in 1230 and created a large park around it at about the same time. The King gave him some deer from Savernake Forest to stock it. So Mortimer may have held sporting parties there when at the Royal Court in Windsor. In 1250, his widow, Princess Gwladys of Gwynedd, was certainly given permission to keep her hunting dogs at Stratfield. However, the rest of the family appear not to have made much use of the manor and it was eventually leased out to the Bishop of Winchester for a 'rose rent'. Even so, it is just possible that Edmund Mortimer, the 3rd Earl of March, may have stayed there prior to his wedding. He was married, at Reading Abbey in 1359, to Princess Philippa, only daughter and sole heiress of Prince Lionel, Duke of Clarence, the third son of King Edward III.

Figure 106: King Edward III & his War Horses

For a short period in the early 14th century, the manor was confiscated from the great rebel, Roger Mortimer, the 1st Earl of March, by King Edward III. It was during this period that a royal stud farm was established at the Manor Farm, adjoining the manor house. In 1330, four foals and three big cart horses are recorded there: 'Ellen' was black with a white star on her forehead, 'Cesse' was dun with a similar star, 'Cappe' was chestnut coloured. By 1336, there were six colts, twelve carthorses and nineteen warhorses, one given by Sir John Brocas of Clewer, the man in charge of all the royal studs. These beasts would have fought in the Hundred Years' War during the King's attempt to claim the French Throne. The stud was probably wound up at the beginning of the following century.

By 1430 the manor house was in an extreme state of decay but, twenty years later, large sums of money were spent on its restoration. The keeper, John Flegge, appears to have been expecting a visit from the then owner, Richard, Duke of York, the heir of the Mortimers. It is not known whether he turned up or not. However, by 1460, the Duke was dead: killed in battle while trying to wrest the Throne from King Henry VI during the Wars of the Roses. His strong claim was through his ancestress, the aforementioned Princess Philippa, and his son eventually did succeed in becoming King Edward IV.

During the Tudor period, the manor was one of the minor lands granted to each of the wives of Henry VIII in turn (save for Anne of Cleves). In 1535, the keeper, Lord Sandys, had cause to complain of illegal hunting in the park at Stratfield by Thomas Trapnell, the brother-in-law of Sir Thomas Englefield of Englefield House. When he sent his brother to investigate, he was attacked and injured by Trapnell and his six servants. Sandys wrote to the King for redress but whether he got it or not is unclear.

Stratfield Mortimer probably saw troops from both sides passing through the village during the Civil War with major activity centred on the besieged town of Reading and the two battles fought on the important highways through Newbury. As royalist troops used the area as their route between Oxford and the besieged Basing House, the parliamentary army considered stationing a unit in the village in 1644, but eventually decided on Aldermaston instead.

On 2nd February 1787, an old labouring man from Stratfield Mortimer, called William Billimore, was brutally murdered on the local common by two idle lads from Ufton Nervet who wanted some money to spend at the Reading Fair. They bludgeoned the poor man with a lead weighted club and took his pocket watch but were too flustered to search properly for his money. They escaped to Hare Hatch and then Maidenhead, where they sold the watch, but were captured when they decided to return home. They were condemned to death at the Reading Assizes and hanged at Gibbet Piece (which is just within Ufton parish) on Mortimer Common.

Figure 107: The Horse & Groom opposite the Fairground

Mortimer Common, where the villagers once freely grazed their livestock, was enclosed for cultivation in 1802, mostly with the consent of the parish residents, although the vicar protested. A small open area was retained for the holding of annual cattle and horse fairs in November. This is the existing Fairground, opposite the appropriately named Horse and Groom pub, now used as a public recreation ground. The ponds there were used for watering cattle by Welsh drovers who passed through the village down Welshman's Road. The settlement of Mortimer Common, or simply Mortimer, began to slowly grow up soon afterwards, although there was no organised building programme until the 1870s. In the 1850s, a wise woman or witch lived there. She was thought to have bewitched several people in the village. One of her victims bore a scar that he covered with black silk to prevent further misfortune. Until 1866, Mortimer West End was part of Stratfield Mortimer, although, being a parish that crossed the county boundary, it was always in Hampshire.

Streatley

This place-name is Anglo-Saxon for Street Clearing, the street being the north-south Roman road from Calleva (Silchester) to Dorcic (Dorchester-on-Thames). For many years, misguided Victorian antiquarians actually identified Streatley with the Roman town of Calleva, but the excavations at Silchester in Hampshire in the 1890s produced inscriptions that proved otherwise. There was indeed a Roman settlement in the village, just south-west of the parish church, but it was very small. It was an ideal spot for guarding two trading routes, for there was a second ancient track heading east-west that had a ferry crossing over the Thames where the bridge now stands. The Romans improved the crossing by added a causeway to form a ford. The road is known as the Icknield Way because it took Iron Age man to the land of the Iceni tribe in Norfolk, although it is considerably older, as shown by Bronze Age and Neolithic finds from the parish. The several sarsen stones scattered around the area are perfectly natural but tradition relates that these were originally thrown into Kiddington Bottom by the 'Aldworth

Giants' during a stone hurling competition. The print of a giant hand may supposedly still be seen impressed onto one sarsen.

The Anglo-Saxon settlement is first mentioned in a land charter of AD 687, when King Ine of Wessex granted a parcel of land there to Bradfield Abbey. The ford and ferry became one of the major crossing points between the kingdoms of Wessex (west side) and Mercia (east side). This may have brought much trade to the village but also potential conflict. In AD 871, the Vikings had invaded England and made Reading their base for attacking Wessex. When the two sides set out to clash at the Battle of Ashdown, on the Berkshire Downs (probably at Compton, East Ilsley or Aldworth), the Vikings would have marched through Streatley to join the Ridgeway. An Anglo-Saxon warrior burial, complete with weapon stuck in him, was discovered on the village bowling green in 1932 and may have been a local man who died in the battle.

Figure 108: The Berington Brass in Streatley Church

Before the Norman Conquest, Estralei (as it was then called) belonged to Esgar, the Sheriff of Middlesex, whose main

Berkshire manor was in the west of the county at East Garston (originally Esgar's Town). He was probably killed at the Battle of Hastings, after which King William's army marched through Streatley on their way to Wallingford to cross the Thames and take London. Esgar was certainly succeeded by Geoffrey de Mandeville, Earl of Essex, not only in his appointment, but in his lands as well. Geoffrey mostly lived in Norfolk, although he probably visited Hurley in East Berkshire occasionally, as he founded a priory there. At the time of the Domesday Survey (1086), Streatley village was recorded as quite large, consisting of 18 villeins (tenant farmers), 10 cottars (cottage dwellers), 7 serfs and their families. Not surprisingly, there were 22 acres of water meadow, a mill and two fisheries. Some years later, the last two were granted to Goring Priory. The weir that was built to provide the mill with a large head of water caused problems for the river traffic however. In the mid-13th century, King Henry III had to issue a number of decrees preventing the miller from holding up the important watercraft. Eventually a flash lock was constructed which held back some of the river water so it could be released in a 'flash' to carry boats over the weir.

Figure 109: Streatley Bridge & Mill (burnt down in 1926)

The manor of Streatley continued to be owned by non-resident great lords, although in the early 15th century it was purchased on behalf of William de la Pole, later Duke of Suffolk, who lived not far away at Ewelme Manor and Wallingford Castle. The original manor house at Streatley is thought by some to have been Place Manor in the High Street, near the crossroads. It has a 16th century core and a beautifully preserved dovecote of the same date. At this time, it was owned by the Earls of Derby, who seem to have leased it to the Berington (or Buriton) family who have a brass memorial in the parish church. They were a Welsh family who had settled in Herefordshire. They probably made their way to Reading to work with their uncle, Walter Barton, a rich merchant who has a memorial brass in St Laurence's Church there. One might surmise that he had connections with Reading Abbey and its daughter house, Leominster Priory.

In 1607, an inventor called William Bush made an attempt to travel in a single vessel, by air, land and water through Berkshire. He started by descending from the tower of Lambourn Church in his 'ship'. Giving this a series of wheels, he travelled on across the Downs to Childrey, Aldworth and down to Streatley. There, the vessel entered the River Thames but Mr Bush was so harassed by a group of local bargemen that, in fear for his life, he was forced to flee to his lodgings in the village. The bargemen, meanwhile, scuppered his ship with staves, hooks and pikes. It took the poor man a month to make repairs but he did eventually manage to sail his ship to London, where he was greeted with great celebrations.

Less strange, but more dangerous, the village would have seen many troops passing by during the Civil War: particularly royal units travelling between Wallingford and Reading, especially when the troops left Reading following the famous Siege. In the late 17th century, Captain Thomas Harwood RN (died 1713), who had fought valiantly in the Dutch Wars, retired to Streatley Farm, a handsome brick house dated 1673, where his descendants lived for several generations. His family came from East Hagbourne but his father had also owned land in Goring. Thomas became Sheriff of Berkshire. He also acquired land in Maryland in the United States, where his son, Richard, has many descendants. Another fine property, Streatley House, opposite the lane to the church, represents the Rectory estate. It was built in 1765 for the Stone family and later passed to the Morells. This latter family owned almost two-thirds of the village and dominated life there for most of the early 20th century. However, double death duties due in quick succession eventually forced them to sell up. The Royal Veterinary College was evacuated there when they bought the house in 1940. They left in 1958.

Figure 110: The Swan at Streatley, 1970s showbiz hub

The backwater in front of the medieval mill at Streatley is said to have been the setting for Mole and Ratty's picnic in the opening scene of 'The Wind in the Willows', although it is more likely that it was the inspiration for EH Shepard's illustrations, as the author, Kenneth Grahame, was by that time living in Pangbourne. He wrote the book in Cookham Dean. The mill was a famous beauty spot for centuries but it burnt down in 1926, shortly after being converted for electricity generation. Streatley and the Bull Inn (formerly the Turnpike post house) feature in Jerome K Jerome's 'Three Men in a Boat' and Richard Adams wrote 'Watership Down' whilst living in the village. Oscar Wilde is said to have stayed at the famous Swan Inn, on the river, and been inspired to name characters in his play, 'An ideal Husband', Lord Goring and the Earl of Caversham. The Swan dates back to the 15th century and was first turned into a pub in 1698 by Francis Swan who gave it his family name. He was the grandfather of architect, Sir John Soane, who changed the surname slightly in order to sound more aristocratic. In the 1970s, it was owned by entertainer, Danny La Rue, and saw many visitors from the world of show business.

Sulham

Sulham is an Anglo-Saxon phrase meaning Gully Home. The name fits well, for the old parish (since combined with Tidmarsh) follows a small stream, stretching from Purley down to Theale, at the foot of the ridge covered by Sulham and Boxgrove Woods. The valley may have been the site of some conflict between the Anglo-Saxons and the Vikings around the time of the Battle of Englefield in AD 870, as suggested by the surviving field names, Breaches and Deanfield (or Danefield). The old parish contains two small settlements, Sulham and Nunhide, both based on ancient manors. A third smaller estate, mentioned in the Domesday Survey (1086) as held under Miles Crispin of Wallingford, probably merged into that of Purley Hall. The parishes of Purley, Sulham and Pangbourne once met in the dining room there. The Wilders of Sulham bought the hall in 1773 and it remained a popular home with them into the 1830s.

The poetic name Nunhide is a corruption of One Hide, a hide being a measure of land; although the current form may have been influenced by the fact that it was owned by the nuns of Goring Priory in the Middle Ages. An erroneous legend suggests, however, that it was named after the secret retreat of a nun who ran away from the Anglo-Saxon Nunnery in Reading. At the time of the Domesday Survey (1086), it was one of the Berkshire properties of Theodoric the Goldsmith, centred on Hampstead Norreys. A German immigrant, this man was the finest gold and silver craftsman in London both before and after the Norman Conquest. He mainly lived at Kennington in Surrey but, in Berkshire, he also held five manors with good woodland, like at Sulham, for smelting his precious metals.

Wilder family legend states that the manor of Nunhide was given to Nicholas Wilder in April 1497 by King Henry VII in thanks for his valour in battle against King Richard III at Bosworth Field twelve years before. If true, either there was an early Nicholas who has left no record, or he survived to a great age, dying in 1542. By that time the Wilders were living in Sulham parish, almost certainly at Nunhide which they leased from the owners of Aldermaston House. Thomas Wilder eventually purchased the estate in 1632 and the present house there largely dates from his time, although the building has an earlier core. Wilder's Folly on Nunhide Hill is traditionally said to have been erected by Reverend Henry Wilder in 1768 as a token of his love for his future wife, Jane Thoyts, from Sulhamstead House. There was once an outside wooden staircase to the windowed meeting room and the building was supposedly positioned so the two lovers could both see it from their respective homes. Some people think it is of an earlier date, built as a folly for Reverend John Wilder in the 1730s. Others favour a later date, being built as a beacon or look-out tower during the Napoleonic Wars. It was also said to have been converted into a dovecote in Victorian times, but where the doves would nest is something of a mystery.

Figure 111: The Garden Cottages on the Sulham Estate

In 1712, the Wilders purchased the newly rebuilt Sulham House and switched residences. This house still remains hidden behind the present façade which encased it in 1839. Much of the village was also then rebuilt in the idyllic cottage ornée style for which it is now well known. The Wilders lived at Sulham House for nearly two hundred years. Five members of the family over five generations, throughout the 19th century, were also rectors at the church next door which they rebuilt in 1836. The last of their number died in 2009, but the estate is still owned by their descendants, the Scutt family.

The manor of Sulham had been one of those owned by Godric, the Ealdorman (or Sheriff) of Berkshire during the reign of King Edward the Confessor. It would have made a convenient stopping place between Wallingford and Reading, the two major towns under his control. William the Conqueror gave the place to William de Cailly but he rented it out to an unnamed man-at-arms (or cavalryman). There were six smallholders and four villagers and their families, along with two serfs also in residence in the manor in 1086. By the early 13th century, it belonged to a family who took their name from the village, the De Sulhams. Their heirs appear to have been the St Philibert family. Sir Hugh St Philibert served with King Edward I in Scotland and Flanders and his son, Sir John (who was born at Sulham) served with Edward III in Scotland and Gascony where he became Mayor of Bordeaux. They seem to have been a pious family, fond of pilgrimage. Sir John travelled to Saintiago de Compostela in Spain to see the body of St James, whose hand he had, no doubt, already viewed at Reading Abbey. His son, another John, was illegally arrested in Pisa whilst on a pilgrimage to Rome at the age of only twelve. He later joined the retinue of the Black Prince and was made Lord St Philibert, but he sold Sulham in 1352.

Sulhamstead

The name Sulhamstead means Gully Homestead and was given to the area by the first Anglo-Saxon settlers. Note that there is no 'p' in the name. There is supposed to have been a Viking camp of some sort there during the troubled times before King Alfred's reign. Perhaps it was an outpost from their Reading headquarters.

The place has always historically consisted of two manors with two separate villages and parishes: Sulhamstead Abbots and Sulhamstead Bannister. They were only united in 1782. The main village of today is in Sulhamstead Abbots, although the church is some way to the south. This is now the parish church for both manors. Once dedicated to St Bartholomew, it may have been given its present dedication to St Mary during the time of the Black Death. A plaque in the church commemorates Robert Venn, the man who improved and hybridized the potato in the century that saw the tragedy of the Irish Potato Famine. He lived at Cottage Farm which was later transformed by Sir Edwin Lutyens into the Arts-and-Crafts architectural masterpiece now called Folly Farm.

Figure 112: Lutyens' Folly Farm at Sulhamstead

Sulhamstead Bannister is split into two parts. The Upper End is the main village of Sulhamstead Bannister. Straddled by Sulhamstead Abbots land on both sides, the area is now little more than a farm alongside the old churchyard. Detached, near Grazeley, between Burghfield and Spencers Wood, is Sulhamstead Bannister Lower End, which retained the parish name for some time after the Upper End merged with Sulhamstead Abbots.

Banister was the name of the lords of the manor from the early 12th century. They still held lands there three hundred years later and had another important manor in Finchampstead. The Upper End was, however, often called Meales which is a contraction of St Michael's, the dedication of the church whose remains stand next to the reputed manor house at Meales Farm. The last church was pulled down in 1966 but some of its fittings can still be seen in the church at Sulhamstead Abbots. It wasn't a very old place, having been built by the lords of the manor in 1914 to replace a charming little building only a hundred years older. For a very short time, the two stood side by side. The Rector of Sulhamstead Bannister in 1625 was the father of Sir Samuel Morland, the great 17th century inventor who demonstrated a calculating machine, a speaking trumpet and various pumps and engines before King Charles II. However, he was particularly famous for sorting out the plumbing at Windsor Castle, which he flamboyantly showed off with a fountain spouting red wine.

The Abbots who owned the other manor throughout the Middle Ages were, of course, the Abbots of Reading. Their old manor house survives in the large cottage called Brazenhead (named after the old door-knocker), a fine old timber-framed place on the edge of the village. It was apparently favoured as a summer residence, presumably because of the nearby river. Along with Burghfield, it was purchased by John, Lord Williams, after the Dissolution of the Monasteries and he kept the house as a hunting lodge before renting it out to the Weldon family. The Weldons entertained Queen Elizabeth I there and delivered to her some important news from Ireland. As a reward, she granted them a coat-of-arms featuring a royal lion and a 'cinquefoil' which is not dissimilar to an Irish shamrock.

Figure 113: The Three Kings Jack's Booth (now the Spring Inn)

The hilltop Sulhamstead House later became the local manor house. It is now the Thames Valley Police Training Centre and Museum. This beautiful white porticoed building is easily seen from down on the Bath Road. It is erroneously said to be a twin to Beenham House, across the valley. Sulhamstead was built by Daniel May between 1744 and 1748, just after his marriage to one of the Tippings from Woolley Park in Chaddleworth. In 1714, Daniel's father, Charles, had bought the manor from Lord Williams' heir, the Earl of Abingdon, having made his money making malt for beer production in Basingstoke. He became the mayor there but lost his life along with most of his children in a smallpox epidemic. Hence, when Daniel died childless in 1753, there were no Mays to inherit and Sulhamstead passed to his young nephew, John Thoyts, whose family lived there until 1910. They united the two manors of Abbots and Bannister in 1774. Their memory is kept alive on numerous plaques in the church, along with their coat-of-arms in stained glass and two hatchments (or heraldic funerary boards).

The Old Bath Road (or A4) has, of course, played a major part in shaping Sulhamstead life. It was first converted into a reliable routeway and turnpiked as a toll road from Reading in 1714. This initially stopped at Sulhamstead but was extended to Newbury in 1728. The Three Kings – Jack's Booth was one of its most popular roadside pubs and was a stop off point for the famous Flying Coach which travelled between London and Newbury in twelve hours flat. The unusual name has, in more recent years, regrettably been changed to the Spring Inn. The old suffix supposedly stems from the legendary Newbury clothier, Jack O'Newbury, who used to undertake business dealings on the premises during his visits to Mid-Berkshire. Alternatively, a local innkeeper called Jack Jones is said to have made the place famous by arranging bareknuckle fist-fights there. Thomas Stackhouse, the Vicar of Beenham, was such a regular visitor in the 1730s that he wrote most of his famous 'History of the Bible' there.

Swallowfield

The name Swallowfield has nothing to do with birds but is Anglo-Saxon for Swirling River Field. In King Edward the Confessor's reign, Swallowfield manor was owned by a Viking 'huscarle' (or royal bodyguard) named Sexi. However, throughout most of the Middle Ages, it was owned by the St John family from Stanton St John (Oxfordshire) and Lagham (Surrey). Roger St John seems to have liked Swallowfield Manor and King John visited him there in both 1205 and 1206. Roger's daughter-in-law, Emma, and her second husband, Geoffrey Le Despenser from Beaumys Castle near Beech Hill, were also often in residence. In 1253, Emma was made governess to the newly-born Princess Katherine by her father, King Henry III. The poor little girl was a deaf-mute and had frequent bouts of poor health. During one of these episodes, at the age of two, Emma brought her to Swallowfield to recover. She had other children for company and her father sent her a baby goat from Windsor Great Park to play with. Katherine only lived for another year.

Figure 114: Duchess of Gloucester does penance for 'witchcraft'

Emma's rebel son, John Le Despenser, later lived at Swallowfield in his half-brother's house. He gained permission from the Pope to build the church on the edge of his estate, so he didn't have to travel all the way to the mother-church at Sonning every Sunday. His grave was found under the church floor during Victorian restoration work. John lay in a stone coffin with a large flat cross upon it. He was surrounded by cloves and a wooden dish, probably for salt, rested on his chest. John's contemporary neighbours, the Blount family, created a deer park at Sheepbridge Court on the River Loddon and probably dug the moat, that can still be seen, around their house there at the same time. The present farmhouse only dates from the 16th century however.

Swallowfield manor also gained a deer park in the 1350s after it had passed into royal hands. King Edward III turned the place into a stud farm that supplied war horses for the Hundred Years'

War, under the watchful eye of Edmund Rose and Sir John Brocas. In the late medieval period, Swallowfield continued to be owned by various absentee Royals and, eventually by the wives of King Henry VIII. It was, however, sometimes granted out to their servants such as the mid-15th century Groom-Usher of the Chamber, John Martin. He was probably ancestor of the Martins of Wokingham and Shinfield but is best remembered for having escorted the Duchess of Gloucester to imprisonment at Chester Castle after having done penance for having supposedly used witchcraft against King Henry VI. Martin's Corner in the park, near the church, was named after him.

In 1553, the manor passed into private hands again and the deer were removed from the park. By 1582, it was in the hands of Samuel Backhouse, a London merchant who wanted a country estate near his wife's family home in Marlow (Buckinghamshire). Fourteen years later, after a series of bad harvests, the leading villagers drew up the 'Swallowfield Articles', a list of rules that tightened control of the locals in an attempt to lessen burdens on the parish purse, such as unmarried mothers or vagrants. These are upheld by historians as a symbol of the transition of community government away from the medieval manorial system. As Sheriff of Berkshire in 1601, Samuel entertained Queen Elizabeth I on her visit to Reading and endeared himself to everyone by embracing the pomp and ceremony that he was unaccustomed to. His two sons followed him at the Park. Sir John was a royalist during the Civil War and, in consequence, Swallowfield was confiscated by the Parliament and he had to go and live on a small estate at Worldham near Alton (Hampshire). While he was away, much of the parliamentary army camped in Swallowfield Park in October 1644, on their march from Basingstoke to join the Second Battle of Newbury. Sir John's brother, William, was a linguist, inventor, chemist, astrologer and 'Rosicrucian' philosopher who studied metaphysics, mysticism and alchemy. He invented the pedometer and gave farms in Sindlesham and Arborfield to Jesus College, Oxford on the understanding that the farmers installed there could speak perfect Welsh.

Figure 115: Swallowfield Park & Diamond Pitt

William's daughter and heiress, Flower, married three times. Her last husband was Viscount Cornbury, the eldest son of the former Lord Chancellor, the 1st Earl of Clarendon. The Earl spent his last years in exile abroad where he wrote his famous 'History of the Rebellion and Civil Wars in England' despite his attempts to come and live at Swallowfield with his son. Cornbury succeeded as the 2nd Earl of Clarendon in 1674. His sister was married to the Duke of York (later King James II) and her daughters, who later became Queen Mary II and Queen Anne, probably stayed at Swallowfield as children, for their aunt was Anne's governess. King Charles II is known to have visited in 1680 and would, no doubt, have enjoyed the beautiful Dutch style gardens described by the diarist, John Evelyn, shortly afterwards. There were two orangeries, walks, groves, 'parterres' of low box hedges, a bowling green, an ornamental canal and fishponds: one with white and one with black water. The 2nd Earl's son joined the supporters of his cousin, Queen Mary II and her husband, King William III, when they pushed Mary's father off the Throne. However, the Earl himself refused to swear his allegiance and had to retire from the Royal Court to the Berkshire countryside. From 1689, he spent his time totally rebuilding Swallowfield Place (as the house was then called) but he consorted with rebellious Jacobites and was sent to the Tower of London a number of times. Around the same time, his son was made Governor of New York, where he demonstrated transvestite tendencies much to the disapproval of the Government at home. His father died soon after his recall and the 3rd Earl sold Swallowfield in 1719 to Thomas Pitt.

Figure 116: Mary Russell Mitford's Grave in Swallowfield Churchyard

Pitt was a successful merchant who became the President of Fort Madras in India for the British East India Company. While there, he was given the nickname of Diamond Pitt after acquiring the now famous Regent Diamond (then called the Pitt Diamond) in 1701. Being the largest diamond in the World at the time (now the 15th largest), there were naturally many rumours concerning its origins. The most popular story declared that the diamond was found by a slave who hid it in a wound in his leg. Having made a fateful pact with a ship's captain, the poor man was murdered and the diamond sold on to Pitt for £1,000. Thus, the poet, Alexander Pope, who grew up in Binfield, wrote of him:

Asleep and naked as an Indian lay,
An honest factor stole a gem away;
He pledged it to the Knight, the Knight had wit,
So kept the diamond, and the rogue was bit.

Thomas, however, claimed that he had legitimately purchased the diamond for £20,000 from a reputable Indian diamond merchant. He eventually sold it to King Louis XV of France and it became part of the French Crown Jewels. Napoleon used to wear it in the hilt of his sword, but today it is safely on display in the Louvre Museum in Paris. With the proceeds of the sale, Pitt bought Swallowfield Park. He was the grandfather of William Pitt the Elder, Earl of Chatham and Prime Minister, who also lived at Swallowfield for about a year before his father's death. The house is now split into retirement flats. One of the estate barns (now a private house) has an interesting old dovecote.

Due to its ruinous state, Swallowfield Church was almost pulled down in the 19th century but Charles Kingsley, the Vicar of Eversley (Hampshire) and a close friend of Lady Russell of Swallowfield Park, saw its merits and had it restored. Lady Russell was also friends with Charles Dickens and took on his dog after his death. It has a little gravestone in the small pet cemetery in the park where it is buried. Another friend was Mary Russell Mitford, the author of 'Our Village'. She retired to Swallowfield (which gains a mention in her book) so the two could be close to one another. Locals long remembered the books from her private library being pushed through the Berkshire lanes in a handcart, all the way from her previous home at Three Mile Cross. She died at Swallowfield and is buried in the churchyard under a large stone cross by the back gate into the park.

Theale

Just west of North Street in Englefield parish, a small 1st century Romano-British village has been excavated. Ditch-enclosed small fields or gardens were found where wheat was grown and cattle grazed, but no evidence remained of the, presumably wooden, buildings.

The name Theale is a simple Anglo-Saxon word meaning a Plank. This was probably a plank bridge, either over the River Kennet or just across a marshy gap in the gravel terraces on which the settlement stands. However, it has also been suggested that it could refer to a plank-built hall where the local hundred court met. A hundred was a small English administrative unit, a bit like a district council with judicial powers. Theale Hundred was created in the 12th century and stretched from Bradfield to Stratfield Mortimer and Purley to Aldermaston (minus Sulhamstead Abbots in the middle). Historically (before 1894) Theale was in Tilehurst parish which, bizarrely, was not part of the Hundred. Perhaps it was chosen as the meeting place because of its good communications. The court was often held at the Bull Inn. Hundreds lost their powers in 1867 but officially still exist.

After the First Battle of Newbury, the royalist army is known to have fled back to Oxford as soon as possible. Prince Rupert and his cavalry officers were not best pleased and, at a council of war, he punningly declared that "Although the Roundheads are marching into Reading, we will make calves of them before they come into Veale". The prince was as good as his word and there was indeed an armed skirmish at Theale shortly afterwards. Many soldiers died in the fighting that ensued and their bodies are said to have been later buried in Deadman's Lane.

Figure 117: The Bull Inn & Draper's Brewery in Theale

The village had always been a wayside ribbon settlement along the old Bath Road (now the High Street and Church Street) which, though more disjointed then, was known as the King's Street to the West Country even back in the Middle Ages. From 1632, King Charles I had the route upgraded, for the postal service, to a proper continuous thoroughfare known as the Great West Road. It is therefore not surprising that, as a convenient stopping place just outside Reading, Theale became famous for its coaching inns. Both the Falcon and the Crown date back to this time and have probably always been hostelries. In 1714, Reading to Sulhamstead, via Theale, became the first section of this major highway to be turnpiked, and this was extended to Newbury fourteen years later. This meant the road was then kept in good repair but travellers had to pay for the privilege of using it. The Kennet and Avon Canal was built through the area in 1810 and Theale had a busy quay until the railway arrived thirty years later. Things have picked up again since the age of the motor car.

Highwaymen were attracted to the area by the rich travellers on the road and, in the 1730s, Dick Turpin (perhaps, in reality, some other forgotten bandit) is said to have hidden out many times in a secret room at the thatched Old Lamb Hotel. Later, in 1809, the roundabout just south of the village was the scene of a recorded daring robbery. A certain horse dealer from Hungerford, named Hazell, fell into conversation with a fellow rider on the road, while on the way to Henley Fair. Shortly after the two parted company, Mr Hazell found himself being robbed by the same man and a masked accomplice. A more light-hearted story tells how, in January 1795, a certain Mr Skuse of Keynsham (Somerset) placed a considerable wager with friends that his horse could reach Hyde Park Corner from Bristol in only 15 hours. However, finding the attempt impossible, he gave up at Theale.

The Lamb claims to have been built in 1487 although it may only be 17th century. Its life as an inn has been rather fragmented. The first one on the site closed in 1791 but re-emerged in the late 1850s in the building next door, as a simple beer seller's that later became a pub. There were once ten alcohol establishments in Theale (and one in North Street) that gave the village the nickname of 'The Ale', but these were also mostly beer seller's rather than pubs. The other three major inns were the Castle (previously the Black Boy), the White Hart (under the motorway) and the Bull. The present Bull was built about 1800 on the site of an earlier building. It became part of Draper's Brewery complex next door sometime before 1830. Sold to the Blatches in 1854, the brewery continued production until 1965. Its old creeper-clad offices survive with Brewery Court behind, an attractive cobbled courtyard surrounded by other related buildings including the maltings and cooper's house.

As a tithing far from the parish church at Tilehurst, Theale had its own chapel dedicated to St John from at least 1291. It stood near the entrance gates of the present church and belonged to the nuns of Goring Priory (Oxfordshire). After its dissolution in 1542, the chapel with associated land was passed around a number of Berkshire gentlemen. It may have been trashed by passing soldiers during the Civil War. By the end of the 17th century, it was certainly in ruins and had completely disappeared by the Victorian era.

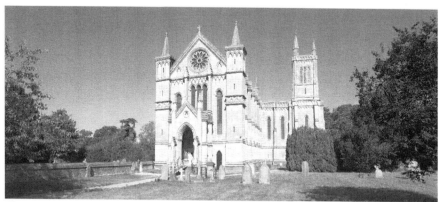

Figure 118: Theale Church, a Georgian Gothic Revival Masterpiece

At the request of her late husband, the first incumbent of a new temporary chapel at Theale, Mrs Sophia Sheppard built a superb new church, with octagonal chapter-house-like vestry, between

1820 and 1822 to save everyone walking all the way to Tilehurst on Sundays. It is an unusual neo-Early English style building, the details replicating those found at Salisbury Cathedral. The tower was added by the topographical artist, John Buckler, in 1827-32. The ensemble was much appreciated by John Constable, who painted the place soon afterwards, while he was working at Englefield House. The chantry chapel of 1486 on the north side of the chancel is that of Bishop William Waynflete, from his foundation, Magdalen College, Oxford. It was acquired by Mrs Sheppard's brother, Doctor Routh, the president there, when the college chapel was restored in 1830. It serves as a cenotaph to the lady and houses a fine figured brass by Augustus Pugin to her memory.

Three Mile Cross

Three Mile Cross grew up around a prominent crossroads in Shinfield parish on the main road to Basingstoke, three miles outside Reading. Since the time of the Norman Earls of Salisbury, this area of the parish, along with Spencers Wood, was a detached part of Wiltshire but was united with Berkshire in 1844. There was a small settlement there as far back as the Iron Age, with associated slag heaps indicating iron smelting somewhere very close by.

The place is best known for having been immortalised in Mary Russell Mitford's "sketches of rural character and scenery" called 'Our Village'. It was first published in a popular magazine from 1822 and then in 5-volume book form two years later. For most of her life, Miss Mitford lived in Three Mile Cross, next to the 16th century Swan pub. She had been reduced to living in this cramped labourer's cottage with her well-to-do parents, after her father had gambled away all their money and had to sell their elegant home at Poundgreen. Most of her books and plays were written at Three Mile Cross:

- Julian (1823)
- Our Village (1824-32)
- The Foscari (1826)
- Rienzi (1828)
- Charles I (1834) and
- Belford Regis (1835)

Mary became firm friends with the poetess, Elizabeth Barrett Browning, who helped gain her a civil pension of £100 a year; but financial worries continued even after the death of her father and his debts had to be paid by public subscription.

Figure 119: The Swan Inn & Mary Russell Mitford's Cottage (centre left)

Just north-west of Three Mile Cross, adjoining the M4 motorway, is the area of Shinfield parish known as Hartley, meaning Stag's Clearing. The area was anciently split into five small manors, probably carved out of the medieval Spencers Wood: Hartley Court, Hartley Dummer, Hartley Battle, Hartley Amys and Hartley Pellitot. The last four were, for many years, owned by the Woodcock family who lived at Hartley Pellitot. The road in

Three Mile Cross called Woodcock Court commemorates their residence, as does Woodcock Lane alongside the A33. They were relatives of Doctor Robert Huick, Queen Elizabeth I's Chief Physician, who also had an estate in Shinfield. Its exact site is unknown, but he probably rented one of the Hartley manors. Hartley Court is the only manor house to survive. It is an early 16th century house with an 18th century façade. It was probably built for Thomas Beke, the grandson and namesake of a mayor and MP for Reading. There is apparently a fine wooden mantelpiece in the house featuring the colourful Beke coat-of-arms dated 1509. The family had other properties at Whiteknights in Earley and at Haddenham in Buckinghamshire. Thomas' grandson, Henry, has a superb monument in Shinfield Church. King Edward VII is said to have rented Hartley Court from the Benyon family around 1900, and it was to there that his mistress, Lillie Langtry, retired in her later years.

Tidmarsh

Just to the west of Tidmarsh, straddling the motorway, sits Maidenhatch. A Roman villa was excavated there prior to the building of the M4 in 1970. This consisted of a seven-roomed corridor type dwelling of the late 2nd century and an outbuilding that was replaced, a hundred years later, by a large agricultural aisled building with corn driers and colourful plaster walls.

Mention of the roadside settlement of Tidmarsh is first found in 1196. It is almost certainly an Anglo-Saxon village which grew up along what is now the A340, but this is supposedly, in origin, an old Roman road running north from Silchester to a river crossing at Pangbourne (although the southern portion of this highway has been artificially straightened in more recent times). The place-name has a number of suggested meanings. Tithe

Marsh is appealing but sounds more medieval than Anglo-Saxon. Being named after a man called Tydda is a rather dull suggestion, although this could be a variation of Dydda, the Anglo-Saxon King of Northern Wessex and father of St Frideswide. Common Marsh seems to be the most likely derivation. However, a Celtic alternative could stem from Tyddyn-March meaning Small Farm for Horses, perhaps referring to a Roman roadside hostel.

Figure 120: The 12th century Greyhound at Tidmarsh

The most famous building in the village is the ancient Greyhound Inn (formerly the Grid Iron). A fine example of 12th century cruck construction, this little thatched cottage became a wayside public house in 1625. The old house called Bere Sizes is said to have belonged to the monks of Reading Abbey. It may have been associated with the vineyard which they are recorded to have tended to in the parish in the mid-13th century. The Abbot certainly had his favourite Summer residence at nearby Pangbourne and was the overlord of Tidmarsh Mill. The house, then called Wynhird, and its associated garden at the vineyard, was, however, given to a certain Gunnora de Bendenges in 1239.

This lady was embroiled in a shocking 13th century court case in which she claimed to be the widow of the lord of the manor, John de Tidmarsh; despite the fact that, Maud de Berners, the mother of John's son and heir, Geoffrey, was already enjoying all the rights and privileges of that position. Maud claimed that Gunnora's marriage was a sham and her daughter, Juliane, illegitimate. But, when she failed to turn up to the second hearing, the court proclaimed in Gunnora's favour and she was given a third of the manor.

Figure 121: Carved Norman Doorway to Tidmarsh Church

The old manor house stood on the site of Tidmarsh Grange, next to the parish church, but was transferred to the hill above the village in the 19th century. It was part of the Honour of Wallingford and held in return for providing a knight to help garrison the castle there for forty days in time of war. From early times, Tidmarsh Manor had its own fishery and this was later joined by other means of providing sustenance: a rabbit warren and a dovecote. The Tidmarshes had lived there until 1407 when it was sold, eventually coming into the hands of the Rothwells and their heirs, the Leynhams, whose fine brass memorials can still be seen in the church.

Tidmarsh Church is an unexpected treasure. It is dedicated to St Laurence, who was martyred on a grid iron, the symbol once used by the local pub. It has one of the most superbly carved Norman zig-zag doorways in the county. There is a fine Norman font to match which was found buried in the churchyard in Victorian times. The building is also unusual in having a polygonal apse. Some think this 13th century structure may be built over an Anglo-Saxon original, as its plan is similar to the existing Anglo-Saxon example at Wing in Buckinghamshire.

Between 1917 and 1924, Tidmarsh Mill was the home of the artist, Dora Carrington, and the author, Lytton Strachey. Strachey, who was a member of the Bloomsbury Set of intellectuals, wrote his biography of 'Eminent Victorians' there. The couple were socially unconventional Bohemians and were joined by Ralph Partridge in a bizarre three-way relationship when he married Carrington in 1921. Regular visitors included Virginia Woolf and EM Forster.

Tilehurst, Kentwood and Norcot

Today Tilehurst is a divided settlement. Modern Tilehurst parish in West Berkshire District is only a very thin sliver on the western boundary of the ancient parish. This once covered all of Reading Borough west from the Brock Barracks, Prospect Park and Calcot Place. The original village, which was little more than a hamlet, stood around St Michael's Church at what is sometimes called Churchend. It was first called Tigel-Hurst by the Anglo-Saxons, referring to the well-known local tile and brick making industry, although it does not appear in the Domesday Survey (1086) and is only first recorded in the 1160s. If the tiles were made by the Anglo-Saxons themselves, then it means Tile-Makers' Wooded Hill. However, it may mean Tile-Finding Place on a Wooded Hill, the tiles being older Roman ones. At the very least, it is known that kilns have been making tiles from the Thames Valley Clay there since the 1340s and probably much earlier.

King Alfred's men are said to have fought the Vikings in Dark Lane, once known as Deadman's Lane after the numerous bodies of the enemy slain there. The story may hold some truth, for, when Alfred was still a prince in the late 9th century, the Vikings made Reading their Southern English headquarters and, when they burst out to face the Anglo-Saxons at the Battle of Englefield in AD 871, they are believed to have travelled there over the ridge on which Tilehurst sits and out across Little Heath.

Figure 122: Dutch Diamond merchant Sir Peter Vanlore. Need I say more?

The manor house of Tilehurst may have stood on the site of the old rectory, next to St Michael's Church, from at least Norman times. It seems to have been given to Reading Abbey as an agricultural grange soon after its foundation but the rector they appointed to the church may also have resided there. When sold after the Dissolution of the Monasteries, the manor house was rebuilt some distance away in the relative privacy of Calcot Park. Memorials to its owners may still be seen in the church which, though largely rebuilt in the 1850s dates in part from the late 13th century. The tower is of Georgian Berkshire brick but the spire is later. Most notable amongst its monuments is the superb Renaissance one to Sir Peter Vanlore, who purchased the manor of Tilehurst in 1604. It bears the inscription:

When thou hast read the name "Here lies Vanlore"
Thou need'st no story to inform thee more.

Sadly, however, this man's great achievements have been largely forgotten, even amongst the locals. He was a Dutch diamond merchant, banker and money lender who lent extensively to the King but received little thanks in return. His many children who predeceased him are shown holding skulls along the front of his monument. A false legend tells how they were murdered by the black servant shown on the family crest at his feet. Vanlore's grandson-in-law, Henry Zinzan, lies in the centre of the chancel. He was from a family of well-known horsemen who took part in many royal jousts. His heraldic ledger stone was only rediscovered under the floor in 2012. There is also a disappointing tablet to the Victorian Blagraves of Calcot Park that does nothing to indicate the large areas of Reading they once owned. They also donated the Blagrave Recreation ground to the local community. Other local parks are named after Reading entrepreneurs, Arthur Newbery, the furniture seller, and William McIlroy, the department store owner.

William Lloyd, Bishop of Worcester, was born in 1688 in the old rectory behind the church, where his father, Richard, was rector, as well as being Vicar of Sonning. However, the present building on the site, now called Iris Court Rectory, only dates from the early 19th century. Lloyd's career was not without controversy in a time of religious upheaval. As one of the famous 'Seven Bishops', he was imprisoned and tried (but acquitted) for opposing King James II's attempts to promote Catholicism by bringing freedom of religion to the country. He was a staunch supporter of the Protestant King William III and assisted at his coronation. In later life, he proclaimed himself something of a prophet.

Figure 123: Sir John Kentwood captured a Prince at the Battle of Poitiers

Although today's Tilehurst is a single urban area, it was originally several disparate hamlets spread over four manors: Westwood Row, the Gutter, Harmoor (now the Lower Armour Road area), School End (now the Triangle), Chapel Hill, Little Heath, the City, Norcot, Kentwood, Calcot Green, Calcot Row, Horncastle and, later, Honey End, Langley Hill and Grovelands. Kentwood (from Kennet-Wood) was a minor manor in the parish and there were two others in Calcot: Pincent's and Beansheaf. In the 14th century, Kentwood House (on the site of the present 1723 building in Kentwood Mews) was owned by Sir John Kentwood, a good friend of the Black Prince who captured the son of the King of France at the Battle of Poitiers in 1356 and was paid a 'King's ransom' for his troubles. His son, Reginald, became the Dean of St Paul's Cathedral in London.

S and E Collier moved their brick production from Coley to near Grovelands Farm (in Grovelands Road) in 1870. The site is now covered by Collier's Way. When the clay was exhausted, they moved extraction to the Lawrence Road area of Norcot (hence nearby Pottery Road) but had to convey the clay back to the kilns at Grovelands by aerial cableway. They mostly produced handmade bricks and were famous for 'Collier's Reading Red' but also made flower pots and construction pottery and terracotta. At its height, the site had sixteen kilns, one of which could fire 200,000 bricks at one go. The Shakespeare Memorial Theatre in Stratford was built with their brown burnt bricks. The Silchester Ware studio pottery was also located there in the early 20th century. Production did not recover after the Second World War and ceased in 1967. Another company, Tilehurst Potteries, on Kentwood Hill specialised in roofing tiles. They produced 20 million a year in the 1930s and roofed places like Radley College, the Middle Temple and Sydney Sussex College, Cambridge. It was founded by Samuel Wheeler in 1885. Following a fire in 1966, the pottery closed due to lack of available skilled labour.

Tutts Clump, Rotten Row and Bradfield Southend

The Blue Pool at Kimberhead Farm (formerly Upper Frogmoor Farm), north-west of Rotten Row, was once a famous local tourist attraction; but, sadly, it is now hidden away from visitors because of problems with the water quality, which has led to the closure of the surrounding watercress beds that were active for a hundred years. The intense blue colour of the water is produced by its unusual suspension of clay particles. The prefix of Kimberhead could mean St Kyneburga's but is probably a corruption of the Celtic word, 'gwrm', often used for a stream. This literally means Dark or Dusky or indeed Blue, and indicates how the spring has been an important watering place, possibly a holy one, since the Iron Age. The head [of the spring] has been added later.

Figure 124: Bradfield Hall, built in 1763 for an illegitimate Royal

Perhaps it was the spring which attracted a rather important visitor to the area. In the AD 630s, St Birinus brought Christianity to the Anglo-Saxons then living in Berkshire and local legend says that, whilst passing through Bradfield parish, he rested in the shade of the trees at Tutts Clump. He sat down and, when he struck his sword into the ground, it burst into light, drawing people from miles around to be converted from paganism. However, the village is supposed to be named after another visitor, a General Tutts who, during the Civil War, tied his horses to the clump of trees there while having a drink in the Traveller's

Rest pub opposite. This was probably three days before the indecisive Second Battle of Newbury in October 1644, when the unwell Earl of Essex and his army spent the night in this area. The following day, the Earl was too ill to continue and returned to Reading, while his men carried on to rendezvous with the rest of the parliamentary army near Chapel Row.

Bradfield Hall at Rotten Row is an Adam-style house built in 1762-3 by John Barrington, an illegitimate son of King George II. The associated farm next door was one of those in the parish attacked by a 200-strong mob marching from Thatcham during the Swing Riots of November 1830. The men were desirous of an agricultural pay increase alongside the destruction of the machines that were putting them out of work. Ironically, Jethro Tull, the inventor who had begun this Agricultural Revolution, grew up in Bradfield some 150 years before. At nearby Frogmoor Farm, Farmer Lailey managed to lock his barn doors when he heard the rioters' horn blowing but they still smashed up his portable threshing machine in the yard.

Southend, as the name suggests, is the southern end of Bradfield parish. However, before 1900, there was little there in the way of a settlement. At the dog-leg Cock Lane/Admoor Lane crossroads on Southend Road below Southend Farm, there was a smithy and the pub, the Queen's Head – which dates from the 1860s and still survives – and a couple of cottages. A few houses then began to be built in the Heath Road area and things spread from there. The War Memorial, at the Copyhold Farm triangle, was designed by the sculptor and Reading brewer, George Blackall Simonds of Bradfield House. Sadly, his only son is commemorated on it. In more recent times, HRH the Duchess of Cambridge spent her early years in Southend and was christened in Bradfield Church.

Twyford

Twyford was first established as an early Anglo-Saxon settlement around an important river crossing. In the lower Loddon Valley, the river splits into two smaller channels, making it easier to cross. So, the place called Two-Fords or Twyford was born. It was across this double ford, that King Aethelred and his brother, Prince Alfred, fled whilst being pursued by the Vikings after the AD 871 Siege of Reading. Similarly, King James II's Irish Catholic troops also fled this way back to London, via Maidenhead, after being routed by William III's Protestant Dutchmen at the Battle of Broad Street in Reading during the Glorious Revolution of 1688.

Figure 125: Twyford & some of its many Coaching Inns

Until it became a separate ecclesiastical parish in 1876 (and a civil parish in 1895), Twyford was part of the manor of Hinton Pipard in the parish of St Nicholas Hurst. By 1166 it came into the hands of the Earl of Salisbury who ran the manor through his hundred (like a district council) court at Amesbury in Wiltshire. The area thus became one of the detached parts of that county surrounded by Berkshire, which lasted until 1844. In the early 18th century, the village stocks were placed on the border between the two counties. At some point, a medieval chapel dedicated to St Swithun was built in Twyford, but this burnt down in 1710. There was already a mill in the village by 1168, where the miller had the Anglo-Saxon name of Wimund; and in 1250 King Henry III granted Ralph FitzNicholas the right to hold a fair at Twyford on the Feast of the Assumption on 15th August.

Twyford always stood on an important road for the wool merchants of Berkshire, taking their cloth from Reading to London and abroad. At some point in the early Middle Ages, hostelries began to be set up there for travellers to stop and refresh both themselves and their horses, and where they could stay when the fords were too deep to cross. In the early 17th century, the main road was transformed into the Great Road to Bristol (later called the Bath Road), passing through the village along London Road and the High Street. The local hostelries on the latter road quickly prospered on the back of it: the Bull, the Bell and the Rose and Crown. The King's Arms later became the most important coaching inn. In 1718, the Maidenhead to Twyford stretch of the road was turnpiked and Twyford was given its own gate and toll house at the junction with the road to Sonning. The toll keeper collected revenues for those who paid for the road's upkeep.

During the Civil War, the villagers complained to Parliament that they were pillaged by one side or another almost daily. In 1643, seven hundred parliamentary troops were stationed near Twyford. The royalist captains, Fawcett and Ashton, marched out from Reading to attack them. Armed with two cannon, they entrenched themselves on Twyford Green. Captain Turner took just over a hundred of the roundheads to push them back. Bloodshed followed but, when parliamentary reinforcements arrived, the cavaliers quickly retreated.

Figure 126: Twyford Mill, built 1800 as Billinges' Silk Factory

An old story tells of how on Christmas Eve, about 1666, a poor destitute young lad was found on the steps of the Rose and Crown Inn and taken in by the landlord, who clothed him and fed him up, and sent him on his way to London. The boy, called Edward Polehampton, made his fortune there but never forgot the kindness of the Twyford landlord. Though the lad in fact appears to have come from a wealthy Twyford family (with no connection to the inn), when he died in 1721, he certainly left a large sum of money to build a school, a new chapel and a house for the chaplain in the village. The chaplain was to teach ten poor Twyford boys to read and write, to clothe them and to preach to the locals every morning and afternoon. Twyford Library is named after Polehampton and, though the Wee Waif Inn at Charvil is not, the name is an appropriate reminder of the story. The chapel closed when the present church was built in 1847.

Another charity, the almshouses on the London Road, were built for Richard Harrison of Hurst House in 1640, and include the manor court room. Other notable residents have included Doctor Anthony Addington (1713-1790) one of the doctors who treated mad King George III, the Earl of Barrymore (1769-1794) the theatre patron from Wargrave who had his stud farm in Twyford, Doctor William Gordon Stables (1837-1910) the children's author, Captain Frederick George Coleridge (1838–1923) the watercolourist and Llewelyn Treacher (1859-1943) the geologist, antiquarian and local historian.

The railway arrived in Twyford in 1839 and it was given a station on the main line to the West Country and later a junction with the Henley Branch Line. Although Twyford has always largely been an agricultural community, the village centre attracted other industries too and had pretensions of becoming a town. A more modern Twyford Mill was built in 1800 as a silk factory by the Billinge Brothers of Macclesfield. After 1845, it became a corn mill and later made cattle cake. It burnt down in 1891 only to be rebuilt and burnt to the ground again in 1976. Until 1937, there were five silk-weavers' cottages nearby with large third-storey windows in which the weavers sat at their work. Later in the 19th century, lace making and basket making became important to the local economy too.

Ufton Nervet and Ufton Green

The Roman road from Silchester to Dorchester-on-Thames once ran through Ufton Nervet and there are several sections of the sub-Roman 'Grim's Ditch' still surviving in the parish. This was built to protect the Roman town at Silchester from the unpredictable Anglo-Saxons settling in the Thames Valley. One of these men was called Offa. He was not the famous King of Mercia, but he did give his name to the area: Offa's Town.

It would be much better if this parish were called merely Ufton, for the parish church of St Peter is not the church of Ufton Nervet at all, but that of Ufton Robert, a separate manor. It is unclear where the name came from, presumably an early owner. His manor house stood within the moat just west of the church and it acquired a deer park in 1338. The place came into the hands of the Perkins family around 1411, and it was there, a hundred years later, that Sir Humphrey Forster of Aldermaston House broke in with ten armed men, intent on murdering the owner, Richard Perkins, who had defied him in local administrative matters. He was saved only by the pitiful pleading of his wife.

Ufton Nervet, or Ufton Richard as the manor was also known, was at Ufton Green. It had its own church of St John the Baptist, the ruined walls of which can still be seen today. The place was named after Richard Neyrnut or 'Black Night', later corrupted to Nervet. He owned the manor in the 13th century and presumably had a somewhat unsavoury reputation. By 1435, the church was in the hands of the Knights Hospitaller from Greenham, who agreed with William Perkins that the two parishes should combine. This was probably due to a considerable decline in the local population which had been decimated by the Black Death a hundred years earlier. St John's became a mere chapel and, by the 18th century, seems to have been converted into two cottages. These were mostly pulled down in 1883.

The beautiful Elizabethan Ufton Court was originally the centrepiece of a minor manor, possibly split off from Ufton Robert in the late 14th century and called Ufton Pole. Some of the present house still dates from the 15th century, including the hall and its cross-passage with original buttery and pantry doors. It was largely rebuilt by the Perkins family who moved over from Ufton Robert in 1567. They were well known Roman Catholics who were persecuted by the local magistrates in the 16th century. They had to pay heavy fines for refusing to attend the parish church and Ufton Court was raided at least twice by officials looking for priests in hiding. In 1586, a Sulhamstead tailor ran the family in but, although three servants were imprisoned, the expected ecclesiastic was not found. Sir Francis Knollys Junior found some of the priests' hiding places and a small fortune in gold plate in 1599 but, again, the priests had gone. Several impressive priests' holes and a slightly later painted 'oratory' chapel still remain today, as well as traces of an escape tunnel leading into the woods.

Figure 127: Ufton Court dates back to the 15th century

Several Perkins family monuments decorate the church they tried so hard to stay away from. They have been badly damaged, perhaps by the parliamentary soldiers who are known to have moved through the area around the time of the two Civil War

Battles of Newbury. The building itself is now redundant and there are hopes that it will become a community centre. Doctor Henry Beke, rector there in the late 18th century, was the government financial consultant who invented income tax. A Victorian rector, Reverend James Fraser, was one of the few clergymen ever to have been elevated directly from a parochial living to a bishopric. He just got a letter in the post from Prime Minister Gladstone offering him the See of Manchester.

Figure 128: The 'Rape of the Lock' – Lord Petre & Miss Fermor

The Perkins family's most practical memorial is the Ufton Bread Dole which is distributed every year from the most southerly window in the Court's hall. Elizabeth, Lady Marvyn, widow of Richard Perkins, left the money for the dole in her will (1581) in thanks for the villagers having helped her find her way home after getting lost in the woods. A later lady of the manor was the beautiful Arabella Fermor, who married Francis Perkins, in the early 18th century, in order to get away from London society. She had been the toast of the City until Lord Petre had secretly cut a lock from the lady's hair at a society ball. The scandal, of what now seems such an innocent act, led to huge animosity between the two families. The Binfield poet, Alexander Pope, tried to heal the rift by writing his 'Rape of the Lock' poem making light of the incident, but just ended up making things worse. In the middle of the century, Bonnie Prince Charlie is said to have visited the family on one of his forays into the country incognito. The Perkins family finally sold up in 1802 and the house was left in a somewhat run-down state until restored by Miss Mary Sharpe, a tenant in Victorian times, who also wrote the house's history. The building is currently owned by the Benyons of Englefield House but is leased to an independent children's educational charity in which the family are actively involved.

On 2nd February 1787, prompted only by want of money, two idle lads from Ufton conspired to waylay and kill an old labourer called William Billimore. They took the poor dead man's silver watch and, too frightened to search properly for the money they had hoped to find, made their escape. They sold the timepiece in Maidenhead but were later caught upon returning to the scene of the sale. They were tried at the Reading Assizes and condemned to death, being hanged on a piece of land on Mortimer Common, but just within Ufton parish, now called Gibbet Piece.

Upper Basildon

Upper Basildon, as the name suggests, forms the village and farmland on the higher ground of Rush Down above Basildon Park and the River Thames. This is the original Basildon as Lower Basildon was previously called Basilford. Several of the estate cottages in Upper Basildon were built by the well-known Arts-and-Crafts architect, Sir Edwin Lutyens, after the original architect went off to fight in the First World War. This includes Harley House in Park Way Lane, a fine small country house in Queen Anne style, built as the estate office. Next door is the 18th century Godwin's Lodge opposite the western entrance to the park, an attractive architectural mixture with Gothic revival windows and shaped gables almost in the Dutch style. In 1917, Lutyens was also commissioned to build a red brick Italian-style war memorial church with a large tower. The complex was to include a vicarage, a men's institute, a school and almshouses with a communal kitchen and laundry. However, the plans were abandoned because, as Lutyens recorded, using the same space, "women quarrelling ... makes the scheme impossible".

Figure 129: Godwin's Lodge & Nobes' Tomb

Wood Green Farm in Mead Lane was almost certainly the birthplace of the famous 18th century agriculturalist, Jethro Tull, in 1674. He is revered as the 'Father of the Agricultural Revolution' because he wrote a highly influential farming manual called 'Horse Husbandry' and invented the British seed drill. Although Tull was the son of a Bradfield farmer, his mother was a member of the wealthy sheep farming family of Buckeridge whose large estate was centred at Wood Green. Tull was certainly baptised in the parish church at Lower Basildon soon after his birth. He is also buried in the churchyard. Until Victorian times, anyone descended from William Buckeridge and Elizabeth Kibblewhite, who married in Basildon in 1562, could have applied for a founder's kin scholarship to St John's College, Oxford: as their son, John Buckeridge, Bishop of both Rochester and of Ely, did in the early 17th century.

In November 1830, Wood Green became the last of several farms in Upper Basildon targeted by a mob of 40 'Swing' Rioters from Ashampstead. They were farm labourers protesting about poor pay and increased agricultural mechanisation, largely brought about by Tull's innovations. This group wanted to be paid to leave whilst still smashing threshing machines before they went. They forced many men to swell their numbers in return for avoiding a beating, but the local wheelwright – who had already protested that he was a tradesman not a farm worker – managed to run off and hide in the bushes on the common. By the time they reached Wood Green Farm, the local militia had been turned out and eleven men were arrested.

While most of the population were employed in agriculture or estate management, back as far as at least the 18th century there were also brickworks in Basildon. The first was at the top end of Park Wall Lane where a 17th century timber-framed cottage used to be called Claypits. In the 1870s, the Osborne family from Emery Farm established their brickworks in the area immediately west of Kiln Corner and Kiln Ride, on the site of Old Stocks Court. A pond just to the north was one of the old claypits. This eventually became the Basildon Brickworks Company whose four kilns could produce nearly 110,000 high-quality facing bricks at one firing. During the Second World War, the site was taken on by Tenaplas Ltd, plastic extruders, who stayed until 1999.

The farmer and wheelwright at Tomb Farm, in the late 17th century, was a nonconformist named Thomas Nobes. The modern farm name derives from the once prominent but now ruinous Berkshire curiosity, 'Nobes' Tomb', which stood in the grounds. This strange little building, inscribed with the date 1692, was where Mr Nobes had himself interred after he was refused burial by the Church of England. He was recorded in the parish registers as having died but "was not buried". His ghost is said to ride the area on his white horse. Being some distance from the old parish church, Upper Basildon was popular with such religious rebels. It only gained its modern Anglican place of worship, dedicated to St Stephen, in 1964. It is supposedly built in the shape of the Christian symbol of a fish.

For Basildon Park see Lower Basildon

Whistley Green

Whistley stands in the parish of St Nicholas Hurst, but is an older and bigger settlement than Hurst itself. Its name means Marshy Meadow Clearing, as it stands by the Loddon on the western edge of Windsor Forest. After the siege of Viking Reading in AD 871, the Norsemen chased King Aethelred, his brother Alfred and their men away to Whistley; but the Anglo-Saxons had local knowledge and escaped through the shallows on the Loddon at Twyford, while the stumped Vikings were forced to retreat.

A hundred years later, in AD 968, Whistley manor (later called Hurst manor) was granted by King Edgar as a personal gift to Abbot Osgar of Abingdon (via a thane called Wulfstan). The grant included the bizarre clause:

"If any man should have the stupidity and temerity to infringe this my gift, let he be tied with heavy chains to the neck among the multitude of devilish flames"

Figure 130: The Elephant & Castle at Whistley Green

The area had great potential for the exploitation of the River Loddon and, after Osgar left the manor to his abbey, Whistley became one of their granges. It included a fishery, which supplied the monks with 550 highly prized eels every year, and the mill north of Whistley Bridge, as recorded in the Domesday Survey (1086). In the 18th and 19th centuries, the mill was used for paper making. The growing of osiers on the little islands in the River also provided much local industry. These coppiced willow trees provided long flexible shoots (or withies) that could be used for making basketwork and hurdles, a business that lasted into the early 20th century. The manor also supplied other farm produce and timber from woodland whose oaks were used to build Abingdon Abbey's choir stalls in the mid-13th century. It had a resident steward who reported directly to the Abbey's kitchener (or catering manager) until the Dissolution of the Monasteries.

The old grange house was called Whistley Court because the manor courts were held there. It stood towards the River Loddon, along the path heading west from Lodge Road, about a third of a mile south of the village. After it was confiscated from the Abbey, the manor was granted to Richard Warde of Winkfield, who built himself Hurst House in the 1540s. Whistley Court was turned into his 'park house' for relaxing by the River. Elegant gardens and avenues of lime and chestnut trees were planted there and enjoyed over several generations. The old house was rebuilt in the 17th century but eventually pulled down two hundred years later.

The actual green at Whistley was located on the land sandwiched between Lodge Road and Broadwater Lane where all the village houses now stand. Lodge Road was the main road through the area. This stretch of Broadwater Lane was then just a path. The earliest houses stood on the green's southern edge. Over the years, many parish amenities came to be located there: the pound for holding stray animals sat at the south-east corner and the stocks for minor infringements of the law were on the green from at least the 18th century. A hundred years later, Whistley was particularly known for its pubs. The Halfway House was supposed to be a very ancient pub, once frequented by highwaymen who gleaned information there about rich pickings to be had on the Bath Road. However, it does not seem to appear on local maps before 1841. It closed in early 1915 due to its poor position on a dangerous bend and its proximity to the Elephant and Castle, the only pub which has survived.

Whitley and Whitley Wood

Whitley is the area of Southern Reading, between the town and Shinfield, from the high ground alongside the Shinfield Road right down to the Foudry Brook and the River Kennet. The area around Northumberland Avenue on Marshall's Hill is thought to be the home of prehistoric Reading. A late Bronze Age mini-hillfort or ringwork has been identified there beneath the later housing.

Figure 131: The old Four Horseshoes with the Monastic Long Barn behind

Whitley was an Anglo-Saxon hamlet settled on a small area of land cleared from the woodland on the edge of Windsor Forest. The name means White Clearing, perhaps referring to the white sand found within the geological Reading beds. The manor appears in the Domesday Book of 1086. Before the Norman invasion, it had been owned, along with other Berkshire manors, by a certain Edward. By the time of the invasion, it was held by Theodoric the Goldsmith. He was a German immigrant who had been living in London for some years, making jewellery for the Royal family. His chief country estate became Kennington in Surrey, but the Conqueror also gave him five wooded Berkshire manors where charcoal could be made for smelting metal. The main one was at Hampstead Norreys, but he may have visited

Whitley occasionally. Living there were two villeins (tenant farmers), two bordars (cottage dwellers), two serfs and their families. As well as the usual agricultural land, there were twelve acres of meadow (presumably along the Kennet) and a fishery.

In the 12th century, Whitley was given to the monks of Reading Abbey. It was one of their closest manors and so a deer park was quickly established around the manor house in the 1160s. It was there that the abbot would entertain his guests with a day's hunting. The park and its house were up on the high ground adjoining the Shinfield Road, but there were also monastic granges on the manor, like Whitley Park Farm. Their produce was apparently collected at the 'Long Barn' that once adjoined the Four Horseshoes pub at the junction of Long Barn Lane and the Basingstoke Road. After the dissolution of the Abbey, Whitley Park was granted to various well-known Reading families: the Englefields, Knollyses and Vachells. They did not live there but seem to have leased the place out to the Watlington family. Richard Watlington was at Whitley Park from around the 1560s and was Mayor of Reading, like many of his descendants. However, it seems likely that the great house in the park may have been destroyed during the Civil War Siege of Reading when there was much fighting around the small fort established at Harrison's Barn on Whitley Hill. Sometime before 1679, the park was rented to the Kendrick baronets who may have built a new house. The first of the family there was a grandson to the brother of the philanthropist, John Kendrick of Oracle and Kendrick School fame. The great heiress, Frances Kendrick – known as the 'Berkshire Lady' – was the last to live there before moving on to Calcot Park shortly before 1707.

Whitley remained a series of scattered farms and cottages until the 18th century, when proper hamlets began to emerge along the road from Basingstoke into Reading: around the World Turned Upside Down pub at the Manor Farm Road junction and further north near the Bourne Avenue junction. The local pound for lost cattle and the smithy were near the World Turned Upside Down. Great and Little Lea Common and Whitley Wood Common, in the south of the manor, were enclosed in 1858. The Rose Kilns in what is now Rose Kiln Lane were built on the land of Manor Farm, owned by the diplomat Sir George Rose from Lyndhurst in Hampshire. They were run by the Billing family from about 1838 and, later, by the Philbricks from the Katesgrove Tannery.

Figure 132: The original Whitley Pump with Christ Church behind

By the 1870s, there was a small hamlet at the junctions of Whitley Wood Lane and Whitley Wood Road, and this grew to become what we today call Whitley Wood. By the 1890s, another hamlet was developing around the Four Horseshoes and, within twenty years, this had joined up with the houses spreading south from

Whitley Pump. After the First World War, Reading contributed to the National campaign to provide council housing for the returning soldiers by building steadily over most of Whitley and Whitley Wood.

Whitley Hill

Whitley proper starts south of the junction of Elgar Road with the Basingstoke Road. The Mount is the area north of Christchurch Road and Southern Hill is the area to the south, with Whitley Hill (or Rise) on its western edge. Reading Abbey had a conduit on Whitley Hill, over a spring that supplied the monks with fresh water. A serious outbreak of plague visited Reading in 1638 and the Corporation decided that victims should be banished to specially built 'boarded houses' on the remoteness of Whitley Hill. Four years later, during the Civil War siege of the town, Harrison's Barn in the same location (now the corner of the Basingstoke Road and Christchurch Road) was made a royalist outpost from Reading's main defences, guarding this major southern route into town. Many soldiers were stationed there. They created a small fort, digging huge banks and ditches with diamond-shaped bastions around the barn. It would have been the first place to fall when the parliamentary army eventually overran Reading.

A fine gentleman's villa called Highgrove was built at the top of Whitley Hill around 1840. It stood at the top end of Mount Pleasant, right at the fork, and its extensive gardens stretched out behind Whitley Street. This is where the well-known Reading solicitor, John Jackson Blandy, lived. He liked to grow exotic plants there. However, by the late 1890s, his house had been demolished and Highgrove Street built in its place. One of the old entrance lodges survives as the Reading Bowling Club in Kendrick Road.

Figure 133: Cintra Lodge (demolished) in Christchurch Road

Christ Church was built in 1861-2 by architect, Henry Woodyer, in order to accommodate the increasing congregation at St Giles'. It features an extraordinary latticework screen high up in the chancel arch. During the same period, more country villas for the town's gentry began to be built along Christchurch Road. Sutherlands was home to one of the Breedons from Pangbourne. Cintra Lodge was the home of Martin Hope Sutton of Sutton Seeds and others. Both are now gone. Slightly later is the surviving brick and terracotta Hillingdon Prince Hotel built for the brickmaster, William Poulton, from the Adamantine Brickworks at Katesgrove. Next door, on the corner of Kendrick Road, is Kirkland/Bergheim which was another Blandy house. Further villas were built on Whitley Hill, south of the junctions of Basingstoke Road, Christchurch Road and Whitley Street: Whitley Lodge, Whitley Grove, Whitley Place and Whitley Hill (later called Whitley Rise). The area would eventually become known as Whitley Pump after the popular watering hole that replaced the old conduit at the road junction. The pump in the middle of the roundabout today is a copy of the original and was erected in 1999.

Winnersh and Merryhill Green

Winnersh was originally one of the four liberties of the old parish of Hurst. It was called a 'liberty' rather than a manor because it was under the direct jurisdiction of the Bishop of Salisbury. It was the northern part of his personal hunting chase at what was called Bishop's Bearwood on the edge of Windsor Forest. He would bring his guests out hunting there from Sonning Bishop's Palace. By the time the bishops sold Sonning in the 16th century, their Winnersh estate had already been broken up into Sindlesham Manor and Hurst Wynhurst, which was attached to Hurst Manor. Wynhurst, or Winnersh, means Water Meadow Wood, reflecting its position on the banks of the River Loddon, although the main settlement is the ribbon development that grew up on the higher ground further along the main road between Reading and Wokingham.

Now called the Reading Road (or the A329), this major routeway was originally known as King Street, a name that was adopted by the settlement itself by the 18th century. It consisted of a post office and the Pheasant pub and a few other houses like Kingstreet Farm, Winnersh Lodge, Winnersh Grove and Winnersh Farm, immediately east of the Winnersh Crossroads. It was really centred on the, now hardly noticeable, dog-leg crossroads beneath the motorway flyover. Winnersh Lodge was the dower house to Newland Lodge near Arborfield Cross and was the home to Emma widow of the Reading banker, John Simonds, after his death in 1881.

Figure 134: Loddon Bridge, where King Richard's Barons gathered

Winnersh became part of the ecclesiastical parish of Bearwood in 1846. The North Downs Railway was laid just north of the village in 1849 but Winnersh Station, then known as Sindlesham and Hurst Halt wasn't built until 1910. It was as a direct result of this that the village as we know it today was built during the subsequent decade. There was a huge expansion to the west of the crossroads, with houses down Robinhood Lane, that joined Winnersh to the little hamlet of Merril Green, now Merryhill Green, on the Old Forest Road to Binfield which has all but disappeared in this area.

At the western end of Winnersh stands not only a large cinema complex but also Loddon Bridge. It was an important crossing point and meeting place in times past, as it stood on the border between the Earley region of Sonning parish and the Winnersh area of Hurst and was an entrance point to Windsor Forest. In 1191, when King Richard the Lionheart went off on Crusade, he left the country in the control of his unpopular chancellor, William Longchamp, Bishop of Ely. Longchamp's subsequent actions led to the Barons inviting him to a great open-air gathering in the meadows adjoining Loddon Bridge at Winnersh, on 5th October that year. The gathering had been encouraged by Prince John and was essentially a trial. So Longchamp shut himself up in the safety of the Tower of London instead. There he was besieged and later sent into exile.

Wokefield

The name Wokefield reminds us that this area was settled by the Anglo-Saxon Woccingas tribe from Woking in Surrey in the 5th century. Their main Berkshire settlement was at Wokingham. Wokefield is mentioned in the Domesday Survey of 1086 and was historically part of the parish of Stratfield Mortimer.

Figure 135: Wokefield Park, dating from 1720

Wokefield Park is recorded as a deer park belonging to the prominent Mortimer family as early as 1319. As such, however, it was presumably attached to their manor of Stratfield Mortimer rather than on the site of the present park which then belonged to the Danvers family. The present Wokefield House contains some ancient vaulting in the cellars which may possibly date from the time of Sergeant Edmund Plowden who purchased the house in 1569 and made it his home. He was a prominent Tudor lawyer who rose to great office under the Catholic Queen Mary I, being Treasurer of the Middle Temple at the time that its magnificent hall was built. However, under the Protestant Elizabeth I, he was banned from such positions because of his Catholic beliefs. She had wanted him to be Lord Chancellor.

The core of the present house was built around 1720 for Charles Parry, the brother-in-law of the 4th Duke of Bolton from Hackwood Park near Basingstoke. The Brocas family, who had owned the property back in the 14th and 15th centuries when they lived in Clewer, repurchased the house in about 1750. It then became their most popular home. Widow Brocas commissioned alterations by Sir John Soane (who went to school in Reading) in 1788-9 but it was her step-grandson, the last of many Bernard Brocases, who had the building expanded to the 17 bays that we see today. The house was later the home of the Allfreys for a hundred years. After 1900, it became the home of Alfred Palmer, Director of Huntley and Palmer's Biscuits in Reading, but it is currently part of an hotel and golf complex.

Just north of Wokefield Park is the similarly named Oakfield House (formerly Oakfield Lodge). The house retains very little of its 18th century origins as it was almost completely rebuilt after a devasting fire in 1986. A Roman pottery kiln was discovered (and largely destroyed) when the kitchen garden was laid out in 1902. This was an important producer of 1st century coarse 'Silchester Ware' that fed that Roman town's insatiable appetite for crockery – mostly jars. It was around this house that the small hamlet of Oakfield or Wokefield Green grew up with its own mill and mill pond. It was originally in the detached part of Sulhamstead Bannister parish called Lower End.

Wokingham

There is sparse evidence of any sort of settlement in the Wokingham area prior to the arrival of the Anglo-Saxons: a few Neolithic tools, a possible flattened Bronze Age barrow, a Roman cremation burial. This is not really surprising, since Wokingham is and always has been forest land. In the early years of Anglo-Saxon settlement, the followers of a man called Wocca, who had made their home at Woking in Surrey, set out across the Berkshire Moors in search of new lands to settle. They cleared themselves some land on the edge of the forest and so began Wocca's People's Home or Wokingham. Some of them even went a little further and stopped at Wokefield in Stratfield Mortimer. For a long period through the 17th to the 19th centuries, Wokingham was known as Oakingham, but this was a corruption that has now been dispensed with.

Wokingham does not appear in the Domesday Survey of 1086. The first actual mention of the place in extant records comes in 1146 when "Sonning, with Dunsden and Wokingham" is recorded amongst lands owned by the Bishop of Salisbury. These Bishops, originally Bishops of Sonning, had had a residence at Sonning since the early 10th century. The special reference to Dunsden and Wokingham may indicate that they were the only other villages in the large minster-parish with their own chapels. The names of Wokingham chaplains are known from around 1160 and what is now the parish church was certainly standing by 1190 when Bishop Hubert Walter (later Archbishop of Canterbury) visited and dedicated the building to All Saints. It still retains small parts of this Norman chapel today. Wokingham

Chapel had the right of baptism and burial, so the villagers did not have to make the long trek to Sonning.

Because half of Wokingham was owned by the Earl of Salisbury, that section was always officially a detached part of the county of Wiltshire and not in Berkshire at all. At the corner of Rose (or Rows) Street and Wiltshire Road can be seen an inscribed post that reminds us of this peculiar situation that gained the latter road its name. It used to stand in Cross Street and marked the boundary between the two counties until 1844, when all of Wokingham fell to Berkshire.

Figure 136: Medieval 'Wealden' hall houses in Rose Street

By 1219, Bishop Richard Poore decided to found a 'new town' at Wokingham in order to boost his income. He was about to start work on building the present Salisbury Cathedral and so, no doubt, was in sore need of the funds. He extended the village sited around the chapel, having burgage plots laid out along two parallel streets heading south-west (Peach and Rose Street) to a triangular market place (where the town hall now stands). He then gained permission to hold a market there every Tuesday. Forty years later rights to hold a fair on St Barnabas' Day and All Saints' Day were added. Broad Street and Denmark Street (aka

Down Street) were established shortly afterwards and the market moved into the former's wide avenue. The scheme seems to have worked well and Wokingham grew into a thriving medieval centre for Windsor Forest folk, full of commerce and industry. Wokingham became particularly noted for its Bell Foundry. As early as 1383 the industry was well established in the town and many local churches ring out on Wokingham Bells. Only Bell Foundry Lane now remains where the owners held a farm. The foundry itself was in the centre of the town but, by the late 16th century, it had relocated to Reading.

Figure 137: The Old Town Hall in Wokingham Market Place

There are still many interesting and historic buildings in Wokingham dating back to medieval times. In Rose Street are a remarkable series of medieval 'Wealden' (Kent/Sussex-style) hall houses, some of which date back to the late 14th century. One of these you can even visit, as it is currently the Fifty-Six wine bar (formerly the Metropolitan pub). A slightly later house in the same street was the childhood home of chimney sweep, James Seward, in the 1850s. He eventually became the inspiration for 'Tom' in Charles Kingsley's 'The Water Babies'. A sculpture outside the library commemorates his life. The 15th century Overhangs, in Peach Street, were once the Windsor Forest Verderers' Court. Cases of offences committed within the bounds of the royal forest were heard there. The judges could extract fines for minor offences, but more serious cases had to be referred elsewhere.

Queen Elizabeth I is said to have visited Wokingham a number of times, whilst riding out from Easthampstead Park. Inside the parish church, there is a fine and rare Royal Arms of her reign (1582) featuring the Welsh Dragon in place of the Scottish Unicorn. In the vestry is a memorial to a local man, Thomas Godwin, whose preaching skills had persuaded Elizabeth to make him Bishop of Bath and Wells in 1584. Archbishop William Laud's parents also lived in Rose Street a few years before his birth. In 1583, Queen Elizabeth granted Wokingham its first charter, although it did not finally rid itself of the Steward of Sonning's influence until James I granted a more wide-ranging version in 1612. Fines and court profits now went to the town, rather than Sonning manor. Wokingham instituted an 'alderman' (mayor), nineteen burgesses and a high steward, and erected a fine guildhall with a many-pillared ground floor, which was unfortunately demolished in 1858. The best surviving 16th century building in the town is the Tudor House looking directly up Broad Street, with its superb timber-framed façade – but this part is not original. It was brought from the ruinous Billingbear Park (in Waltham St Lawrence) in the 1920s. At about the time of Elizabeth's charter, Flemish weavers fleeing from religious persecution made Wokingham famous for its manufacture of silken goods. The industry flourished, dominating the town until the early 19th century, when trade declined due to cheap French imports. Then the townspeople turned to alternatives. The market became well-known for its 'fatted fowls', which were bought for resale in London. Then there was leatherworking, wool-dealing, brewing and coach-building. The Lush Brothers made coaches for King Edward VII, Prince Christian of Schleswig-Holstein and Eugenie, Empress of the French.

During the Civil War, Wokingham was mostly a roundhead town. At one stage, the royalist garrison from Reading arrived on the scene, demanding the townspeople fill eight carts full with firewood and bedding. When they refused, the troops burnt four town houses to the ground. The occupiers were told to take themselves off to parliament-supporting Windsor. Much of the local gentry, however, was royalist in its sympathies. Tales of woe brought on by the Civil War are recounted on a most extraordinary block of Portland stone at the entrance to the parish churchyard. This monument to the wife and nephew of one Benjamin Beaver (1761) gives a complete (though somewhat dubious) family history, including the story of how a Beaver ancestor, along with his brother-in-law, Richard Harrison of Hurst, were almost ruined raising three troops of horse for the King at their own expense. By the time of the Restoration, about twenty percent of the town had been destroyed in the upheaval. This, despite the fact that the commander-in-chief of the Berkshire troops was himself a Wokingham man. Major-General Sir Richard 'Moses' Browne grew up in the town. He was the man who led King Charles II's triumphant procession into London at the Restoration. Not many years afterwards, however, things were looking up for Wokingham and it benefitted from a number of rich bequests. In 1664, Richard Palmer provided for a curfew bell at the church to be rung at 4am and 8pm between September and March. This was so that strangers, lost in the surrounding countryside, could know the time and receive some guidance as to the right way to go.

At heart, Wokingham remained a rough tough kind of a place. Cock fighting was popular and there was once a famous cock-pit at the end of Cock Pit Path. This was also the scene of female wrestling, where topless women fought until one dropped the penny that they each held in one hand. There was also a big prize fight in the town in 1787, when Tom Johnson beat Bill Warr for the title of Champion of England. However, the place was best known for its bull baiting.

Figure 138: Wokingham was once famous for its Bull Baiting

Having been once mauled by a bull, in 1661 a local butcher, named George Staverton, left the rent from his house to provide such a creature for the townsfolk to bait in the Market Place every St Thomas' Day. This horrible 'sport' continued in the town until banned by the Corporation in 1821. Despite the Nation following suit six years later, the last bull baiting in England took place there in 1832. The bull was still provided as beef for the poor but before the unfortunate creature could be slaughtered, an excited mob seized the animal and set the dogs upon it, as of old. People came from miles around to see these spectacles and the vast crowds often got out of hand. In 1794, Elizabeth North was found dead after the baiting and the parish register also records:

Martha May, aged 55,
who was hurt by fighters after the Bull-baiting,
was buried December 31st, 1808.

Wokingham's unsavoury forest reputation was further enhanced by the criminals who frequented the town and, by 1675, the authorities were forced to build a lock-up there. The gallant French highwayman, Claude Duval, worked this area and is said to have owned a cottage in Highwater Lane at that time. More thieves appeared in the following century. In 1723, a white paper was passed in Parliament, making it a criminal offence to undertake blacking, the painting of one's face black in order to commit unlawful acts. It was known as the Black Act and was so called after the infamous Wokingham Blacks, a band of footpads who infested Windsor Forest. They began as mere poachers, but soon expanded their list of nefarious activities to encompass such crimes as robbery, blackmail and even murder. Their little base at one William Shorter's house in Wokingham soon controlled nearly all criminal activity in Eastern Berkshire. The locals were afraid to speak out against them, for retaliation was swift and merciless. Even the local magistrates were not safe. Eventually, the custodian of Bigshotte Rayles (now Ravenswood in Crowthorne) called in the Bow Street Runners (early policemen) to entrap the leading miscreants. Two disguised officers arrived and made friends with three of the Blacks at Wokingham Fair.

They convinced them that there was plenty of easy money to be had by becoming professional witnesses in London. Meeting some days later, in a Holborn tavern, the unsuspecting Berkshire lads were quickly taken into custody. Their arrest led to a major round up and the gang was broken.

Figure 139: The Elms, built 1730 as a Dower House to Swallowfield Park

Wokingham does not show much evidence of the great profits of the 18th century being turned into fine town houses. Although Broad Street does feature the superb 'Elms', a dower house built around an older building for the Pitts of Swallowfield Park about 1730 and Montague House of about the same date but named after a Presbyterian schoolmaster who lived on the site in the 1690s. The magnificent Baptist Church was first built in 1774 but rebuilt in 1861. So there were certainly also more genteel people frequenting the town. Businesses must have benefitted, however, from the establishment in 1759 of the improved turnpike toll road from Reading to Sunninghill, and onwards to London. William Heelas arrived at Buckhurst Lodge (now St Anne's Manor) sometime in the 1790s and set up business as a linen draper in the town. Over the centuries the shop expanded to become a department store covering most of the north side of the Market

Place. There is no longer a Heelas in the town but their second branch has, of course, become Reading's greatest department store, now under the name of John Lewis. One of the old Wokingham buildings is now a popular chemist's shop.

It was during this period that Wokingham's pubs and inns came into their own. The Duke of Wellington frequented the Rose Inn in the 1820s, on his way to Stratfield Saye; but a hundred years earlier it was already famous as the residence of the much-celebrated barmaid, Fair Molly Mogg. She was the publican's daughter who had been brought to public attention through a ballad written for her by the well-known writers, Alexander Pope, John Gay, Jonathan Swift and John Arbuthnot. Being a local man, Alexander Pope often visited the inn and, finding themselves stranded there one day, during a violent storm, he and his friends set about extolling the virtues of their beautiful hostess. The obsessive suitor, mentioned in the rhyme, was said to have been the young lord of Arborfield manor, whose advances she rejected. Some claim there was a case of mistaken identity and the poem was really about Molly's sister, Sally, who was even more beautiful. The Rose, at that time, was not the one which we see today, but an older building which again stood on the site of the chemist's mentioned above.

The Railway arrived in Wokingham in 1849 and the following two decades were a time of great civic pride and much public building work, including the present town hall and the old police court (with prison). This all culminated in the creation of the Borough Council in 1885 and the replacement of the Alderman (the last one in the country) with a mayor; and, since then, the town is proud to have risen to the top of the list of the Nation's most favoured places to live.

Woodley and Sandford

Woodley is a modern suburb of Reading, but the fact that it still forms part of Wokingham Borough serves to remind us that it was anciently part of the parish of Sonning. The liberty of Woodley and Sandford consisted of part of the manor of Sonning in the north, along with the smaller manors of Bulmershe in the west and Haywards (around Coleman's Moor Farm) in the east.

Figure 140: Woodley Lodge, home of Prime Minister Henry Addington

The name Woodley means Wood Clearing and the area was originally heath and moorland cleared at the edge of Windsor Forest. This is reflected in the names of Bulmershe Heath, Hadleigh Heath and Coleman's Moor, but the area was soon taken into agricultural use. The locals supplemented their diet by fishing in the fish ponds at Coleman's Moor Pond and the 'New Pond' (from the mid-18th century) on Bulmershe Heath. Farms and farm workers' cottages were widely scattered, largely rented from the Palmers at Holme Park in Sonning or the Addingtons at Woodley Lodge.

Woodley Lodge or House, also known as Woodley Park, was built about 1790, soon after the Speaker of the House of Commons, Henry Addington MP (later Viscount Sidmouth) purchased the Bulmershe estate from the executors of George Blagrave. His father had been a Reading doctor and he made Woodley his chief country seat until he became Prime Minister in 1801. In the lead up to the Napoleonic Wars, in 1798, Addington established the Woodley Cavalry as a very early form of the territorial army. Along with other Berkshire units, they were reviewed the following year by King George III on Bulmershe Heath. Unfortunately, this great honour turned into something of a farce, when the Queen turned up early and the King late, having spent most of the day at Billingbear Park (in Waltham St Lawrence) awaiting his wife.

In 1801, Addington moved to White Lodge in Richmond and sold Woodley to a Roman Catholic, James Wheble. He built a small Catholic Chapel at the house and later poured large sums of money into the founding of St James' Roman Catholic Church in Reading. The family lived at Woodley Lodge for another two generations, selling up in the early 1920s. It was used by the Ministry of Defence during the Second World War and subsequently fell into a ruinous state. It was pulled down in 1964 to make way for Bulmershe College (later part of Reading University and now a housing estate).

Woodley Lodge was also sometimes known as [New] Bulmershe Court which has made for much confusion with the previous manor house, [Old] Bulmershe Court, which stood to the north-east and is now called Bulmershe Manor. The Blagraves had lived at this former grange of Reading Abbey since it was purchased by their step-ancestor, William Grey, after the

Dissolution of the Monasteries. Another branch of the family lived at Southcote House. Bulmershe Manor's survival can be attributed to it having been converted into farm workers cottages during the time of the Whebles. In the late 1920s it was restored by HE Budd using architectural details from the burnt-out Billingbear Park.

Figure 141: George Aldridge & his nephew Walter Ford at the Bakery

The common grazing land of Bulmershe Heath was once characterised as a "marshy wilderness frequented by gypsies". From 1727 until 1814, the highly popular Reading Races were held at its centre each Summer. There was quite a party atmosphere, with additional revels and sporting matches, like cudgel-play, surrounding the Chequers Inn. However, when the unpopular Earl of Barrymore was steward in the 1790s, owners shunned the meets and his lordship was obliged to enter his own horses under his friends' names.

Concentrated hamlets soon began to emerge at Woodley Green and Sandford (where the mill was mentioned in the Domesday

Survey of 1086), later followed by Wheeler's Green and Cobbler's City around the beginning of the 19th century. Wheeler's Green had a Congregational Chapel as early as 1834, an offshoot of St Mary's Castle Street in Reading. The village name Woodley switched between a number of areas, as recorded on old maps, and was presumably just a general name for anywhere in the liberty. By 1847, nine farmers, three other tradesmen and six publicans were listed in the liberty. However, of the latter, all except those at the Chequers, the Bull and Chequers and the George (at Loddon Bridge), were probably merely taking advantage of legislation allowing them to sell beer from home. They certainly didn't last. Local pubs could be rough places even when the races were not in town. In April 1839, a man named George Greenaway was killed in a fight outside the Bull and Chequers pub by his colleague, John Siddall, whilst being egged on by thirty fellow railway workers. Siddall was let off with a fine and a short stay in prison.

The village school was opened at Woodley Green in 1854 under the patronage of the Palmer family. Miss Caroline Palmer took a particular interest in the local children and visited often. The Palmers also built St John's Anglican Church in 1873, and Woodley became its own parish in 1881.

Cobbler's City, previously Headley Corner, at the most easterly end of Headley Road East, may have gained this nickname as it was the most enterprising region of the liberty. The Sonning Workhouse was built there in 1821, but was soon described as, "an ill-conducted establishment, and more like a disorderly and over-crowded lodging house than a useful public institution". George Aldridge Senior set up a bakery in this area about 1875. The family sold locally famous 'Zilvo' flour with its secret ingredient. His son, George Aldridge Junior, expanded the business into a grocery store and pig farming enterprise, selling pork and bacon, and also opening a second bakery. The original bakery and shop was, unfortunately, demolished in 1969.

Figure 142: Inside the Museum of Berkshire Aviation

In 1913, French aviator, Henri Salmet, landed an early aeroplane in a field in Woodley as part of an air circus touring the country. Shocked villagers were taken for flights or allowed to sit in the plane, including Gladys Aldridge, daughter of the baker. Perhaps this was the inspiration for the opening of Reading (later Woodley) Aerodrome, with a flying school, at Sandford Farm in 1929. Two years later, the heroic aviator, Douglas Bader, had his infamous flying accident there, which led to his losing both his legs at the Royal Berkshire Hospital. Other famous visitors, in happier circumstances, included Amy Johnson and Charles Lindbergh. In 1932, Phillips and Powis, later renamed Miles Aircraft, built an aeroplane factory at the aerodrome. It was an important centre of the British war effort, with huge aircraft hangars and temporary accommodation for over 500 Royal Air Force personnel. The first Biro pens in Britain were also manufactured for them there by the Miles Martin Pen Co. In 1948, the aviation assets of the bankrupt Miles Aircraft were taken over by Handley Page and production of just under 6,000 civil and military aircraft continued until 1962. The Museum of Berkshire Aviation stands on part of the site today.

There was also a bookbinding machinery and actuator side to the Miles company, taken over by the Western Manufacturing Estate Ltd. They later merged with the Adamant Engineering Co to become the Adwest Group. Adwest was taken over by Magal Engineering in 2002 and they still operate from one of the old aeroplane factory buildings. Other industries also moved into the area. Huntley, Boorne and Stevens, the Reading tin box manufacturers, moved there from their London Street/Crown Street/Southampton Street site in 1967. They were taken over by Linpac in 1985 and largely turned to aerosol can manufacture before closing in 2003.

Woosehill and Limmerhill

These are the south-eastern suburbs of Wokingham. Woosehill was historically the southern part of Toutley Common (itself part of Bearwood Common) where the people of Wokingham could graze their animals. This extended down the Reading Road, the eastern end of which, around Rotherfield Avenue, was called Hughes' Green. After its enclosure in 1817, this became agricultural land surrounding Baker's Farm (in the Brookside area) and later Bearwood Farm (in the Diamond Way area). The woods to the west of Limmerhill, around Round Hill and Fox Hill, stretching to the Bearwood Road, were further areas of common land. Limmerhill was originally a small hamlet located at the end of Limmerhill Road. Both housing estates were chiefly built in the 1980s.

Ye Olde Leatherne Bottle on the southern edge of Limmerhill is so named because, at the end of the 19th century, there was also a New Leather Bottle quite nearby. The site has been a pub since 1737, although the present building only dates from 1766. For many years the license was held by a survivor of the 1943 People's Pantry bombing in Reading. The name is appropriate for a pub just down the road from an old tannery.

Figure 143: Philbrick's 'Tanhouse' Tannery on the edge of Woosehill

Across the Reading Road from the Rifle Volunteer at Emmbrook, there was a brickworks, in the late 19th century, owned by Joseph George Ford, from Winnersh Farm. His steam rolling contractor company, JG Ford and Co (later John Allen and Ford), laid most of the roads in the local area. Windmill Pond nearby indicates the site of an old windmill, although the pond itself only dates from the early 19th century. Simon's Lane on Woosehill's western border was originally called the Drift Road and went all the way through to the Bearwood Road. Emmbrook House stood on the site of Brookside. It was the home of Charles Marsh Vialls who, as a young man in the 1840s, had rowed for the Cambridge Team in the famous University Boat Race. Later, the Philbricks from the Tanhouse (Wokingham) and Katesgove (Reading) Tanneries lived there.

Tanhouse Lane, on the far side of Barkham Road from Woosehill, is named after the former tannery and woolstapler's on the Emm Brook which it once led to. This business is believed to have been first established by James Twycross in 1820. He often won prizes for buying the most wool at the famous East Ilsley Sheep Fair and was, at one time, the Alderman (Mayor) of Wokingham. James was from an old Godalming tanning family. He also had a wool staple branch in Bradford in Yorkshire and his sons extended the business to Melbourne in Australia, always following the wool – although only one stayed there. He became a rich wool merchant and is well remembered for his wide-ranging collection of objets d'art, now in the Melbourne Museum, which he purchased at the two international exhibitions held in that city. In 1858, the Tanhouse Tannery was rented to the Philbricks from the Katesgrove Tannery in Reading and they bought the place eleven years later. George Philbrick and his wife made nearby Emmbrook House their family home in 1911 but closed the tannery and moved away upon George's retirement in 1920. As with the Twycrosses, his brother managed tanneries in Australia.

On the Woosehill side of the Barkham Road, the buildings of the old Wokingham Workhouse were built by the local Poor Law Union in 1848-50. The union covered most of the modern borough of Wokingham and transferred over from its old building in Wargrave. It could house 250 of the local destitute in a three-storey T-shaped block with men on the west side and women on the east. There were separate infirmary, fever and vagrants' wards. The designer won a prize of £50 (about £4,000 today). It is now part of Wokingham Hospital, currently providing rehabilitation, physiotherapy and children's mental health support.

Footnote

On the following pages is a family tree showing just a few of my ancestors from Mid-Berkshire and some of their relatives who are mentioned in this book. My father always said that if, on a map, you drew a circle of 15 miles radius around Burghfield Common, all his paternal grandfather's ancestors would have lived within the circle.

Space has meant that not all dates, marriages and siblings are shown. Siblings are also not necessarily listed in chronological order of birth. Preference has also been given to the inclusion of associated residences or businesses in Mid-Berkshire. However these are not necessarily the chief residence or business associated with any individual.

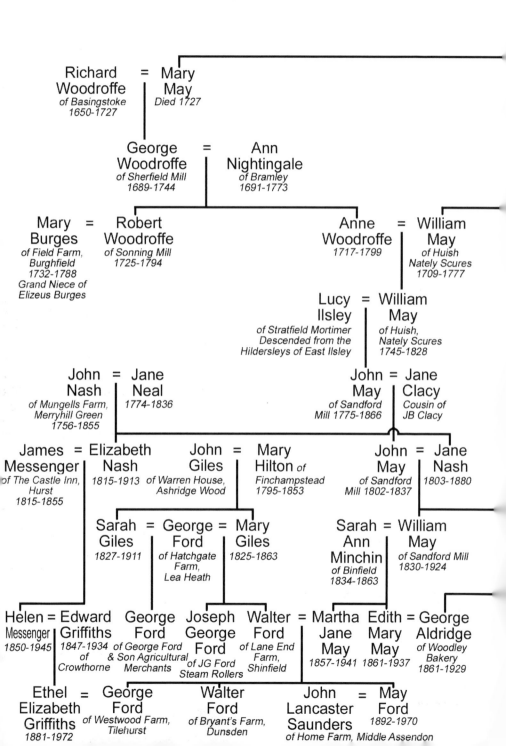

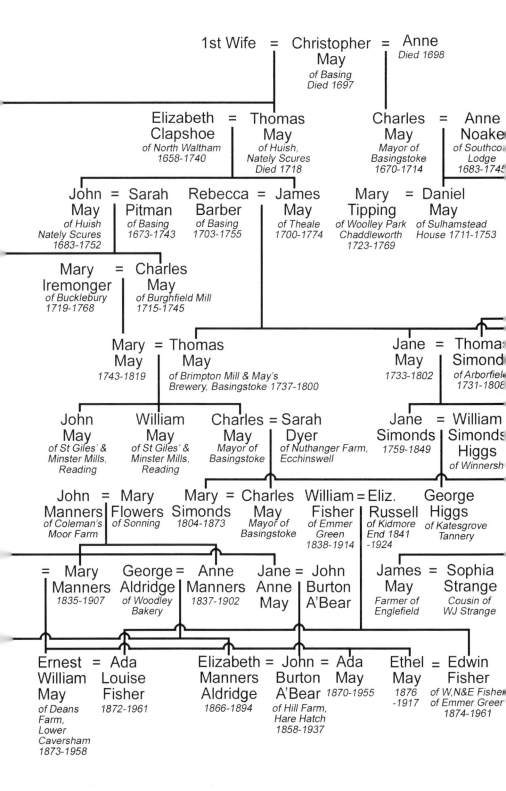

1st Wife = Christopher = Anne
May *Died 1698*
of Basing
Died 1697

Elizabeth = Thomas   Charles = Anne
Clapshoe May   May Noake
of North Waltham *of Huish,*   *Mayor of* *of Southco*
1658-1740 *Nately Scures*   *Basingstoke* *Lodge*
Died 1718   *1670-1714* *1683-174!*

John = Sarah   Rebecca = James   Mary = Daniel
May Pitman   Barber May   Tipping May
of Huish *of Basing*   *of Basing* *of Theale*   *of Woolley Park* *of Sulhamstead*
Nately Scures *1673-1743*   *1703-1755* *1700-1774*   *Chaddleworth* *House 1711-1753*
1683-1752   *1723-1769*

Mary = Charles
Iremonger May
of Bucklebury *of Burghfield Mill*
1719-1768 *1715-1745*

Mary = Thomas   Jane = Thoma:
May May   May Simond
1743-1819 *of Brimpton Mill & May's*   *1733-1802* *of Arborfiel*
Brewery, Basingstoke 1737-1800   *1731-180£*

John   William   Charles = Sarah   Jane = William
May   May   May Dyer   Simonds Simonds
of St Giles' & *of St Giles' &*   *Mayor of* *of Nuthanger Farm,*   *1759-1849* Higgs
Minster Mills, *Minster Mills,*   *Basingstoke* *Ecchinswell*   *of Winnersh*
Reading *Reading*

John = Mary   Mary = Charles   William = Eliz.   George
Manners Flowers   Simonds May   Fisher Russell   Higgs
of Coleman's *of Sonning*   *1804-1873* *Mayor of*   *of Emmer* *of Kidmore*   *of Katesgrove*
Moor Farm   *Basingstoke*   *Green* *End 1841*   *Tannery*
1838-1914 *-1924*

= Mary   George = Anne   Jane = John   James = Sophia
Manners   Aldridge Manners   Anne Burton   May Strange
1835-1907   *of Woodley* *1837-1902*   *May* *A'Bear*   *Farmer of* *Cousin of*
Bakery   *Englefield* *WJ Strange*

Ernest = Ada   Elizabeth = John = Ada   Ethel = Edwin
William Louise   Manners Burton May   May Fisher
May Fisher   Aldridge A'Bear *1870-1955*   *1876* *of W,N&E Fishe*
of Deans *1872-1961*   *1866-1894* *of Hill Farm,*   *-1917* *of Emmer Greer*
Farm,   *Hare Hatch*   *1874-1961*
Lower   *1858-1937*
Caversham
1873-1958

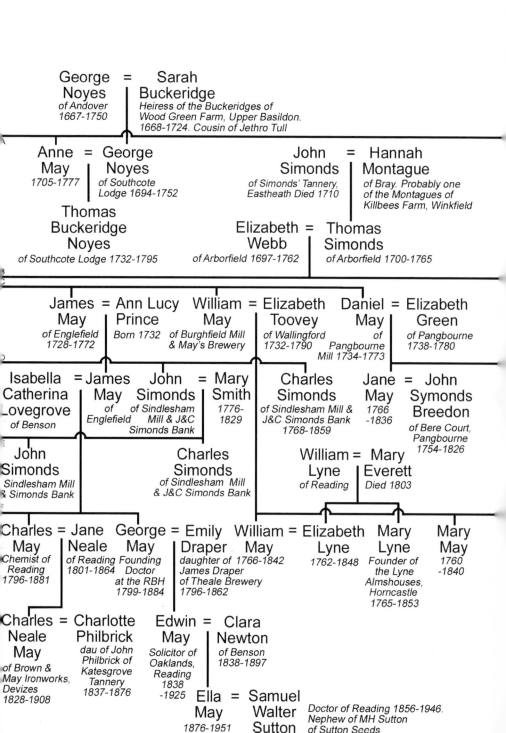

George Noyes = **Sarah Buckeridge**
of Andover 1667-1750 | *Heiress of the Buckeridges of Wood Green Farm, Upper Basildon. 1668-1724. Cousin of Jethro Tull*

Anne May = **George Noyes**
1705-1777 | *of Southcote Lodge 1694-1752*

John Simonds = **Hannah Montague**
of Simonds' Tannery, Eastheath Died 1710 | *of Bray. Probably one of the Montagues of Killbees Farm, Winkfield*

Thomas Buckeridge Noyes
of Southcote Lodge 1732-1795

Elizabeth Webb = **Thomas Simonds**
of Arborfield 1697-1762 | *of Arborfield 1700-1765*

James May = **Ann Lucy Prince**
of Englefield 1728-1772 | *Born 1732*

William May
of Burghfield Mill & May's Brewery

= **Elizabeth Toovey**
of Wallingford 1732-1790

Daniel May = **Elizabeth Green**
of Pangbourne Mill 1734-1773 | *of Pangbourne 1738-1780*

Isabella Catherina Lovegrove
of Benson

= **James May**
of Englefield

John Simonds = **Mary Smith**
of Sindlesham Mill & J&C Simonds Bank | *1776-1829*

Charles Simonds
of Sindlesham Mill & J&C Simonds Bank 1768-1859

Jane May = **John Symonds Breedon**
1766-1836 | *of Bere Court, Pangbourne 1754-1826*

John Simonds
Sindlesham Mill & Simonds Bank

Charles Simonds
of Sindlesham Mill & J&C Simonds Bank

William Lyne = **Mary Everett**
of Reading | *Died 1803*

Charles May = **Jane Neale**
Chemist of Reading 1796-1881 | *of Reading 1801-1864*

George May
Founding Doctor at the RBH 1799-1884

= **Emily Draper**
daughter of James Draper of Theale Brewery 1796-1862

William May = **Elizabeth Lyne**
1766-1842 | *1762-1848*

Mary Lyne
Founder of the Lyne Almshouses, Horncastle 1765-1853

Mary May
1760-1840

Charles Neale May = **Charlotte Philbrick**
of Brown & May Ironworks, Devizes 1828-1908 | *dau of John Philbrick of Katesgrove Tannery 1837-1876*

Edwin May = **Clara Newton**
Solicitor of Oaklands, Reading 1838-1925 | *of Benson 1838-1897*

Ella May = **Samuel Walter Sutton**
1876-1951 | *Doctor of Reading 1856-1946. Nephew of MH Sutton of Sutton Seeds*

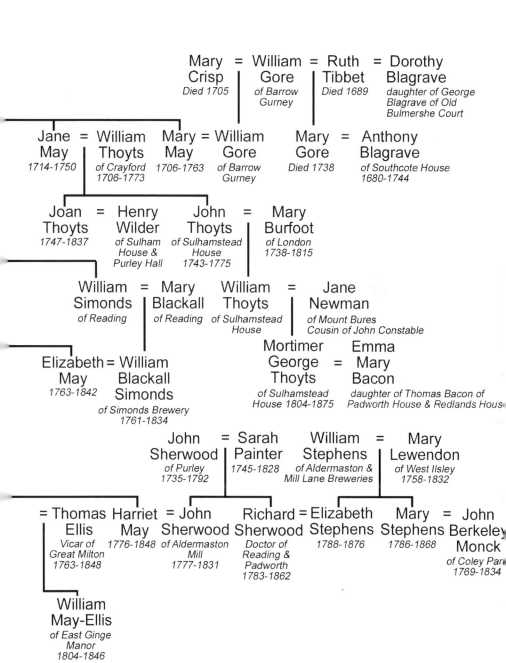

Mary = William = Ruth = Dorothy
Crisp | Gore | Tibbet | Blagrave
Died 1705 | *of Barrow* | *Died 1689* | *daughter of George*
| *Gurney* | | *Blagrave of Old*
| | | *Bulmershe Court*

Jane = William Mary = William Mary = Anthony
May | Thoyts May | Gore Gore | Blagrave
1714-1750 | *of Crayford* *1706-1763* | *of Barrow* *Died 1738* | *of Southcote House*
| *1706-1773* | *Gurney* | *1680-1744*

Joan = Henry John = Mary
Thoyts | Wilder Thoyts | Burfoot
1747-1837 | *of Sulham* *of Sulhamstead* | *of London*
| *House &* *House* | *1738-1815*
| *Purley Hall* *1743-1775*

William = Mary William = Jane
Simonds | Blackall Thoyts | Newman
of Reading | *of Reading* *of Sulhamstead* | *of Mount Bures*
| *House* | *Cousin of John Constable*

Mortimer Emma
Elizabeth = William George = Mary
May Blackall Thoyts Bacon
1763-1842 Simonds *of Sulhamstead* *daughter of Thomas Bacon of*
of Simonds Brewery *House 1804-1875* *Padworth House & Redlands House*
1761-1834

John = Sarah William = Mary
Sherwood | Painter Stephens | Lewendon
of Purley | *1745-1828* *of Aldermaston &* | *of West Ilsley*
1735-1792 | *Mill Lane Breweries* | *1758-1832*

= Thomas Harriet = John Richard = Elizabeth Mary = John
Ellis May Sherwood Sherwood Stephens Stephens Berkeley
Vicar of *1776-1848* *of Aldermaston* *Doctor of* *1788-1876* *1786-1868* Monck
Great Milton *Mill* *Reading &* *of Coley Park*
1763-1848 *1777-1831* *Padworth* *1769-1834*
1783-1862

William
May-Ellis
of East Ginge
Manor
1804-1846

Printed Resources

This is a list of some of the major works consulted over many years and revisited more recently. Primary sources in the Berkshire Record Office and the National Archives are not listed. Various articles in the 'Reading Mercury', 'Berkshire Chronicle', 'Berkshire Archaeological Journal', 'Berkshire Old and New', 'The Wokingham Historian', 'The Twyford & Ruscombe Local History Society Journal' and publications of Thames Valley Archaeological Services are not listed individually.

Amos, Katie (2016) The Mansion House: Its History and its Occupants. Reading: Scallop Shell Press

Appleby, HM (1948) The Kendrick Book. Reading: Bradley & Son Ltd

Astill, Grenville G (1978) Historic Towns in Berkshire: An Archaeological Appraisal. Reading: Berkshire Archaeological Committee

Ashampstead, Parishioners of (1990) Ashampstead: A Berkshire Parish. Ashampstead: Ashampstead Parish Council

Ayres, Dennis & Hunter, Judith (1994) The Inns & Public Houses of Wokingham. Reading: Berkshire Books

Babbage, T (1976). Tylehurst Described. Reading: Reading Libraries

Babtie Group Ltd's Public Services Division (1994) Prehistoric Berkshire. Shinfield: Berkshire County Council

Babtie Group Ltd's Public Services Division (1995) Bastions of Berkshire: Medieval Castles. Shinfield: Berkshire County Council

Babtie Group Ltd's Public Services Division (1995) Roman Berkshire. Shinfield: Berkshire County Council

Babtie Group Ltd's Public Services Division (1996) Medieval Berkshire. Shinfield: Berkshire County Council

Barham, Tony (1973) Witchcraft in the Thames Valley. Bourne End: Spurbooks Ltd

Barnes-Phillips, Daphne Joyce (2202) The Top of Whitley. Reading: Corridor Press

Baxter, Ron (2016) The Royal Abbey of Reading. Woodbridge: The Boydell Press

Bayley, Michael (1990). Personal Correspondence. Nash Ford Manuscript: M Bayley

Beckinsale, RP (1972) Companion into Berkshire. Bourne End: Spurbooks Ltd

Beenham Group, History of (1999) Beenham: A History. Beenham: History of Beenham Group

Berkshire Federation of Women's Institutes (1939) The Berkshire Book. Reading: Berkshire Federation of Women's Institutes

Berkshire Local History Club (1893) Berkshire Local History Club Vols 1-6, 8 & 9. Berkshire LSL Manuscript: Berkshire Local History Club

Betjeman, John & Piper, John (eds) (1949) Murray's Berkshire Architectural Guide. London: John Murray

Brain, John A (1904) Berkshire Ballads & Other Papers. Reading: Thomas Thorp

Breedon, Victor (2007) Bere Court: History of an English Manor House. Ste- Anne-de-Bellevue: Shoreline

Butts, Dennis (2008) From Abbey to the Office. Reading: Two Rivers Press

Caversham Court Gardens, Friends of (2013) Caversham Court Gardens: A Heritage Guide. Reading: Two Rivers Press

Chambers, Jill (1999) Berkshire Machine Breakers: The Story of the 1830 Riots. Letchworth: Jill Chambers

Chapman, John (ed) (1999) Purley on Thames at the Millennium. Purley: Project Purley

Childs, William Macbride (1905) The Story of the Town of Reading. Reading: William C Long

Clark, Gillian (2009) Down by the River: The Thames & Kennet in Reading. Reading: Two Rivers Press

Coates, Charles (1802) The History & Antiquities of Reading. London: J Nichols & Son

Cooper, Mike (2016) Southcote: An Historical Introduction. Reading: Reading Libraries

Cooper, Mike & Bond, Janet (2001) A Hamlet called Harmour. Tilehurst: Armour Road History Group

Cope, Esther S (1992) Handmaid of the Holy Spirit. Ann Arbor: University of Michigan Press

Corley, T Anthony B & Simonds, Raymond E (2009) H & G Simonds Ltd: The Story of the Bridge Street Brewery, Reading 1785-1980. Chiswick: Simonds Family

Corporation of the County Borough of Reading (1956) Reading: Official Town Guide. Reading: Corporation of the County Borough of Reading & Reading Chamber of Commerce

Costin, Diana (1999) Grave Tales from Berkshire. Seaford: SB Publications

Cram, Leslie (1988) Reading Abbey. Reading: Reading Museum & Art Gallery

Crane, Bill (1994) A Walk around Charvil. Twyford: Twyford & Ruscombe Local History Society

Cripps, Mary (ed) (2009) Memories of Beech Hill. Winchester: Hampshire Printing Services

Cusden. Phoebe E (1977) Coley: Portrait of an Urban Village. Reading: Reading Branch of the Workers' Educational Association

Curtis, Audrey (2016) Twyford & Ruscombe through the Ages. Twyford: Twyford & Ruscombe Local History Society

Dils, Joan (ed) (1980) Redding 1540-1640: A Portrait of a Community. Reading: Extramural Department, School of Education

Dils, Joan (2019) Reading: A History. Lancaster: Carnegie Publishing Ltd

Dils, Joan & Yates, Margaret (eds) (2012) An Historical Atlas of Berkshire. Reading: The Berkshire Record Society

Ditchfield, PH (1920) Byways in Berkshire & the Cotswolds. London: Robert Scott

Doble, Douglas (1961) A History of the Parish of Shinfield, Berkshire. Shinfield: D Doble

Doran, J (1835) The History & Antiquities of the Town & Borough of Reading in Berkshire. Reading: Samuel Reader

Dormer, Ernest William (1912) Erleigh Court & its Owners. Reading: GA Poynder

Dormer, Ernest William (1929) Watlington House, reading. Reading: Poynder & Son

Dormer, Ernest William (1944) The Parish & Church of Saint Peter Earley. Reading: C Nicholls & Co Ltd

Dumbleton, Michael (1984) Brickmaking: A Local Industry. Bracknell: Bracknell & District Historical Society

Dunlop, Lesley & Greenaway, Dick (2011) Around the Three Valleys. Theale: The Friends of the Pang, Kennet & Lambourn Valleys

Durrant, Peter & Painter, John (2018) Reading Abbey & the Abbey Quarter. Reading: Two Rivers Press

Earley Local History Group (2001) Earley Days: An Illustrated Account of Our Community's Development. Earley: Earley Local History Group

Earley Local History Group (2006) Suttons Seeds: A History 1806-2006. Earley: Earley Local History Group

Eddleston, John J (2009) Foul Deeds & Suspicious Deaths in Reading. Barnsley: Wharncliffe Books

Elliott, Colin (1978) A Brief History of Sulhamstead & Ufton Nervet. Sulhamstead: Sulhamstead & Ufton Nervet Parish Councils

Farndon, Doris, Mayne, Miranda, Millward, Joyce, Perkins, Angela, Shorland, Eileen & Stirling, Brends (eds) (1979) The Old Berkshire Village Book. Newbury: Countryside Books & Berkshire Federation of Women's Institutes

Farrar, Henry (1984) The Book of Hurst. Buckingham: Barracuda Books

Fasham, Peter & Hawkes, John (1983) Reading Abbey Rediscovered. Maidstone: Trust for Wessex Archaeology

Fasham, Peter & Hawkes, John (1986) Reading Abbey Waterfront. Maidstone: Trust for Wessex Archaeology

Finchampstead Society (1998) Finchampstead in Old Pictures. Finchampstead: The Finchampstead Society

Finn, Margot & Smith, Kate (2018) The East India Company at Home 1757-1857. London: UCL Press

Ford, David Nash (2009) Berkshire in the Reign of Henry VIII. Wokingham: Nash Ford Publishing

French, David & Firth, Janet (2000) Barkham: A History. Barkham: Barkham History Association

French, David (2013) The Ancestry of the Balls of Berkshire, Northamptonshire & Virginia. Barkham: D.J. French

Gelling, Margaret (1974-82) The Place-Names of Berkshire Parts 1-3. Cambridge: The English Place Name Society

Gillespie, Emily (2011) Ufton Court: Nine Hundred Years of History. London: Pitkin Publishing & Ufton Court

Glover, Catherine (ed.) (2016) More from Our Village of Spencers Wood. Spencers Wood: Spencers Wood Local History Group

Goring & Streatley Local History Society (1986) Picture History of Goring & Streatley. Goring: Goring & Streatley Local History Society

Goring & Streatley Local History Society (2000) Millennium Exhibition: Life in Goring & Streatley in the Second Millennium. Goring: Goring & Streatley Local History Society

Green, Roy & Brown, Jonathan (2010) Barrett, Exall & Andrewes: The Firm & its Products. Andover: The Road Locomotive Society

Greenaway, Dick & Ward, Dorcas (eds) (2002) In the Valley of the Pang. Ashampstead Common: The Friends of the Pang & Kennet Valleys

Griffin, Sarah (1996) The Siege of Reading. Bristol: Stuart Press

Hadland, Tony (1992) Thames Valley Papists. Buckland: Tony Hadland

Handscomb, Sue (1989) Saint Michael's, Tilehurst: The First 800 Years. Tilehurst: Tilehurst PCC

Handscomb, Sue (1995) Tilehurst. Stroud: Alan Sutton Publishing

Handscomb, Sue (1998) This was Tilehurst. Tilehurst: Sue Handscomb

Harrison (c. 1890) Englefield. Berkshire LSL Manuscript: Harrison

Hartley, Mary C, Hine, Pauline & Marr, Peter (1971) Guide to the Parish of St Giles-in-Reading. Gloucester: British Publishing Company Ltd

Hill, Mick (2016) Berkshire's Bareknuckle Battles 1777-1881 Peterborough: Fastprint Publishing

Humphreys, AL (1926) Caversham Bridge 1231-1926. Reading: E Poynder & Son

Hurry, Jamieson Boyd (1901) Reading Abbey. London: Elliot Stock

Hurry, Jamieson Boyd (1921) The Octocentenary of Reading Abbey AD 1121- AD 1921. London: Elliot Stock

Hylton, Stuart (1992) Reading Places, Reading People. Reading: Berkshire Books

Hylton, Stuart (2007) A History of Reading. Chichester: Phillimore & Co

Hylton, Stuart (2015) Reading 1800 to the Present Day. Stroud: Amberley

Ingram, Christine & Tony & Ridley, Pamela (1976) The History of Some Berkshire Inns & their Signs. Reading: Berkshire Federation of Women's Institutes

Ingram, Christine (1985) (ed) The New Berkshire Village Book. Newbury: Countryside Books & Berkshire Federation of Women's Institutes

Ingram, Christine (1990) (ed) Hidden Berkshire. Newbury: Countryside Books & Berkshire Federation of Women's Institutes

Jessel, Anne Green (2017) A Road of Distinction: A Noble History of Southcote Road Parts 1 & 2. Reading: Reading Libraries

Josten, CH (2000) Elias Ashmole. Oxford: Ashmolean Museum

Keddie, Barbara Young (2014) Evidence of a Monumental Investigation: The Beaver Monument in Wokingham, Berkshire. Wokingham: Barbara Young Keddie

Kemp, Brian (1984) The Monuments in Hurst Church, Berkshire. Hurst: St Nicholas Hurst Church

Kerry, Rev Charles (1883) A History of the Municipal Church of St Lawrence Reading. Reading: Rev Charles Kerry

Keyser, Charles Edward (1916) Notes on Excavations carried out on the Site of the Palace of the Bishops of Salisbury at Sonning. Reading: Berkshire Archaeological Society

Kift, Mary (1980) Life in Old Caversham. Caversham: Mary Kift

Lack, William, Stuchfield, H Martin & Whittemore, Philip (1993) The Monumental Brasses of Berkshire. Piccadilly: Monumental Brass Society

Lea, John (ed) (1995) Wokingham from Elizabeth I to Cromwell. Wokingham: Wokingham Society Local History Group

Lea, John & Lea, Rosemary (1990) Wokingham: A Pictorial History. Chichester: Phillimore & Co

Leach, Arthur Francis (1900) A History of Bradfield Collage. London: Henry Frowde

Lloyd, Frances (1977) Woodley in the Nineteenth Century. Reading: Reading Libraries

Long, Roger (1990) Murder in Old Berkshire. Buckingham: Barracuda Books Ltd

Long, Roger (2011) Haunted Berkshire. Stroud: The History Press

Lyon, William (1895) Chronicles of Finchampstead in the County of Berkshire. London: Longmans, Green & Co

Malpas, John (1997) Caversham Park & its Owners. Caversham: John Malpas
Man, John (1816) The History & Antiquities Ancient & Modern of the Borough of Reading. Reading: Snare & Man
MacNaghten, Angus (1986) Haunted Berkshire. Newbury: Countryside Books
Markham, Sarah (1984) John Loveday of Caversham 1711-1789. Wilby: Michael Russell Publishing Ltd
McLoughlin, Ian (1992) Berkshire Murders. Newbury: Countryside Books
Millson, Cecilia (1977) Tales of Old Berkshire. Newbury: Countryside Books
Millson, Cecilia (1986) Old Berkshire Tales. Newbury: Countryside Books
Mitchell, Anne (1972) Ghosts along the Thames. Bourne End: Spurbooks Ltd
Money, Walter (1884) The First & Second Battles of Newbury & the Siege of Donnington Castle during the Civil War. Newbury: WJ Blacket
Money, Walter (1893) Stray Notes on Basildon. Newbury: WJ Blacket
Morley, HT (1924) Monumental Brasses of Berkshire. Reading: Electric Press
Morris, John (ed) (1979) Domesday Book: Berkshire. Chichester: Phillimore & Co Ltd
Mortimer Local History Group (1994) Mortimer through the Ages. Stratfield Mortimer: Mortimer Local History Group
Mullaney, John (2014) Reading's Abbey Quarter: An Illustrated History. Reading: Scallop Shell Press
Neave, Jack (1988) The History of All Saints' Church, Wokingham. Wokingham: the Wokingham Society
Neave, Jack (1989) The History of St Mary's Church, Shinfield. Wokingham: J Neave
Neave, Jack (1993) The History of All Saints' Church, Swallowfield. Wokingham: J Neave
Neave, Jack (1995) The History of St James' Church, Finchampstead. Wokingham: J Neave
Nicolls, Jeff (1985) Our Mysterious Shire. Slough: Corinthian Publishers
Noel-Perkins, Peter (1990) Tidmarsh Grange. Unpublished Manuscript: Peter Noel-Perkins
North, Leslie (1979) Royal Reading's Colourful Past. Peppard Common: Cressrelles Publishing Co
Ormonde, Margaret (2001) Emmer Green: Past & Present. Emmer Green: Emmer Green Residents' Association
Over, Luke (1990) The Parish Church of St Peter, Caversham. Caversham: Caversham Parochial Church Council
Padley, F.C. (1983) A Village in the Town. Reading: Workers' Educational Association
Page, William; Ditchfield, Peter Hampson & Cope, John Hautenville (1923) The Victoria History of the County of Berkshire Volume 3. London: St Catherine Press
Paterson, Christopher (2015) St Mary's Church & the Aldworth Giants: A New History & Guide. Upper Basildon: Sarum House Press
Paulden, Sydney (1977) Finchampstead Past, Present & Future. Finchampstead: Finchampstead Society
Pawlisch, Hans S (1985) Sir John Davies & the Conquest of Ireland. Cambridge: Cambridge University Press
Pearson, Hugh (1890) Memorials of the Church & Parish of Sonning. Reading: Edward J. Blackwell
Perkins, Angela (1977) The Book of Sonning. Chesham: Barracuda Books
Petyt, Malcolm (1993) The Growth of Reading. Stroud: Alan Sutton Publishing Ltd
Pheasant, Pam (2003) The Grotto House. Lower Basildon: The Institute of Leisure & Amenity Management

Phillips, Daphne (1980) The Story of Reading. Newbury: Countryside Books

Phillips, Daphne (1983) The Great Road to Bath. Newbury: Countryside Books

Phillips, Daphne (1993) Berkshire: A County History. Newbury: Countryside Books

Pugh, Charles (2002) Basildon Park. Bromley: National Trust (Enterprises) Ltd

Read, Mike (2015) Caversham Park & its People BC to BBC. Bognor Regis: Woodfield Publishing

Redlands Local history Group (1990) Old Redlands: The Story of the Redlands Area of Reading, told by Local People. Reading: Redlands Local History Group

Rotheray, Brian (2010) A History of Caversham Park. Caversham: BBC Monitoring

Rosevear, Alan (2004) A Booklet on the Turnpike Roads around Reading. Kingston Bagpuize: Alan Rosevear

Rudd, John & Sheila (1984) Old Inns & Alehouses of Twyford. Twyford: Twyford & Ruscombe Local History Society

Russell, Constance CEL (1901) Swallowfield & its Owners. London: Longmans, Green & Co

Salter, Martin (ed) (1995) Newtown, Reading: The Inside Story. Reading: Newtown Local History Project

Sharp, Mary (1892) The History of Ufton Court, of the parish of Ufton & of the Perkins Family. London: Elliot Stock

Sharp, Mary (1911) A Record of the Parish of Padworth & its Inhabitants. Reading: Bradley & Son

Shilham, PR (2011) Emmbrook: More Unfinished History. Wokingham: PR Shilham

Shilham, PR (2016) Emmbrook: Still More Unfinished History. Wokingham: PR Shilham

Simonds, Beatrice M (ed) (1947) The History, Stories & Customs of the Parish of Arborfield& the Liberty of Newland. Arborfield: Arborfield & Newland Women's Institute

Slade, Cecil (2001) The Town of Reading & its Abbey. Reading: MRM Associates Ltd

Smith, Ernest (1957) A History of Whiteknights. Reading: The University of Reading

Southerton, Peter (1975) The Story of a Prison. Reading: Osprey Publishing Ltd

Sowan, Adam (2012) Believing in Reading: Our Places of Worship. Reading: Two Rivers Press

Stokes, Penelope (2005) Free Rein: Racing in Berkshire & Beyond. Hamstead Marshall: Penelope Stokes

Storry, Guy (1991) The Church of Saint Andrew, Sonning. Sonning: Sonning Parochial Church Council

Stout, Adam (ed) (1997) RISC: Of Books, Stones, Friends & Visions. Reading: Two Rivers Press

Streatley PCC (1985) Streatley 1086-1986. Streatley: Streatley PCC

Summers, Malcolm (2014) History of Greyfriars Church, Reading. Tilehurst: Downs Way Publishing

Sutcliffe, Nigel (2010) Reading: A Horse-Racing Town. Reading: Two Rivers Press

Thorne, Ellie (2016) St James the Less, Pangbourne 1966-2016: Then & Now. Pangbourne: Pangbourne Parochial Church Council

Thoyts, Emma Elizabeth (1888) History of Sulhamstead Parish. Sulhamstead: EE Thoyts

Thoyts, Emma Elizabeth (1893) Annals of a Country Churchyard during 150 years (1602 to 1750). Sulhamstead: EE Thoyts

Thoyts, Emma Elizabeth (c. 1890) History of Sulhamstead Parish Volumes 1 & 2. Berkshire LSL Manuscript: EE Thoyts

Tomkins, Charles (1805-10) Views of Reading Abbey. London: J Whiting

Tucker, Joan (2011) Ferries of the Upper Thames. Stroud: Amberley

Tyack, Geoffrey; Bradley, Simon & Pevsner, Nicholas (2010) The Buildings of England: Berkshire. London: Yale University Press

Vincent, James Edmund (1931) Highways & Byways in Berkshire. London: MacMillan & Co Ltd

Ward, Dorcas (2011) History of Bradfield. Frilsham: Dorcas Ward

West, David Marshall (1983) The Parish Church of St Nicholas, Hurst. Hurst: Hurst Parochial Church Council

Wilcox, Joan (1992) Pangbourne: An Illustrated History. Stroud: Alan Sutton Publishing Ltd

Williams, Clive (1994) Basildon, Berkshire: An Illustrated History of a Thames-side Parish. Reading: Clive Williams

Williams, Clive (2010) The Nabobs of Berkshire. Purley: Goosecroft Publications

Wokingham Society Local History Group (1977) Wokingham: A Chronology. Wokingham: The Wokingham Society

Wood, Dennis (2017) Views from the Hill: The Story of Whitley. Caversham: Scallop Shell Press

Wykes, Alan (1970) Reading: A Biography. MacMillan & Co Ltd

Yarrow, Ian (1974) Berkshire. London: Robert Hale & Company

Online Resources

Apart from my own Royal County of Berkshire History Website *www.berkshirehistory.com*, there are a number of good websites currently covering local history in Mid-Berkshire:

Arborfield Local History Society *www.arborfieldhistory.org.uk*
Berkshire Turnpike Trusts *www.turnpikes.org.uk/Turnpikes in Berks.htm*
CD-ROM of Hurst *history.woodedhill.org/hurst*
Coley Park and Beyond *www.coleypark.com*
East India Company at Home 1757-1857 *www.uclpress.co.uk/products/88277*
Englefield History *englefieldhistory.net*
East Court, Finchampstead *eastcourt.org.uk*
Huntley and Palmers Collection *www.huntleyandpalmers.org.uk*
Mortimer Village History *www.mortimervillage.org.uk/history*
Project Purley: History *project-purley.eu/history*
Reading Abbey Quarter *www.readingabbeyquarter.org.uk*
Reading Museum: Our Collections *www.readingmuseum.org.uk/our-collections*
The Story of the Bridge Street Brewery *simondsfamily.me.uk*
The Whitley Pump *whitleypump.wordpress.com*
Wokingham Remembers *www.wokinghamremembers.com*
The Workhouse: The Story of an Institution *www.workhouses.org.uk*

Index